W9-DFK-772

DISCARDED

DISCARDED

A PSYCHOLOGY
OF ORIENTATION

A PSYCHOLOGY
OF ORIENTATION

Time Awareness Across
Life Stages and in Dementia

ALLEN JACK EDWARDS

PRAEGER

Westport, Connecticut
London

FLORIDA GULF COAST
UNIVERSITY LIBRAR

Library of Congress Cataloging-in-Publication Data

Edwards, Allen Jack, 1926–
    A psychology of orientation : time awareness across life stages and in dementia / Allen
Jack Edwards.
        p.   cm.
    Includes bibliographical references and index.
    ISBN 0–275–97556–8 (alk. paper)
    1. Time perception.   2. Time perspective.   3. Time—psychological aspects.   4.
Dementia—Treatment.   I. Title.
    BF468.E36   2002
    153.7'53—dc21   2001036686

British Library Cataloguing in Publication Data is available.

Copyright © 2002 by Allen Jack Edwards

All rights reserved. No portion of this book may be
reproduced, by any process or technique, without the
express written consent of the publisher.

Library of Congress Catalog Card Number: 2001036686
ISBN: 0–275–97556–8

First published in 2002

Praeger Publishers, 88 Post Road West, Westport, CT 06881
An imprint of Greenwood Publishing Group, Inc.
www.praeger.com

Printed in the United States of America

The paper used in this book complies with the
Permanent Paper Standard issued by the National
Information Standards Organization (Z39.48–1984).

10 9 8 7 6 5 4 3 2 1

FLORIDA GULF COAST
UNIVERSITY LIBRARY

For Joel
Who still makes good things happen

Contents

Illustrations

Preface

Time has been a subject of interest to psychologists throughout the twentieth century. In research, time has served as an independent variable, as witnessed in the plentitude of reaction time studies. In contemporary research, time also has been used as an intervening variable in some studies. Most frequently the implication has been that time is whatever is measured by clocks, to paraphrase the old saw about intelligence testing.

Yet there have been thrusts toward explaining the nature and influence of time. Proposals of this sort are found in theoretical papers published in a variety of journals and books that explore time's influence on the lives of humans. These have been focused, usually, within a context such as psychiatric conditions, physical circumstances such as medical illnesses, or social climates such as environment.

To date, there have been limited attempts to consolidate findings and proposals into a cohesive ensemble and draw conclusions about time's ultimate presence and meaning. That is the purpose of this book. Not only does it include a brief consideration of the history of time measurement, but it also surveys selective portions of the study of time throughout the life cycle. Since time and space are the integral components of orientation, there is a major impetus in this direction, eventually focusing on what has been called *dis*orientation. This latter condition has been defined in terms of the reality created by the greater portion of social orders. In this book, the term is used in a less pejorative sense: what we have called disorientation must be considered instead as an alternative form of orientation. This must mean, then, that time and space are as much a part of the orientation of those called disoriented as they are to the rest of us. To demonstrate this view, dementia has been chosen as the illustrative condition:

an outcome of physical changes in the brain combined with the effects reflected in our measures of orientation (largely memory-based) and behavioral effects in such executive functions as planning and problem solving.

It is the contention in this book that the traditional concepts of present, past, and future are as applicable to disorientation as they are to orientation. A model to include this view is the matter of a final chapter.

I wish to acknowledge the cooperation and assistance of those who made the work possible. Dr. Carol Grove read and commented on the manuscript, contributing ideas and questions that helped me clarify ideas and proposals. My wife, Jean, supported my efforts and made a significant contribution by creating graphics that illustrate basic points of the conceptions of time used in this work. As always, there are the librarians at Southwest Missouri State University and the University of Missouri at Columbia who provided resources and sought copies of works that were not available locally. To these and any others whom I have overlooked, my heartfelt gratitude is expressed.

PART I

The Nature of Time

Time is not measured by a watch, but by moments.
                                        —From a fortune cookie

CHAPTER 1

The Substance of Time

We have become so accustomed to the pervasive and urgent nature of time that it seems natural to us that references to it are to be found in every segment of our lives. Certainly the mechanical means to measure time have become a substantial force in our actions and plans. Timepieces are everywhere: on the walls of public buildings, the towers of churches, the facings of business structures, even sometimes on stanchions in public streets, certainly in air terminals, even in our cars, on our wrists, and by our bedsides. We read the numerals of these timepieces even when we have no real need to know the hour. We are so subservient to schedules that we look forward to retirement when we need no longer care about the time, although we continue to do so, of course.

Nor is this dependence on time and its measurement unique to the sophisticated societies of today. Being aware of time has had significance to humankind for thousands of years, beginning with observations of the heavens to determine when to plant and when to reap, continuing to the hours to say prayers and chants, and finally focusing on the workplace to assure that shifts fulfilled their demands while guaranteeing that a change in shifts would permit continued maximum production. Time must have been an element influencing behavior even in the time of the caveman. With recorded history, it became apparent that time had been a seminal element for generations and had even reached sophisticated levels that proved unexpected.

Nearly 4,000 years ago, for example, astronomical observations were a commonplace among the educated, and by 1000 B.C., competent students were able to calculate the movements of the planets and consequently correct the calendar used by the royal house in Mesopotamia (Kramer, 1967,

p. 125). The scholars of that day used a lunar year in which there were 12 months. Since errors occurred because the movements of the moon were not consistent with other natural events, every three years or so it was necessary to add an extra month. The scholars of the day were thus gainfully employed and important to the proper functioning of political decision making.

In China, astronomy had become the major science in ancient times, being used as the basis of control over man and nature (Schafer, 1967, pp. 125–126). Available for use only by the ruling family, it functioned for astrological predictions and guidance as well as the systematic plotting of the heavens. Around 3,000 years ago, the architect Wen Wang designed and constructed an observatory tower that permitted the astronomers of the day to develop an almanac that permitted setting the dates of the spring and autumn equinoxes and the summer and winter solstices. With other observations, it was possible to determine the date of the New Year, the principal occasion in Chinese society since life began anew on that date and all days were counted until the time for the next new year. The problem of length of the year occurred here as well, being first set at 366 days and later corrected to 365.25 days in the fourth century B.C. The new year was conceived to begin at the winter solstice (about December 21 in our calendar). At this time of the year the energy of *yang* (the sunlit, warm, male, aggressive and dominant force) was at its lowest ebb, while *yin* (the cool, female, submissive and regressive force) was at its highest. As the year wore on, *yang* warmed the earth and permitted sowing and growing of crops until gradually *yin* returned to greater dominance. These characteristics gradually became applied to everything in life. It is no distortion to point out that the features are found today and are not restricted to Chinese religion and life.

More recently, around the beginning of the common era, the Druids, priests of the Celtic religion found throughout Europe from Ireland to the Baltics, were leading their ceremonies based upon religious calendars that they memorized. Seldom were such calendars recorded since that might have detracted from the power of the Druids. An exception to the rule was found in the Coligny calendar, found in France and dated to a period from the beginning of the first century B.C. to the end of the first century of the common era. (Green [1997] dates it in the first century B.C. on page 37 and the first century A.D. on page 89.) This bronze plaque contains 64 months and is believed by scholars to have been used for calculating the most auspicious days for ceremonies, festivals, and political events (pp. 37, 164–165). Interestingly, the calendar had been deliberately broken before being buried, a testimony to the secrecy with which Druidic symbolism was subject.

The focus of the religion was the central role of nature and the pivotal feature of the seasons. The resulting Wheel of the Year endlessly rotated through eight cycles. These eight periods consisted of the summer and winter solstices, the autumn and spring equinoxes, and the midpoints between them. The Celtic new year (called Samhain) ran from October 31 to November 2 in our calendar and corresponds to Halloween. In this period, the Celts concentrated on the culling of livestock. The Yule period was at the winter solstice (December 21 and 22) and corresponds to our Christmas. Imbolc was February 1 and 2, the time of lamb birthing. The spring equinox was March 20 and 21. Beltane fell on May 1, when livestock were taken to hill pasturage. Midsummer came at the summer solstice, June 21 and 22. Lughnasadh was harvest time, August 1. Finally, the autumn equinox fell on September 22 and 23. As with the other societies surveyed here, the role of accurate astronomical observation is marked and essential.

There have been attempts to build science to the service of religion. Perhaps the most notable, and most commonly accepted, of such practices occurred in 1654. James Ussher, a Protestant archbishop in Ireland, was persistent in his search for religious authenticity and became a noted scholar for his collection of manuscripts and his exhaustive distinctions between those that were authentic and the ones that were spurious (Boorstin, 1983, p. 451). Eventually, he concentrated on determining the exact date of Creation—and found it. By his calculations, based only on the most rigorous of holy documents, he announced that God had created the earth on October 26, 4004 B.C. at 9:00 A.M.! Rather than discourage, the dogmatic nature of his statement and the desire to add authenticity to the biblical theory of Creation led to wide acceptance. Even Isaac Newton, in his later years, accepted the dogma proposed by Bishop Ussher and thereby increased the appearance of scientific validity. There are still persons today who faithfully believe that the date proposed is accurate, despite massive evidence to indicate that the earth could not have been created in such a short time period from the present. Duncan (1998, p. 107) tells us that Bede computed the date as March 18, 3952 B.C., but Reiner of Paderborn warned in the twelfth century that such efforts were a mistake due to calendar errors (p. 162).

Whatever the truth about such matters, there is no doubt that an awareness of time and its importance has a long history. (See Grun [1991] for explicit and ample evidence.) Significant refinements in research and theory have made us more sophisticated and precise, although it is clear that the search for truth is not yet over. Consider the momentous work of Einstein on relativity, not only for its theoretical importance but for its practical implications (such as the atom bomb and the ability to travel accurately in space). Refinements continue (and Einstein has been shown to be incorrect on more than one point). Time is an essential element in all these efforts and persists in its pervasive influence. That brings the question: What *is* time?

THE MEANING OF TIME

Many words have synonyms, allowing us to offer variety in our language and thereby avoid excessive repetition and boredom. Some of these same words, however, have no antonym; essentially, there can be no absence of the quality described by the concept. Such a state exists with *time*. Omnipresent and unlimited, time has no commonly accepted beginning or termination in the scientific sense. It may be ignored, but it continues, allowing the events that permit growth, change, expansion, and contraction. Time may bring stress and threat, leading one to discomfort and breakdown at worst or challenge and adaptation at best. There may even be attempts to control time, but the efforts have no effect on the unvarying nature of its passage. It may be viewed as existing in and of itself, independent and autonomous.

The term itself (*time*) comes from the Indo-European expression *dimen*, defined as "to part or divide up." The Anglo-Saxon concept was *tima* and had the same general meaning. There is the implication that time, then, is a period between events. During this period, something may happen and thus restrict the meaning of time to those events that intervened. Implicit, as well, is the implication that there is a measurable quality to time, an issue that has assumed major importance in modern-day science.

Time is so conspicuous and so ubiquitous in our lives that we are apt to assume that there is no need to state its character. Day and night were distinguished in our minds very early in life. More difficult time expressions such as hour, minute, and second were gradually added. A week and a month became meaningful with greater experience. Holidays were easier because of the rewards attached, although it took considerably longer to place their positions within the year. But, almost without exception, we had learned all such dimensions before our childhood was completed.

The operative word here is *learned*. There is no intrinsic basis for awareness of time in any sense except the momentary need to recognize stimulation and to respond in some effective manner to it. Whitrow (1972, p. 9) points out that being able to discriminate time intervals is unique to humans. Every other animal lives in what he calls a "continual present." Because evolution has led to the development of the cortex, we can organize the many experiences we encounter and assess the "relative permanence and succession of changes" (Fraisse, 1981, p. 234).

Having learned the system applied to time relationships in our society, we assume that we have acquired all that is necessary—and even all that is possible. The day consists of 24 hours, separated into daylight and nighttime. Of course, the relationship is not consistent throughout the year, but that seems relatively unimportant. And there is no doubt of the exactness of seconds, minutes, and hours that make up the 24-hour day. Ask yourself, however, why does a day have 24 hours? Where did the 60 in 60 seconds to the minute come from? Why don't we have 24 minutes to the hour and 24 seconds to the minute? That would certainly avoid confusion in some respects. Most persons don't speculate on such matters and would even say that it doesn't matter or that it is a part of some great plan (God's perhaps?) that must not be questioned or changed.

The actual reasons are not nearly so grandiose. As with other matters, in fact, they were adopted as a convenience from past cultures. We can credit the Egyptians with the 24-hour day (Casson, 1965, pp. 146–147). In their system, however, each of the 12 segments of day and night represented one-twelfth of the time between sunrise and sunset. This meant that the length of each segment (an "hour") varied with the season of the year. At one time it might correspond to 52 of our minutes, say, while it could be 64 of our minutes at a different season. Such a system seems unduly confusing so that later, more "civilized" cultures accepted only the equal segments concept: 24 equal "hours" in a day.

This left unaddressed a way to designate the units of time within each of the segments. That issue was solved by accepting Mesopotamian mathematics (Kramer, 1967, p. 159). They had devised a technique that divided the circle into 60 degrees and the hour into the same number of minutes and seconds. (Just why the use of 60 has been lost in time—so to speak.) Being clever enough to recognize a good thing when they saw it, our ancestors simply applied the Mesopotamian math to the Egyptian units and gave us our clear and useful time measurement tools!

Easy enough so far, but only the beginning of a need for definitions if we are to understand what "time" is. In fact, it is necessary to introduce a separate, more complex set of concepts that are essential to appreciating the nature of time. For example, we must learn to distinguish what is "present time" from those experiences that are "past time" and "future time." For many persons, that might seem an easy task. But for those who study time relationships and meanings, the task is not so simple. I may define the "present" as the transitory moment between past and future. It is the *now* of our daily lives. Thus, its existence is so instantaneous as to be almost nonexistent. Further, the present is impermanent and explicitly finite. It lacks reality except as it is compared *to* the past (what was) and future (what will be). The present is the basis for identifying space in time. Indeed, it is what we call "living." As soon as it occurs, life has passed on into the past while we are living in a new present.

The present, in this view then, assumes meaning only in reference to the past and the future. These concepts must be defined as well. For this purpose, I see the past as our permanent record of experience. It is finite in its quality and effect. It is the record against which all experience can be verified. It is reality in the only sense known to human cognition. The past is also the basis for anticipating a future, and it affects the experiences desired and accepted—that is, the interpretations I make of experience and how it is stored in one's memory. It enlarges by encompassing the manifold presents that follow it.

In turn, the future I conceive to be the anticipated present, derived from the prejudiced expectations established by the mind's cataloging of the past. It is infinite within those boundaries but limits the perceived nature of the presents allowed mentally. It can, however, be altered by an unexpected element in experience that then becomes a different present than was expected. However, this new present becomes integrated as a part of the past so that mental equilibrium will be maintained.

An example may help to clarify these definitions, to give them substance that they otherwise lack. I experience at this present moment the stimulation of processing mental information and typing it into the hard drive of my computer, two related but separate actions. Indeed, I now have already had several "presents" in that very process. Those presents are stored in my memory as experiences that I may review (and repeat), should occasion arise. This possibility is necessary in case I reread what I have written at some later time, which is future at the present. However, that "future" will become "past" after all the events ("presents") that precede rereading have become a part of the "past." At the same time, I can anticipate what I need to do next in order to express a continued coordinated sequence to communicate the meaning that I assign to "present," "past," and "future."

Yet other persons would define these concepts somewhat differently. The distinguished psychologist Paul Fraisse (1981, pp. 252–253), for example, speaks of a temporal perspective that is composed of all our stored memories that are used to construct an actual present: a reference basis for such time concepts as a day or week or year. At the same time, he conceives of a perceived present that allows recognition and response to ongoing stimulation. The past, to him, is the basis for all temporal estimations, the "fruit of incessant constructions and reconstructions." The future, in turn, "is sketched out from the perception of time because our present perceptions are signals of what will be happening." Other authorities could be cited with even greater differences than those of Fraisse and this author.

There are many explanations of "time" in the history of humankind, although most are not definitional at all. Consider, for example, the writings of St. Augustine (translated by Pilkington, n.d., pp. 241–242), a revered cleric who grappled with many of the unsolved mysteries of human existence. To him, questions such as one about the nature of time were fruitless because they missed the import of the power of God. To Augustine, time was to be equated to eternity and as such had no independent nature. After describing the misguided attempts by humans to comprehend the eternal, including time, St. Augustine makes comments relevant to our convenient present to past to future trichotomy.

Who shall hold it and fix it, that it may rest a little, and by degrees catch the glory of that ever-standing eternity . . . and let him see that all time past is forced on by the future, and that all the future followeth from the past, and that all, both past and future, is created and issues from that which is always present?

Such a statement may seem unduly confabulated, but the point is one essentially of accepting on faith that a deity is concerned with the eternal, and questions about particulars only separate the unimportant detail from the need to believe.

That point of view may be unsatisfactory, particularly when one considers the concrete explanation of Isaac Newton, a position that was accepted and widely applied (and still is, in the practical sense) from the seventeenth to the twentieth centuries. The central point for this discussion is that Newton proposed that both space and time are absolute and independent. As such, our observations of our world (space) and the experiences we have in it (time) are just as we perceive them. Time is absolute; it flows on in a regular and orderly fashion and is measured by accurate timepieces, wherever we may be located. This seems so practical and logical that it is easy to accept. Indeed, we find that it is quite suitable for our daily lives.

But that assurance was questioned in 1905 when Albert Einstein published his "special theory of relativity." Not an experimentalist, Einstein deduced that there could be no such thing as absolute time (or space or, for that matter, anything else). In fact, everything in the universe is related in a relative sense to everything else. Thorne (1994, p. 72) uses the analogy of a train: "[O]ne can measure a train's velocity only relative to physical objects such as the ground and the air." Motion is relative in this sense. In addition, for our purposes here, time is also relative: there is no way that all of us "must experience the flow of time in the same manner. . . . Each person traveling in his or her own way must experience a different time flow than others, traveling differently." Fortunately, Einstein did not leave us with this dilemma unresolved (but that is a topic to be treated in a later chapter).

Hawking (1996, p. 13) proposes that time had no meaning until the universe began, however that event may have happened. Within that context, an "event is something that happens at a particular point in space and at a particular time" (p. 34). As a result, the event may be specified by its coordinates, three of which are spatial (length, width, and height) and the other of which is time. It really does not matter what coordinates are chosen, since there is no real difference among them. Instead, it is more sensible to think of an event in terms of its position in four-dimensional space, that is, in space and time (pp. 34–35). Perhaps in part because of our reliance on absolute time and space, it is extremely difficult for us to conceive of a four-dimensional spacetime.

DEFINING TIME

So we are still faced with what seems an unsolvable riddle: What is time? In some ways, in over a thousand years we have returned to Augustine's principle: Don't sweat it; believe it. This may seem flippant, but it isn't intended to be. It sets a basis for what Burke (1985, p. 276) has pointed out as the outcome of Newtonian physics.

Newton's universe implied an attitude to knowledge that was at once practical, optimistic and confident. The purpose of science was to investigate reality and to make definitive statements about it. Knowledge advanced certainty. The spread of knowledge was, therefore, desirable.

The position has reaped benefits for 200 years and may still be useful. However, the model is not timeless, and time permits change. Relativity has proven its place in our current lives and will continue to do so until some more needed model requires new vision and enlightened empiricism.

From the practical standpoint, it is more important perhaps to remember that there is no sense of time when we are born, although there is evidence of internal "clocks" that operate in certain behaviors. We must learn what time is and how it impinges on us. Experience influences development on this dimension as in any other. But we may modify our concept of time as we have greater experiences during life. Some persons probably consider time's importance largely in terms of the experiences of childhood and youth. Others, however, encounter experiences throughout adulthood that remold prior learning. The nature of those experiences influences (prejudices) the view held of time. Whether that view is more or less accurate, more or less true, or more or less consistent depends more, then, on which sensations we encounter and respond to than it does to the precise nature of time.

THE CONCEPTS OF TIME

As mentioned earlier, we become acquainted with various dimensions of the expression of time quite early in our lives. We adapt to the environment, and those in it, in terms of the meanings learned for temporal concepts. There would seem no need to define our terms since they are so common. Yet that attitude can be a trap to avoid. Taking the time to give practical, but scientifically accurate, definitions will be helpful in assuring a standard vocabulary as well as an assist in your reading of the remainder of this book.

Time

There seems no better place to begin than with the major construct itself. If we can agree on what time is, it becomes easier to demarcate its dimensions and functions. First, however, we must accept that time is a fundamental element in the physical world, just as height or direction or mass are. Time exists and is continuous regardless of our attempts to control it. We are unable to control or to reverse it, although some physicists today speculate that "time travel," at least to the past, may not be an impossible venture. (This issue I will return to in another part of this book.) You already know time in some of its demands, particularly as it becomes your enemy. Time is of such acute importance that many of us own and wear a wristwatch or pocket watch, with additional reminders of scheduling in our homes, offices, and many public places. I am not alone in the fact that I have a clock with a lighted face next to my bed—and I am retired and don't need to get up to go anywhere! This heavy dependence on time awareness is a relatively recent feature of human behavior. For one good reason, someone had to invent a reasonably accurate measuring device that could be afforded by all who needed or wanted one. This did not occur until the late Middle Ages, with the necessary refinements that resulted in a popular timepiece appearing in the eighteenth century. Swiss watchmaking did not reach a zenith until around 1850. And in this country, affordable (I avoid the term "cheap") and accurate means of telling time became available during the nineteenth century.

Within this history, time has always been a major force, however it might be expressed or judged. A central feature is that time is the dimension *during which* sensations occur. Sensation is the basis for experience, the exact nature of the experience depending on the sensations to which we react, that is, those sensations perceived and responded to. At any moment in time, there are many thousands (perhaps more) sensations that impinge on us. Only a portion of them will be acknowledged by responses, depending on a number of factors. When hungry, for example, we will be most alert to cues about food, whereas an hour later we may direct our attention to sexual stimuli. Meanwhile, the basic element of time proceeds without regard to our preferences, needs, desires, choices. Time is the *medium* in which all life acts, from beginning to end.

The most basic division of time probably always has been in terms of daylight and dark. Behavior during the two differed by adaptation. Certain animals responded more to the environment during the night, avoiding daylight largely and being active only when darkness offered protection. Humans must have been day creatures early in the evolutionary process since the visual system developed in the way it did, buttressed by the other senses, particularly hearing. In any event, the differences between light and darkness assumed more than an interesting departure in time. Activity in the environment was most concentrated in the daylight. During those times, foraging and exploration would have been principally conducted. No doubt the increasing development of the cortex led to greater activity at night, confined though it may have been to observation of the skies rather than of the earth. Krupp (1983, p. 1) has expressed the increasing inclusion of nightly behavior as follows: "Just as the hands of the first people grasped the flints they crafted, so their brains grasped the sky. The regularity of the motions of celestial objects enabled them to orient themselves in time and space." The result of this advancement was to cultivate a sense of cyclical time and the understanding of order and symmetry that pervaded nature and brought predictability. The observations must have assisted the intellectual need to comprehend *why* there are periods of light followed by periods of dark, varying in apparent length with the seasons and the climate. Answers would have been proposed, almost certainly accepted by some and rejected by others, leading to attempts to find even more satisfying answers.

For many millennia, precision in marking time was not a major issue. It was not until the Egyptians, around 2500 B.C., divided the period elapsed in day and night into 12 equal segments each that the variations by time of year had to be confronted. Their solution was to vary the length of each segment (what we call an "hour") according to the season. Not a solution, the Egyptians were nevertheless able to record time on some reasonable basis for relating their history.

Adaptations followed in other cultures with little improvement on precision until the 1600s. Sundials and sand clocks were replaced by mechanical devices with more efficiency and greater portability. Costs were reduced to the point that many persons could own a personal timepiece. But the utility of the devices was negligible if each of them was uncalibrated to a common measure. Today, there are methods to assure that a common and precise system is available for time measurement at any spot in the world.

That fact has emanated from scientific proofs of the relationship of the earth to our solar system. First, there had to be acceptance that the earth (and the other planets) revolved around the sun. The earth was not the center of the universe (even though some religious sects were unwilling to accept that fact for many years, largely because dogma was already in place and hard to resist). Further, the earth itself rotates on its axis and tilts toward and away from the sun, affecting its relationship to the sun from day to day.

Before personal timekeeping became a common activity, the sun and the stars were the markers used to estimate time. As the rotating earth revolves around the sun, the daily pattern of sunrise in the East to sunset in the West helped to define a single day. Further, each "day" was marked by the angle of the sun to any particular point on the earth. Midway in the solar passage, the sun would be directly overhead to the viewer, and that event marked the meridian when the sun has reached its highest point in the sky in the perception of the viewer. We call this point "noon" and have assigned the value of 12 in the 24-hour day. Since different viewers in different parts of the world will have differing lengths of the 24-hour day at different seasons of the year, in the past 200 years the idea of a mean (average) solar day has been used. Thus, differences due to different rates in sun movement are removed. Eco (1994, pp. 187–192) has demonstrated the mental gymnastics involved in solving problems of time and space in former times with a passage that is both amusing and intriguing in its complexity. And he has made the forceful point as well that "[t]he paradoxes of time can indeed unhinge us" (p. 338).

Mean solar time was dependent upon choosing a point in the heavens that permitted accurate measurement. This was accomplished by the use of the vernal equinox, occurring in the spring, usually on March 21 but varying somewhat from year to year due to shifts in the earth's trajectory around the sun. What was done was to establish the equinox by reference to the location of the fixed stars. This "star time" (or sidereal time) became the basis for determining mean solar time. Even so, there is some slight error that leads to a difference between the two. Using mean sidereal time, the earth completes the time for reaching the vernal equinox from one year to the next every 365 days, 6 hours, 9 minutes, and 9.54 seconds. With mean solar time, the earth makes the journey in 365 days, 5 hours, 45 minutes, and 45.5 seconds. The difference is 20 minutes, 24.04 seconds. This is complicated by the fact that the earth does not rotate on its axis in the same motion all of the time *and* that the earth is gradually slowing down. Astronomers today use what is called ephemeris time (using the orbital movements of the earth, moon, and planets) in order to assure absolute accuracy in timekeeping. Fortunately for the rest of us, all the complicated conditions that must be accounted for are unimportant for day-to-day living.

Yet the need to have some accurate demonstration of yearly relationships between earth and heavens has been a practical concern for thousands of years. One of the best examples is the accuracy of the Mayan calendar and the marking of strategic periods of the spring and fall equinoxes and the summer and winter solstices. A dramatic demonstration is found each year at Chichén Itzá in Yucatan when the serpent "walks" down the stairs of the main temple (called El Castillo by the Spaniards). Anyone having the good fortune to experience the event will never forget it. On the March day when I was there, literally thousands of persons were bussed in (or came by other means) to crowd the open terrace in order to see the dramatic happening. Somehow, the Maya were capable of recognizing the relationship of the vernal equinox to the beginning of the spring season. Even more impressive, they were able to design and build a structure that would permit their celebration of the event each year.

Their phenomenal accomplishment is not the only instance of such awareness of time in past civilizations. The Egyptians are a notable example, devising a calendar that reflected the "rhythm of the Nile" (Boorstin, 1983, p. 6). Once in place, the people had a means of knowing the best times to sow and to reap, correlated with the inundation of the river, growth of the crops to maturity, and harvest.

Such ingenious approaches to time expression were more than oddities and geegaws. Indeed, it is "the very purpose of a calendar—a time scheme to hold people together, to ease the making of common plans, such as agreements on the planting of crops and the delivery of goods" (Boorstin, 1983, p. 6). As societies became more complex, the means of measuring time evolved to more sophisticated and accurate levels. The basic elements—making life more standardized—remained at the core of each step.

The Units of Time

Most of us live in a world that treats time as a dimension that still essentially deals with day and night. True, within the daylight hours we must be attentive to our interactions with others, whether in business, social life, or family life. But in many of these interactions, time is only approximate—at least in the sense that a few seconds or even minutes don't matter. When we say that we will meet for lunch about noon, it is not so important that one person shows up at 11:58 and the other at 12:02. "In a few days" may mean only that at some time in the future an action will be carried out.

Time, however, has also become increasingly more precise in many fields of endeavor. Accuracy is more than just convenient; it must be precise to very minute portions of time. This may be seen in the need to calibrate the departure time of a rocket to Mars so that the intersection time will be the most propitious for the purpose. Even in schedules of an earthly nature, however, the need for precision is just as necessary. Airline arrivals and departures constitute an apt example, one of such importance that records are kept and published on the "on-time" performance of each company. Even the lowly appointment can take on an aura of extreme and dire import: if you are notified to be at the Internal Revenue Service office at 8:00 A.M., it seems wise to be there no later than that time. (Of course, you will be left to stew for a while, but you don't dare take a chance.)

In increasing ways, then, precision in time measurement is needed. The familiar and standard units for the purpose remain, but often with a new context added to their definition. The second remains as one-sixtieth of a minute with the lowly role that it plays in daily life. The physical sciences, however, have increasingly refined its expression in ways essential to standardized experimentation. Currently the "second" is represented as 9,192,631,770 periods of the radiation corresponding to the transition between the two hyperfine levels of cesium-133. In case you are not quite up-to-date in your chemistry, cesium is a metallic chemical element that is pliable and tractable. It is the most electropositive of all the elements, and so it is often used in photoelectric cells. Under radiation, wavelengths of electromagnetic energy can be measured precisely. For the purpose of measuring the second, cesium-133 is the preferred medium. As part of the precision currently possible, you might even be interested in knowing that it is possible today to measure at the level of nanoseconds. A nanosecond is one-billionth (10^{-9}) of a second. The next time you make light of a second or so, just remember the scientific importance of your action. And if that's not enough, just think that your great-grandchildren will probably be wearing an atomic wristwatch. Just hope you don't have to pay for it.

The next time element, the minute, puts us on much more secure ground. The term comes from the Latin expression *pars minuta prima*, which means "first minute" and is one-sixtieth of the Babylonian system where there is a division into 60 equal parts (Boorstin, 1983, p. 42). Ptolemy had subdivided the circle into the 60 portions required in the system. In the thirteenth century, the concept was applied to the mechanical clocks that were being produced, primarily for public structures. It was not until the sixteenth century that clocks began to include segments that portrayed the second as well as the minute. What must be remembered is that the measurement of the elemental units (seconds and minutes) is a fairly recent event. Clocks, after all, even as they became more common were features of communities. Initially they did not contain any numbers for the hours since few could have read them even if they were in a position during the day to see them. They *sounded* the time so that one would know when obligations (such as church services) were to be met. It is probable, then, that most people before the seventeenth century had little association with time indicators that became increasingly emphasized as "progress" occurred. Certainly with the beginnings of the Industrial Revolution, clocks assumed an importance never before accorded to them—and people became enslaved (to some degree) by the demands of measured time.

With the concept of the hour there is a continuation in the need for precise measurement but a divergence in the expression of the measure. An hour is composed of 60 minutes and 3,600 seconds, but there are only 24 of them from the time the sun is immediately overhead until it returns to that position. Until the 1700s, the hour was applied only to the period between sunrise and sunset, the "working" time. Since the length of each of the 12 segments would vary by season, no clock would accurately reflect the time unless it was equipped with some means of adapting to the variations. It was not until the Middle Ages that the period from noon to noon (or midnight to midnight, if you prefer) was defined as a "day." Twenty-four equal segments of 60 minutes each was accepted as the criterion (Boorstin, 1983, p. 39). By the eighteenth century the standardization and precision of time measurement were common to civilized nations and almost universal. The nomenclature selected seems to have been arbitrary. Boorstin informs us that the concept "day" comes from the Saxon word that means "to burn," that is, when the sun is warm. "Hour" has evolved from the Greek and Latin, referring to the time between sunlight and darkness as much as the equal units might vary from one season to another (p. 41). Why there should be 24 hours in a day, even in our sophisticated era, is speculative. With such apparent capriciousness in the decisions about the basic divisions of time, it is amazing how much progress has occurred in our ability to use it. Perhaps this tells us more about the inconsequential nature of our labels than it does about the constancy of any dimension of measurement.

The earth rotates on its axis, and the period of time that it takes to return to a particular point in reference to the sun we call a "day." However, that period is not fixed since the earth varies in the time that it takes to complete its orbit. To avoid the problems in differences in time from one day to the next, an average of the times over a year is used as the basis for a definition of the "solar day." Thus, the hour from 3:00 P.M. to 4:00 P.M. is the same as that between 9:00 A.M. and 10:00 A.M. whether it is fall or spring, summer or winter. Such measurement is no more than a convenience but one that "works" for our ordinary lives. Every day is "exactly" 24 hours.

There is a change again when we come to the next temporal segment that is widely used. The label "week" comes from the Latin *vicis*, which my high school Latin teacher pronounced "weekis." The word actually means "change" and was applied by the Hebrews to a unit of time that encompassed the period necessary for the Creation and a day of rest. Other societies did not follow the same nomenclature; for example, the Romans had an eight-day segment, changing it to seven only after the conversion of Constantine and the adoption of Christianity as the state religion. By contrast, the names given to the days in the week are purely pagan. Most are Celtic: Tui (Tuesday), Woden (Wednesday), Thor (Thursday), and Frygga (Friday). In other instances the names of planets are used: Sol (Sunday), Moon (Monday), and Saturn (Saturday). Our week gives us a marker through the year so that certain established ceremonial days (such as church on Sunday) will be continued and work times can be standardized. Other special events may vary, such as vacation time and national holidays (increasingly moving to a Monday in order to permit a longer weekend).

The seven-day week does not fit neatly into a year with 365.25 days. Every four years we have to "catch up" with solar time, and so one day is added. In turn, of course, this throws off track other established days for events: Memorial Day, for example, is always the first Monday in September, but the date will vary. This is one reason calendars remain both viable and eminently helpful. The week has served its purpose, of course, by reflecting the religious concept that the universe was created in 6 days with 1 day for rest. In more recent times, the religious element is only indifferently addressed. Instead, the emphasis is upon the days for labor. Gradually, the push by unions for a 40-hour workweek has limited even some businesses to five days for production and two days for rest. At the same time, shifts became popular so that three eight-hour periods could be used for production. That concept has been extended to service agencies as well. All-night drive-ins and facilities are the mark of progress in small cities as well as large. What this indicates is that the week is the ultimate convenience for social purposes.

As the label would indicate, the month is a tribute to the revolution of the moon about the earth. It takes about 28 days for this event to be completed. But a calendar that uses this unit to reflect the year would require around 13 months. Since 12 months was the already accepted standard for a year, the calendar month varies from 28 to 31 days. It would do no good to use more precise astronomical measures of a month. The lunar month, for example, averages 29.53059 days and is the time needed for the moon to complete all phases. On the other hand, the sidereal month is reflected in the time needed for the moon to make a revolution from a given star back to that same star; this takes 27.32166 days. There are other measures of the month, but the confusion is surely already enough. Imagine what chaos resulted when calendar reform in the sixteenth century required "losing" 10 days (Duncan, 1998, pp. 209–232). It seems best to leave things as they are: an inexact measure of time that has become operational by convenience.

There are just as many different measures of the year astronomically. Depending upon the criteria used, the year ranges from 365 days, 5 hours, 48 minutes, 45.5 seconds to 365 days, 6 hours, 13 minutes, 53.1 seconds. By adjusting our calendars every four years, we manage to overcome some of the difficulties introduced by tradition and convenience. It is interesting to note, however, that Semitic societies have continued to use a calendar for religious purposes that is based upon the lunar month, leading to a year of 354 days. One must accordingly live by one calendar for one purpose and another calendar for other social activities.

Currently there are time dimensions that could not have been anticipated by the ancients. Astronomers today use the light-year to measure the distance that light travels in a mean solar year. Light is known to travel at 186,000 miles per second. In a year's time, a ray of light will cover nearly 6 trillion miles, that is, 5,880,000,000,000 miles. Without much meaning to most of us, the measure is essential to accuracy in measuring objects in space and in space travel. An additional time measure in astronomy is the parsec, equal to 3.26 light-years. The corresponding number is more than 19 trillion miles (19,168,800,000,000).

Now we return to the more blissful state of ignorance. However, remember that atomic watch I mentioned earlier, the one your great-grandchildren might wear? Well, it may turn out to be a refinement on a cesium-133 timepiece such that interstellar communication will be feasible and available—and instantaneous. I wonder if Timex will have a suitable product? And in designer styles and colors?

CHAPTER 2

The Heralds of Time

The sophistication with which we measure time today would be a marvel indeed to those who made significant contributions in the past. Yet, in their own way, the accomplishments of preceding generations are just as astounding and impressive. Full knowledge of the progress of awareness and complexity in recognizing and measuring time is hidden from us by the fact that written records did not begin for thousands of years after the evolution of humankind and that most marvelous of organs—the brain—began.

We can only guess at the steps that led eventually to a means to predict the seasons, the special days important to religious ceremonies, and the proper times to sow and to reap. It seems no stretch, however, to propose that the beginnings were in observations of the heavens. There were activities that could only be accomplished during daylight hours, even after harnessing of fire. But the nights could not be ignored, and there must have been increasing curiosity about the planets that could be observed, even if there was no awareness of what their true nature might be. Certain stars would be found in approximate positions nightly; others would seem to move with time through the year; but all showed some pattern that must have impressed the thinkers of that day.

Events could be calibrated with heavenly sightings early in humankind's development, leading to rationales for their relationships, no matter how far-fetched those explanations may seem to us today. One of the more significant relationships that must have occurred fairly early in prerecorded history was crucial to self-identity and consciousness: the acceptance of orientation in time and space. The sun in the day and the stars at night were surely an essential part of a person's awareness of a conscious nature, acceptance of an *I* that functions to assure meaning to life and purpose to personal actions.

No small part of this accomplishment would have been that orientation to the heavens also brought the knowledge that nature is stable (relatively) despite seasonal changes and transitory aberrations in life. Stability means security, and change provides cues to use for survival. Given such enlightenment, regardless of whether it was understood philosophically or scientifically, the basis for curiosity about all nature and its reflections must have been gradually but inevitably increased. Curiosity leads to conjecture, to experimentation, to trial and error behavior that at times would have been dangerous but also challenging. Over thousands of years humankind would have progressed to the point that skill and invention were recognized and rewarded. Each tiny step made a contribution to freeing the people from the constraints of ignorance and fear. Intellect could develop and allow increasingly significant accomplishments.

There must be countless ways in which this premise was demonstrated. Humans discovered fire, learned its dangers but also its uses. Speech began and made communication possible, at first in concrete and then in abstract ways. Expression in artistic effort became common. Design in implements and practical objects would have allowed both function and beauty. Events could be portrayed on the walls of caves and, later, residences. Grains and vegetables could be cultivated, then improved, and finally made consistent in quantity and quality. Social groupings became more refined. Intercourse between groups reduced the need for conflict and permitted the exchange of goods, ideas, and beliefs. Language would have become the shortcut to communication. The day came when someone invented a symbol for a meaning, a symbol that could be drawn and used by all those who practiced a given language. Now written history was not only plausible, but it became the tool that recorded accomplishments of individuals and societies. This step freed humans from an orientation in time that was largely present to one that included past as well. What is now and what was then could become what will be tomorrow.

For each of the instruments used to measure time, there has been at least one (and often several other) creator. As is true for so many of the great inventions of our history, the visionaries and artisans of the past deserve their share of the actual accomplishment. The names of many of those persons, unfortunately, have not been preserved, partially because the records are incomplete and partially because in much of human history the patron of the act (a king or lord) has been cited as the source. Any history of timekeeping before the Reformation and Renaissance certainly will be spotty at best. That, however, does not reduce our debt to the past nor preclude as much citation as possible in a limited space.

Prehistory is only an educated guess. But there had to be progress made, no matter how slowly, in recognizing the relationship between humans and temporal events. Early on, that would have meant at least dealing with time as it related to natural consequences: when to sow and when to harvest or when to make appeals to certain gods and when to appeal to yet others, for example. Particular and important events, then, would be one way of directing behavior in terms of its time importance. Each day (that is, the daylight hours) would be a seminal basis of time differentiation, followed closely by the year with its cycles of seasons and astronomical observations (Whitrow, 1991, pp. 14–15).

The emphasis upon the heavens as the portender and cause of human events increased steadily, and by the eighteenth to fifteenth centuries B.C., careful observation and charting of the sky was an important function of the priests (p. 31). "Signs" were interpreted for their implications of good and evil. By the fifth century B.C., astrology was extended to forecasting life events, particularly for the leaders of Indo-European societies. The resulting emphasis upon the stars for predicting a person's future contributed to the acceptance of time as cyclical in nature, whereby all things are already experienced and will be reexperienced in future time (p. 31). Calendars were plotted to show the placement of the celestial bodies, with particular emphasis on the phases of the moon.

By 500 B.C. astronomer-priests knew that the year based on seasons did not correspond with that based on astronomical observations (p. 36). Calendars needed to be plotted on that fact and the necessary adjustments made. For example, the equinoxes (days when there are equal daylight and night hours) will vary and be precessed (that is, earlier with each sidereal year). As the earth rotates on its axis there is a slight westward movement of the equinoctial points along the ecliptic. In the course of 26,000 years, this movement will have assumed the function of a cone. The importance of this deviation is that calendars must be revised periodically, as happened with the calendar year of 1582 under Pope Gregory XIII.

TIME IN THE CLASSIC PERIOD

With the development of a written language, records could be accumulated and stored. Our knowledge of individual accomplishments was greatly enhanced, although not completely met, as a result. One center of scientific endeavor worthy of some survey was that of classical Greece and Rome. The accomplishments were both practical and scientific, marking some significant strides on the way to understanding the heavens and humankind's relationships to the "arrow of time."

Vitruvius was a Roman architect who had interest in the manifold ways in which citizens were served by the mechanisms of his age. Around 300 B.C. he described a clock he had observed that had a rotating dial on which were depicted the signs of the zodiac. This dial was part of a clepsydra (water clock) so that it could be moved to reflect the rotations of the signs in the heavens. The movement of the dial was controlled by a float that gradually sank into an outflow opening as time (and water) flowed. Thus, observers could be kept aware of the positions of the planets and stars at all times. Fraser (1987, p. 49) notes that the use of the zodiac as a part of a clock dial would be continued in later eras, even after mechanical clocks were invented. The astrological significance of the heavens continued in popularity and may still be seen even today on clocks, despite that fact that many persons no longer understand or believe in the zodiacal signs as they did in ancient times.

About the same time (around 260 B.C.), a Greek astronomer named Aristarchus of Samos made ingenious observations concerning the actual size of the moon. Brennen (1997, p. 3) describes him as "generally considered the most successful of Greek astronomers," and he certainly was clever in his approach. Since instruments were not available to provide him with tools to his task, he reasoned that an eclipse of the moon could yield the datum he needed to estimate its size. Upon such an occurrence, he noted the size of the shadow thrown by the earth. This gave him the information needed in order to make an accurate estimation. It should be noted as well that Aristarchus proposed that the motions of the heavenly bodies could be judged most accurately if the assumption were made that the earth revolved around the sun, rather than vice versa. This heliocentric hypothesis was correct but, despite its reappearing occurrence in history, failed to receive acceptance for hundreds of years except by a handful of scientists. Instead, the proposals of Aristotle were more acceptable to religious dogma and were imposed uncritically. Even Copernicus and Galileo, in the seventeenth century A.D., felt threatened for their exposition of the heliocentric theory.

Many ancient scholars were talented and original in their attempts to understand and explain the natural phenomena of their surroundings. Eratosthenes (who lived from about 276 to 194 B.C.) is an apt example of such persons. The greatest achievement of Eratosthenes probably was his measurement of the earth, using a method that proved astoundingly close to the true measure. At noon on the summer solstice (June 21), he had been informed that a well in the town of Syene, south of Alexandria, had no shadow, while a shadow was found on that date in his own city. He reasoned that if he could measure the length of the shadow at Alexandria at the same time as no shadow was found in Syene, he could calculate the circumference of the earth. What was needed was the distance between the two points so that he could apply geometry to the problem. Information provided to him by travelers led him to conclude that the actual distance must be about 5,000 stadia (a stadium is about 607 feet in modern measure). He thus calculated the circumference of the earth to be equivalent to 28,700 miles of our measure. His figure was about 15% too high, but it remained as the accepted measure until modern times (Boorstin, 1983, p. 96).

This brings us to the celebrated Archimedes (287–212 B.C.), called by Brennan (1997, pp. 3–4) "the most eminent scientist and mathematician of ancient times." He is noted particularly for his skill in converting theory to practical use. It was he who worked out the principle of the lever and thereby proved mathematically that a small weight at a distance from a fulcrum would balance a large weight near the fulcrum. Thus, the weights and distances were in inverse proportion. He is reputed to have said, "Give me a place to stand on, and I can move the world." Luckily, no one made an offer. Archimedes is also notable for his contributions in movement of water from one level to another (the "screw of Archimedes") and the discovery of the principles of buoyancy.

Cicero wrote of a water clock that Archimedes invented that reproduced the relative motions of the heavenly bodies (Whitrow, 1991, p. 99). Thus Archimedes seems to deserve the mantle of greatness awarded him both for his scientific accomplishments and for his ability to harness them to the practical matters of everyday life.

Before the time of Julius Caesar, Roman contributions to the development of time measurement were limited. The calendar that was in vogue was subject to increasing errors that were compounded by the political manipulations exercised in order to benefit the politicians who were in office. By the time that Caesar became emperor, the confusions in the calendar were so great that the need for reform was evident (Meier, 1995, p. 447). Fortunately, Caesar saw that need and decided to deal with it rather than to use it only to his advantage. He sought the advice of the Greek astronomer Sosigenes and instituted basic improvements.

The Roman calendar was based on the lunar month, with the consequent need to add (intercalate) days in order to keep the calendar in some accuracy with the natural sequence of time. Caesar, in 46 B.C., made corrections in intercalations and added 67 days between November and December. The year was extended to 445 days as a result. The effort was successful enough, however, that the Julian calendar remained in use with only minor changes until gross errors had again accumulated, reformed by Pope Gregory XIII in the sixteenth century.

Ptolemy has earned a reputation by his work in three fields: mathematics, astronomy (and astrology), and geography. Unfortunately, his most basic conclusions have proven to be false. Nevertheless, he exercised considerable influence about such matters until 1600.

Claudius Ptolemaeus of Alexandria, as his parents named him, lived from A.D. 90 to 168. His astronomical observations produced what is still referred to as the "Ptolemaic system." He conceived the earth as a sphere around which the universe revolved and thus proposed a significant error. The heavenly bodies made circular movements, he maintained, and thereby missed the truth of the paths that the stars follow in their sojourn. Despite placing the earth at the center of the universe and declaring that the paths of the planets and stars are circular, he did recognize some significant scientific realities. For example, he proposed the basic tenet of science: When trying to explain phenomena, the simplest possible hypothesis should be stated as long as it is not contradicted by data. He also maintained that when using observations where exactness is necessary, it is best to accept those that have been gathered over longer intervals of time. The result will be stability (reliability) of measurement that is greater than it will be where shorter time intervals are used. With these principles, Ptolemy may be said to have defined and fostered elemental procedures of scientific inquiry.

His writings also were concerned with such matters as the length of lunar months, the construction of the astrolabe (used at the time to find the altitude of a star, significant for navigators as well as astronomers), and the dimensions of the earth, sun, and moon. Ptolemy made significant contributions in geography as well. Using the work of Hipparchus, who had divided the equatorial circle into 360 parts (degrees), Ptolemy mapped the "known world" of his day. Here, too, he made a fundamental error that reduced each degree of latitude and longitude to 50 geographical miles rather than the actual 60. His efforts did allow him to develop a method of conical projection, a feature of map construction, so that meridian circles could be represented as straight lines that converged at a single point: a pole. Latitude, in this system, was shown as a series of circles from a central point, the equator.

Despite the errors, Ptolemy exercised a strong control in astronomy and geography until the revolution in science that came with the Renaissance, particularly during the fifteenth and sixteenth centuries. His record may be said to be "mixed" as a result. "But never since Ptolemy has anyone provided so comprehensive a survey of the whole scientific knowledge of an age" (Boorstin, 1983, p. 20).

As the Christian era expanded its influence in the Western world, church scholars became increasingly influential in scientific belief and practice. Philosophically, explanations about the action and meaning of the deity's power were extended into all areas. St. Augustine (A.D. 354–430), for example, wrote that time and the world must be considered as separate entities. They were, however, to be considered as created together. Before the Creation, there was only a timeless void (Fraser, 1987, p. 102). Time, then, began at a specific point in order to serve particular needs. By inference, when that need has been met (the Lord's plan), time would no longer be useful to His purposes and would apparently be negated.

St. Benedict, in the early sixth century A.D., began the practice of strict scheduling of activities throughout the year. Fraser associates this implementation of rules for monks in the order as an expression of the calendar (pp. 90–91). Orders to be followed by the monks, and the times at which they will be practiced, formed the basis not only for events in holy orders but, in some respects, for society at large. With continuing time, such calendrical expressions were accepted by the Catholic Church and promulgated in the hours of the day, week, month, and year.

THE MIDDLE AGES

The Middle Ages were for many years called "the Dark Ages" because of the apparent lack of progress during the era. Now historians seem to avoid the pejorative term, in large part because the period was not so backward as first believed. Running over a 1,200-year interval (from about A.D. 300 to 1500), there were aspects that were certainly nonprogressive, but that is not the same thing as the regression suggested by use of the term "Dark" (see Cantor, 1993, for a scholarly treatment of this issue).

The influence of time during this era was a limited role. Burke (1985, pp. 93–95) tells us that there was little awareness of time in the modern sense because there were few calendars, almost no clocks, and scant written records. Time was noted by "memorable" events, however those might be defined. In most instances, that would include personal incidents in the lives of people. In the countryside the seasons would be a major cue for behavioral reactions. In towns and cities there might be a sundial or a water clock (but only if there were the wealthy who could afford one), but few persons would pay any attention to them. Instead, there would be a watchman who called the hours from a church steeple. Workers in the fields would relay the calls to their fellow peasants who were further out. There was no need for any time element less than an hour because life moved only at a natural pace.

Given the social structure and political controls of the Middle Ages, it is no surprise that fewer accomplishments related to time occurred than might be expected during a 1,200-year period. There were, however, some results that fitted the tenor of the times.

In Spain, a man called El Sabio (the Wise) encouraged the study of astronomy by sanctioning the development of a set of astronomical tables to denote the occurrence of heavenly events important for various ceremonies and purposes. The scientist responsible for the work was Rabbi Isaac ben Sid of Toledo. The tables were published in 1277 in *Libros de saber de astronomica* (Books of knowledge of astronomy). Included in the volume were descriptions of devices for measuring time, for example, a mercury clock. Unfortunately, the clock had no escapement so that the measurement was subject to considerable error. Whitrow (1991, pp. 102–103) concludes that the escapement feature must have been added to clocks (making them mechanical) between 1280 and 1300.

Originally mechanical clocks had no dial; indeed, for most persons of the era such detail of time measurement was neither required nor wanted.

Instead, the clock rang on the hour—a sufficient marker of time for peasant, monk, and lord. It appears that Jacopo de' Dondi, of Chioggia, Italy, was the first to affix a face so that both sound and sight (or either alone) could be used to tell time (Boorstin, 1983, p. 45).

Jacopo's son, Giovanni, created the usual mechanical representation of the universe but added an intriguing and useful feature. There was a dial that acted as a perpetual calendar, showing all the religious feasts (both fixed and movable) as well as the motions of the sun, moon, and planets (Whitrow, 1991, p. 105).

Filippo Brunelleschi (1377–1446) showed mechanical aptitude from his early youth. His father recognized his talents and enrolled him in the guild of goldsmiths. With time he learned geometry and the means to achieve perspective so that he became an adept sculptor. With added study, he became a proficient engineer.

It is possible that it was Brunelleschi who realized that one could use a coiled piece of metal (that is, a spring) as a means of force. Attached to a machine, the spring, if strong enough, could drive the mechanism for useful purposes. One accomplishment by him using this idea was a clock. The spring-driven mechanism assured more regularity and therefore more accurate timekeeping (Boorstin, 1983, p. 50). The idea was so ingenious and so obviously useful that other engineers began to apply the idea widely, with many sorts of machinery.

Obviously, there was advancement even in the period called the Middle Ages when there was little emphasis on finding ways to improve the quality of life of all persons. In total, however, one would have to conclude that the progress made was slow and hardly impressive.

Other cultures showed similar instances of brilliance that were not always appreciated beyond the transitory and self-indulgent impulses of a ruler or high official. An example of such a condition is mirrored by the widely recognized "heavenly clockwork" created by the Chinese engineer Su Sung. Su lived during the eleventh century A.D. and was a valued servant of the then-current emperor of the Sung dynasty in northern China. The emperors were not mere mortals but gods without peer—and without restraints. Any action ordered must be carried out and could result in reward or penalty with impunity.

Because of faithful and honest service in the past, Su was ordered by his emperor to build an astronomical clock in a design that was to be the most beautiful and practical ever devised: a "Water-Powered Armillary Sphere and Celestial Globe Tower" (Fraser, 1987, p. 53).

Su Sung accepted the task (he really had no choice) and set about creating the clockwork for the emperor's delight and use. When finished in 1090, the clock was a five-story structure, much like a pagoda, and was 30 feet high (Boorstin, 1983, p. 61). The top platform contained a bronze power-driven (by water) armillary sphere that contained a rotating globe of the heavens. On each of the five levels, Su designed sets of manikins that processed carrying bells and gongs set to ring at established times. The clockwork inside the tower was three stories high, driven by water flowing at ground level. A set of scoops, set on a vertical rotating wheel, alternately filled and emptied (p. 61).

There were musical instruments mounted to sound every quarter-hour. The concatenation was sufficient to reverberate throughout the structure. The escapement, responsible for assuring accuracy in time measurement, depended upon the fluid quality of water to provide the motion needed to operate the mechanical timepiece.

The next ruler abandoned Su's monumental timepiece, and it was destroyed. Perhaps the fate of Su Sung's invention is an apt representation of the mentality operating in the Middle Ages in Europe as well. There was great potential in all facets of life but far too few opportunities for expression. There had to be a change in the view of humankind's purpose, meaning, and freedom. That change began during the Renaissance, opening the floodgates that led to the scientific advances of the modern era.

RENAISSANCE AND REFORMATION

Change seldom, if ever, shows a sudden and dramatic turn in history, although there has been an acceleration as communication and sophistication have increased. There has been more change in many areas of life in this century than has ever occurred before. The nineteenth century showed more than the eighteenth, and so on, back into history. The 1,200-year period known as the Middle Ages was replaced by an animus and intent that seemed radical at the time. There certainly was a rebirth in the sense that dormant attitudes toward science and turgid efforts at research began to improve. A considerable part of that effort came about because individual freedoms were fostered. Education was improved and original thought and reason were rewarded. The accomplishments from about 1500 to 1650 were the result of such attainments, particularly by individuals who are still renowned for their creativity.

A major figure of the early Renaissance was Nicholas Copernicus (1473–1543), a scientist who began the "revolution" that moved science from the relatively rigid and restricted techniques and systems of the ancients into a more resourceful and ingenious form. Copernicus proposed that the commonly used tables of planetary positions could be plotted more accurately if the earth revolved around the sun. He followed, therefore, the original proposition of Aristarchus but preceded the proposal of Galileo. Copernicus's most innovative contribution was that he described mathematically how such a system would work. The physical vision was changed: the order of the planets now explained phenomena (such as why Mercury and Venus always appeared close to the sun) that had previously baffled earth-centric science (Brennan, 1997, p. 5).

His proposal also offered a valid explanation for the precession of equinoxes (that is, their occurrence on March 21 and September 21 except in certain years). The earth's tilt on its axis and its journey around the sun were the explanations. The Catholic Church banned his work, titled *De Revolutionibus*, as heretical. This led to its subsequent suppression. But, as always, the effort was not totally successful, and scholars across Europe became familiar with the argument proposed by Copernicus as well as his mathematical proofs that were then subject to test.

Ugo Boncompagni was born in 1502, entering the Church at a young age and taking the vows. He was trained in law and taught for a time at the University of Bologna. He moved up in the hierarchy of the Church, going to Rome in 1539, where he participated in the Council of Trent. His efforts on behalf of the Church led to his becoming a cardinal in 1565. In 1572 he was elected pope and chose the name Gregory XIII.

A major accomplishment was his sponsorship of the reform of the Julian calendar in 1582. Religious holidays had become displaced and difficult to keep in an orderly fashion, particularly Easter with its import for Christian belief and practice. A complicated formula had been devised that allowed the event to be near the equinox (March 21) but separated from Jewish Passover (Fraser, 1987, p. 80). The new calendar was to be put into practice immediately with its acceptance by the pope. If not used, the threat of excommunication was present. Needless to say, Catholic countries put the calendar into immediate use. Since England was Protestant, however, the more accurate calendar was not accepted until 1752. Russia adopted it in 1918 and Turkey in 1927. Fraser notes that in the 1980s there were still at least 40 different calendars in use in some country or other (p. 84).

Tycho Brahe (1546–1601), whose astronomical observatory was an advanced center of discovery, was ingenious in his invention of instrumentation. His tools lacked the precision that would come with later telescopes, yet he managed to gather data that were the most accurate available at the time (Dobbs and Jacob, 1995, p. 40).

After Tycho Brahe moved to Prague, following the accession of Christian IV in Norway and the subsequent loss of royal support, Johannes Kepler became his assistant. Kepler also was gifted and continued the work of Brahe while adding his own influences.

Johannes Kepler lived from 1571 to 1630. Sickly as a child, he was placed in a seminary at age 6 in order to become a theologian. By the time he was 17, his genius was demonstrated in a brilliant examination performance for his baccalaureate degree. As a result, he was admitted to the University of Tübingen. One of his studies introduced him to the work of Copernicus and helped him decide to become an astronomer. In 1594, at age 23, he was awarded the chair in astronomy at Gratz.

His duties in the university required that he have a knowledge of astrology (still a respected basis for horoscopes at that time), so he studied the writings of Ptolemy and Cardan for the purpose. He tested the adequacy of astrological predictions by making applications to experiences in his own life. More significantly, he decided that there must be some "intelligence" that ordered and ruled the solar system and that force must operate to affect our daily lives. His results were published in 1596 and were accepted and praised. One of the outcomes was his contacts with Tycho Brahe and Galileo.

When Brahe died, Kepler became the director of the Prague observatory. He continued work on astronomical tables already partially completed (Dobbs and Jacob, 1995, p. 43), but he also practiced astrology, using it to cast the horoscope of Emperor Rudolph and Baron Wallenstein, among others. He defended his practice by claiming that "Nature" had provided astrology as an adjunct to astronomy. Thus he found grounds for superstition and science to lie in the same bed, perhaps because to do otherwise would have cost him his sinecure if not his life.

Kepler's major contributions lay in his success in showing that physical causation can be discovered and then used to replace subjective, and often irrational, guesswork. The study of optics became his basis for a valid law concerning refraction, as one example. As another, he plotted the orbit of Mars, a major stumbling block to then-current theories of the heavens. The result was his set of the critical principles of astronomy: the elliptical nature of the orbits of the planets and the law of equal areas. He also showed that the tides are influenced by the moon and thereby established the first of several basic truths about gravity.

Kepler completed his astronomical tables in 1627, and they remained the most trustworthy source for computations for the next hundred years. The research proving that the planes of planetary orbits cross the center of the sun and that the sun is the primary source of our solar system has been used to call him the "Father of Physical Astronomy."

Julius Caesar Scaliger (1484–1558) had served as a soldier before he retired and adopted philosophy as his raison d'être. He achieved a reputation as the greatest interpreter of the physics and metaphysics of Aristotle in his day. Scholars such as Gottfried Wilhelm von Leibnitz, during the seventeenth century, praised his work.

Scaliger made another contribution of significant meaning to science. He fathered and nurtured a son, Joseph Justus Scaliger, who has been called the greatest scholar of his day (and thus a worthy successor to his father). Joseph's work with time focused on chronology and astronomy. In 1579 he published a commentary on the astronomical work of ancient scholars, a volume that acted as an introduction to *De emendatione temporum*. In this volume he revolutionized the then-current ideas that only the Greeks and Romans had made important contributions to chronology. His method

used the science of Copernicus applied to the calendars and time computations of the past.

Following the success of *De emendatione temporum*, he continued research and speculation upon his findings. One result was the reconstruction
of Eusebius's *Chronicle*, considered a major resource about antiquity and
the dating and ordering of events in time. The publication of this work in
1606 as *Thesaurus temporum* included the restoration and arrangement of
every chronological relic still available in Greek and Latin.

Clocks had been available in some form for centuries—from sundials to
clepsydras to mechanical. The pocket watch was not introduced until the
sixteenth century, probably by a clockmaker in Augsburg named Peter
Henlein (Boorstin, 1983, p. 68). The new contraption was not an instant
hit, however. Few could afford, or even wanted, the device, so the abundance we know today would take another 200 years to become evident.

A more practical device was devised by John Davis in 1595. At sea,
measurement of latitude during the day was difficult because the sun must
be faced and error could result from its blinding effects. Davis created the
quadrant, an improvement since it allowed the seaman to stand with the
sun at his back as he measured the latitude (Boorstin, 1983, p. 48).

The sixteenth and seventeenth centuries were a time between epochs: a
spirit of science that ruthlessly sought truth over faith and a decadent religious spirit that resisted and suppressed any entry into freedom for the
common man. No figure stands taller during this time than Galileo Galilei,
who had to pay a severe penance for his audacity in thought and experiment. He was the son of a mathematician and musician (a combination
not uncommon among the erudite of the period) who as a child showed
unique talent for mechanical invention. Later he studied medicine at the
University of Pisa at the same time that he continued enlarging his perspectives on life: music, art, philosophy, astronomy, to name only a few.

At the age of 17, Galileo observed a lamp in the cathedral as it swung
after being lighted and released. It seemed apparent to him that, whatever
the range of motion, every arc was completed in the same amount of time.
Experimentation validated his observation. He then applied the principle
to the human pulse, finding confirmation of the rule. Other important discoveries soon followed: hydrostatic balance (related to the pressure of equilibrium of liquids); the center of gravity in solids; the basic principles of
dynamics; a demonstration that objects of different weights all move with
the same velocities. This last was proven beyond doubt by experiments
conducted on the moon by astronaut Gordon Scott. Similarly, Galileo
showed that the path of a projectile is a parabola, the curve formed by the
intersection of a cone with a plane parallel to its side.

From an early belief in the validity of Copernican cosmology, Galileo
produced a telescope with three times the magnification of available models
and continued his experiments until he achieved a power of 32. He man-

ufactured telescopes and found a ready market throughout Europe where the spirit of enquiry about nature was growing rapidly. In 1610 he published *Sidereus Nuncius*, containing descriptions of the mountainous surface of the moon. Further, he was able to demonstrate that the Milky Way is a collection of stars and that Jupiter has satellites.

But these accomplishments were merely prologue. The acceptance of his telescopic findings encouraged him to take a public stand supporting Copernicus—that is, that the sun is the center of our universe, not the earth. The research described, however, was at variance with biblical scriptures and the philosophies of the ancient scholars most acceptable to the Catholic Church. He was warned by Church officials to confine his efforts to physical data. In 1616 the Church decided that his position that the sun is fixed and the earth (and other planets) revolve around it was heretical. Pope Paul V told him to abandon the condemned position, and Galileo agreed.

For several years he kept his promise, but in 1632 he published *Diagolo dei due massimi sistemi del mundo*, a book whose content was in conflict with his promise to remain silent about the heliocentric theory. Widely accepted among scholars, the volume was unacceptable to the Church, sales of the book were forbidden, and he was cited by the Inquisition. In 1633, despite being elderly and infirm, he was forced to go to Rome, where he was questioned by the Inquisition. Threatened with torture, Galileo recanted. He was sentenced to imprisonment at any time the tribunal pleased and was required to recite scripture daily for three hours as penance. Upon his release from examination after several days, he went into retreat at his villa in Arcetri, near Florence. His work continued with a publication in 1636 (*Dialoghi della nuove scienze*) that summarized many of his early experiments and advanced his ideas on the principles of mechanics. This treatise also received great honors. He then made application of the pendulum to the regulation of clocks, work that Christiaan Huygens used later to great effect.

In several ways (inferences of gravitation, the mechanics of force and its interdependence with motion) his theories were the antecedents of major achievements by others, including Newton, in the next century.

Clockmakers became important persons for their skills during the early seventeenth century, a position they were to maintain in the next century. David Ramsey is a good example. His art led to his selection as a Page of the Bedchamber and Keeper of the King's Clocks and Watches under James I. James gave him a pension of £200 a year in 1613 and even increased that sum by £50 during the same year. By 1618 he had become Chief Clockmaker to the crown (Baillie, Clutton, and Ilbut, 1956, pp. 269–270). James I died in 1625, but Ramsey's services were valuable enough that he was retained by Charles I. Ramsey even received the notoriety of serving as the basis for a character in Sir Walter Scott's *The Fortunes of Nigel*. In the book he is described as "the keeper of a shop to the eastward of Temple Bar" (pp. 269–270).

Even more famous and significant was Thomas Tompion (1639–1713). His skill eventuated in the English clockmakers establishing supremacy in the science by the end of the seventeenth century. His first break was an acquaintance with Robert Hooke, who asked him to make an accurate quadrant. The product was so successful that Hooke employed him to help establish Hooke's precedence over Huygens in the development of the spiral balance spring. This effort brought Tompion to the attention of Charles II and subsequent recognition as the leading clockmaker of his time.

Tompion was the first person to make clocks for the Greenwich Observatory in 1676. He was a craftsman rather than an inventor, so he depended on others to employ his skills. From his association with Hooke, he was the first Englishman to apply the spiral balance spring to a watch. His work was so good that his watches were demanded in France, where Huygens's products were already available.

In 1695 he collaborated with others in a patent for an escapement with a horizontal escape wheel, although it was limited to moving in only one direction rather than two. George Graham joined him in his shop in 1695 and married into the family with Tompion's niece (Tompion never married). That same year Tompion made the first clock that showed both solar and mean time. The instrument is still housed in Buckingham Palace (Baillie, Clutton, and Ilbut, 1956). During his lifetime he built around 650 clocks and 5,500 watches. Wisely, he began to number his pieces around 1680, a practice that assured adequate recognition of his work.

RATIONALITY TO ENLIGHTENMENT

The last half of the seventeenth and all of the eighteenth centuries were a time of frenzied scientific activity and advances. One of the leaders was Robert Boyle (1627–1691). At age 17 he began systematic study and research on the sciences, becoming a member of the "Invisible College." This group was dedicated to fostering a modern philosophy of science. His personal research was directed to the properties of air, publishing his findings in 1660. Boyle stated the law that the volume of a gas varies inversely to its pressure.

His interests also included changing base metals into gold and silver, not uncommon as a search in those days. Needless to say, he didn't have much luck—but he wasn't criticized harshly either. Boyle was also interested in chemistry and became active, producing more defensible research in this area. Among his pronouncements was the view that matter is composed of "corpuscles" of several types and sizes, having the ability to arrange themselves in groups, each of which was a chemical substance. The means by which this was accomplished was not explained, but his theory of corpuscular composition was accepted as plausible and remained in some vogue until modern times.

Boyle studied the chemistry of combustion and that of respiration as well. He had interest in physiology as well so that his activity in the sciences was widespread. In his personal life he was a strong proponent of discipline and freedom. This attitude, he felt, must be applied to scientific research and human behavior. Boyle, and other persons with this progressive view, believed that everything in this world was intended for use by humans. There were no constraints, then, on what might or might not be investigated (Dobbs and Jacob, 1995, p. 119).

A contemporary of Boyle's (and his assistant for a time) was Robert Hooke (1635–1703), regarded highly for his study of elasticity. Hooke was an original thinker, but he had difficulty in carrying his products to completion. He is more one who contributed to the advancement of science but not the person usually credited with innovations. He was the first to give a clear conception that the motions of the heavenly bodies could be solved as a problem in mechanics (that is, the relationships of motion and force). His work represented the first steps that led to Newton's discovery of universal gravitation. He did invent the wheel barometer and suggested that applying barometric indicators to meteorological forecasting would improve accuracy. The suggestion that a pendulum could be used to measure gravity was his also. The application vastly improved the accuracy of timekeeping. In 1676 he applied spiral springs to the balances of watches, allowing a smaller but more efficient timepiece.

Hooke criticized Newton's initial explanation of celestial motion (the idea that centrifugal motion was in operation) and suggested that the better rationale was for centripetal (center-seeking) force offset by a tendency to move away from its orbit in a tangent due to inertia. Newton was angered by Hooke's anathema but decided to apply his logic and found it useful. It was only some years later that Newton employed such concepts to refine his theory of gravity, however (Dobbs and Jacob, 1995, pp. 36–37).

The move from using the naked eye to examine the heavens to the refinements of telescopic enlargement developed by Galileo came from several directions. Christiaan Huygens, a Dutchman who lived from 1629 to 1695, was one of those scientists involved in the progression. He found a new way to polish telescopic lenses in 1655, and the resulting product was used to discover one of Saturn's satellites. A year later he observed the constellation Orion Nebular.

In timekeeping Huygens was a major figure. He used the pendulum in the movement of clocks in order to gain an exact measure of time in astronomical observations. The *Horologium oscillatorium* of 1673 described his original discoveries such as the determination of the relation between the length of the pendulum and the time for its oscillation. He is responsible for the theory of evolutes. Evolutes are defined as curves that are either the locus of the center of curvature of another curve, the involute, or the envelope of the perpendiculus, or normals, of the involute. Several theorems on centrifugal force in circular motion, used by Newton to help formulate the law of gravitation, were the work of Huygens as well.

In addition to significant improvements in lenses for telescopic use, Huygens also developed the wave theory of light that had been proposed by Robert Hooke. This helped prove the laws of optics. He accepted Newton's proposal that gravitation is a universal quality of matter at the same time that he accepted Newtonian theory on planetary motions.

The scientific giant of the era was Isaac Newton, still celebrated for his invention of the calculus and his work on optics, mechanics, and gravitation. He was, in fact, the first scientist to be knighted (by Queen Anne) and the first to be enshrined in Westminster Abbey.

Newton attended Cambridge, where the curriculum was based on the philosophy of Aristotle (Brennan, 1997, p. 19), viewing the universe as geocentric and avoiding the ideas of the scientific revolution already under way. For him this was no barrier, however, as he pursued knowledge independently from instructors and course content. On his own he read Descartes, Bacon, Galileo, and Kepler (p. 20). He quickly acquired the mathematics of geometry and algebra, but his independence left him unrecognized when he received the baccalaureate degree in 1665. At this point, fate took a significant hand. There was an outbreak of the plague, and Newton was forced to return to his home while the disease ran its course. He spent the two years of his confinement on the farm to developing the ideas that are the basis for his major findings and contributions.

Although analytic geometry was useful in understanding certain aspects of the cosmos, it was limited to an assumption of a static universe. Newton felt that this idea was too restrictive since the evidence seemed to support the view that the world is always in motion, a dynamic system. Some mathematical technique was needed that would allow quantification for a system of mechanics. He provided the tool for himself: the invention of the calculus. The process allows examining problems where change and fluctuation are common. Newton named this mathematic *fluxions* (Brennan, 1997, p. 23). Had he accomplished nothing else, Newton's name would still be celebrated as one of the greatest in history.

But he did other things. He probably identified at least the basic elements of his theory of universal gravitation while in his two-year hiatus from Cambridge. While the legend of the apple falling on Newton's head may or may not be true, it is a certain fact that there is a force operating throughout the universe that equally affects all elements. Newton proved this by applying fluxions (calculus) to both falling apples and heavenly bodies. So why doesn't the moon fall onto the earth? The answer is that gravitation decreases in its effect according to distance. The moon is 60 times further from the earth than the apple on the tree. The apple is 60 times closer to the center of gravity of this planet than the moon is. This means that the apple has 60 times more gravitational pull than the moon has. That equates to 3,600 times (60 × 60) the pull on the apple as on the moon. In addition, the moon "falls" in its orbit around the earth 1/3600th as far as the apple "falls" in the same time interval (Brennan, 1997, pp. 24–25). During his hiatus, Newton also began work on optics, defining the properties of light and color through the use of prisms.

Part of his honors resulted from the mechanical devices he was so successful in building. He improved the telescope by using a curved mirror instead of a lens to collect light and thereby increased the clarity of view. On request he sent one of these telescopes to the Royal Society, which promptly elected him as a member (Brennan, 1997, p. 27). Pleased by his selection, he submitted a paper on optics, showing that light reflected through a prism is broken down into the color band we call the rainbow. This rainbow returns to white light when reflected through a second prism.

Newton withdrew from active involvement with the scientific community for the next several years (Brennan, 1997, p. 29), he suffered a nervous breakdown in 1678, then his mother's death in 1679. He might have been heard from no more except for the efforts of Edmund Halley (who discovered the famous comet). Halley contacted Newton for help on a problem and visited him in Cambridge. Essentially, his difficulty lay in explaining planetary orbits as elliptical, and Halley consulted Newton as the mathematician most likely to be able to come up with a solution. Newton informed him not only that it was possible but that he had done so years before. Although the proofs were not given to Halley at the time, Newton did send him the proper calculations after some three months (p. 30). Halley, impressed and awed, returned to Cambridge to persuade Newton to organize and publish his many papers. The result was the publication of the *Philosophiae Naturalis Principia Mathematica* in 1687.

There are three parts, or books, that make up the *Principia*. The first deals with the dynamical properties of bodies in a condition where there is no friction or resistance. The second examines the alternative: what happens when bodies encounter friction and resistance. The third book is the most impressive. Here Newton described three laws of motion, the first declaring that a body remains in a quiescent state or continues a uniform motion unless some force changes that state; the second extending the first by declaring that whatever change occurs is in proportion to the force imposed on it. The third law has received the most attention among laymen for its implicit application to life beyond its scientific meaning intended by Newton. Thus, he says "that to every action there is an equal and opposite reaction" (Brennan, 1997, p. 33). These laws became the basis of physics accepted and used in the sciences and technology to the twentieth century. The influence of the work caused Newton to become a public figure, one worthy of rewards and sinecures that otherwise he would not have received.

Sir Isaac Newton lived until 1727, spending his last years in detailed examination of biblical references that represent little more than trivia. Combined with his notes on alchemy, the majority of his life's work is unread and unknown. Yet he must be considered a scientific genius for his findings and their effects on the daily lives of ordinary people, extending to the present.

John Harrison (1693–1776) made a clock with wooden wheels at the age of 22; in 1726, he devised the "gridiron pendulum," which maintained a constant length regardless of temperature variations. He also invented a recoil clock escapement where friction was kept at a minimum. The spring arrangement, which allowed keeping a timepiece going at its usual rate while being wound (called a "going ratchet"), was also his invention.

His ingenuity paid off rather handsomely when the British government announced a competition in 1713. A device was needed that could keep time accurately enough to determine longitude while at sea. Harrison's timepiece was accurate within 18 miles, perhaps not very good today but unheard of in his day. The watch was tested on a sea voyage to Jamaica and back to England. The chronoscope lost only 1 minute, 54.5 seconds. Part of its success was due to the installation of a device to compensate for temperature changes. This "compensation-curb" altered the length of the balance spring in proportion to the expansion or contraction caused by the temperature. For this effort, Harrison won a prize of £20,000—a considerable award. However, he collected only half of it (Boorstin, 1983, p. 52), and the Admiralty did not install the device on ships despite its proven accuracy.

TIME AND THE MODERN ERA

The nineteenth century was a time for applying Newtonian physics to the problems of science and daily life. There was little questioning of the laws that Sir Isaac had proposed, there being even some impression that no further need for theoretical questioning existed. The twentieth century, in turn, became the ground for a major change in model and research, largely because Albert Einstein found reason to question some basic elements of Newton's physics and, by deduction, to introduce an alternative theory that proved more valid.

The major figures of the nineteenth century engaged in proving the reality of Newton's laws and showing applications of their validity. Certainly a major physicist was James Clerk Maxwell (1831–1879), the first professor of experimental physics at Cambridge University. At the age of 15, he was already recognized for scientific efforts, and at age 18 he published a paper that was the basis for his later discovery of a temporary double refraction in viscous fluids.

Maxwell's interest focused on electrical phenomena, and his accomplishments provided the foundation for much of the advances in physics during the twentieth century. He won a prize from Cambridge in 1859 for his essay "On the Stability of Saturn's Rings." His publications included several ingenious papers on color perception and color blindness, receiving the Rumford Medal from the Royal Society for his efforts. He devised his own instruments, noted for their simplicity and convenience as well as their ingenuity.

Maxwell's work on electromagnetic phenomena was built on the research of Michael Faraday. Using this base, Maxwell showed the mathematical relationship between electric and magnetic fields. He moved further into physical reality by demonstrating that light is made up of electromagnetic waves, a finding that had impact on the research of Heinrich Rudolf Hertz. By 1873 he had devised four differential equations that illustrated the nature of electromagnetic fields in terms of space and time.

The work of Maxwell helped move physics from an abstract mathematical science to an understanding of the processes reflected by mathematical symbols (Cannon, 1978, p. 35). As Cannon quotes Maxwell:

The aim of Lagrange [a brilliant French mathematician of the eighteenth century who developed the calculus to a high level] was to bring dynamics under the power of the calculus. . . . Our aim, on the other hand, is to cultivate our dynamical ideas.

To do this, Maxwell says, involves using the mathematical processes of the "language of calculus" in a translation into the language of dynamics. This spirit of moving into an applied field dominated, and still dominates, the role of science. Cannon has called Maxwell "one of [Newtonian physics's] last towering figures" (p. 113).

As suggested above, Heinrich Rudolf Hertz (1857–1894) expanded Maxwell's theory on electromagnetics. His work led to the discovery of the progressive propagation of electromagnetic action through space and then showed that in their operations these waves correspond to the waves of light and heat. Thus, light has an electromagnetic nature. Hertz came close to discovering X-rays with his study of the discharge of electricity in rarefied gases, but W. C. Röntgen made that leap before Hertz reached that point. At the same time, he took a major step on the path to relativity with his publication of the *Principles of Mechanics*.

Most of us are most familiar with Hertz's name through his research that disclosed the nature of sound waves and its subsequent application to radio. Once application began, the ease of communication became manifest. Then it was only with persistence and time that the concepts entered the daily lives of all of us.

By the middle of the nineteenth century, men were being born who would carry the revolution about time and space into the 1900s. One of these was Max Karl Ernst Ludwig Planck (1858–1947), the physicist who proposed the quantum theory. As background, Planck had noted, in studying thermodynamics, that certain phenomena in radiation did not accord with Newtonian physics. Further research established that energy is not a continuous entity; instead, it comes in discontinuous small bundles that Planck called "quanta." These quanta are of different sizes, varying with the frequency of the radiation of which they form a part. He coined a "constant" that he called $\hbar$, a value that reflects that each quantum of radiant energy is equal to $\hbar$ times its frequency.

This quantum theory became the foundation of various subsequent advances. Einstein extended the theory and used it in developing the theory of relativity. Neils Bohr adopted it to explain the known facts of radiation emitted by atomic structures. Planck's work provided the key to the universe *within* the atom where nothing seems to happen as expected from Newtonian physics. The extensions have become known as the science of quantum mechanics.

Planck was awarded the Nobel Prize in Physics in 1918 for his discovery of the quantum. He also received the prestigious Copley Medal from the British Royal Society in 1929, a rare honor considering that he was a German by birth and citizenry. He was even made an honorary member of the American Physical Society. In 1930 Planck was appointed president of the Kaiser Wilhelm Society for Scientific Research.

We are fortunate that Planck wrote a short but telling autobiography, first published in 1949, then reprinted in 1968. He comments on certain facets of his life and work, but even more intriguing he details something of his thinking and beliefs. Incisive and informing are such statements as: "A new scientific truth does not triumph by convincing its opponents and making them see the light, but rather because its opponents eventually die, and a new generation grows up that is familiar with it" (Planck, 1968b, pp. 33–34). Someone who is original cannot expect more than tolerance—and may not receive even that—until the threat that is felt by "newness" has been diminished. Then an objective examination and test of the new truth can begin in earnest. Of course, one could say that the same principle applies to many other expressions of genius, art and music being two easily illustrative fields.

The quantum theory itself was first reported in 1900 (Planck, 1968b, p. 42, footnote) in a paper that Planck delivered to the Physical Society of Berlin. He reports that he tried to incorporate his $\hbar$ into the Newtonian theory but was unsuccessful. A major blow had been struck at the accepted, comfortable view of the universe. Just a few years later, in 1905, Einstein published his "special theory of relativity," and Planck found that he had to consider another alternative to Newtonian physics. What had seemed absolute and exact now appeared to be challenged. Yet it had not been replaced by something that itself was absolute and exact. Even today the paradox has not been resolved. Hawking (1996, p. 18) states that the general theory of relativity (Einstein) and quantum mechanics (Planck) "are the great intellectual achievements of the first half of this [twentieth] century." But they are only partial explanations—and are not even mutually consistent; that is, "they cannot both be correct."

Planck anticipated some of this problem in a lecture published separately in his 1968 *Autobiography* (1968a, p. 97). He notes that the Newtonian theory had its elemental foundation in chemical atoms, whereas the current theories are based on electrons and protons "whose mutual interactions are governed by the velocity of light and by the elementary quantum of action." The former beliefs now appear naive, but Planck points out, from his 1940s view, that the same word may someday apply to the new. Hawking suggests that the eventuality is certain.

Yet validity remains to the Newtonian concepts. Planck (1968a, pp. 98–99) explains this as referring to the "new physics" as a special condition to be added to the old. The only time that Newton's ideas are threatened is when the speed of light is approached at the same time that the quantum of action is near zero, a phenomenon that occurs rarely. In our daily lives, the probabilities are insignificant; increasingly, however, in some areas the probabilities are nearly perfect.

There were publications that disagreed with some aspects, and even a few examples where the theory did not explain adequately, but by and large Newtonian physics remained unchallenged until the twentieth century. The revolution that was to come began with the publication in 1905 of a paper by Albert Einstein. Entitled "On the Electrodynamics of Moving Bodies," it was published in the *Annalen der Physik* and was soon labeled "an affront to common sense" by the London *Times* (Clark, 1984, p. 101). The paper was hardly a bombshell at its appearance, although there were those who were intrigued by its position and who saw Einstein as a physicist to be reckoned with.

Albert Einstein was born in Ulm, Germany, on March 14, 1879. His childhood and youth gave no real indication that he was to become the genius who redefined time and space and established the groundwork that would revolutionize human history. In fact, he was looked upon as a dull student, little motivated, and with few talents. For example, he later wrote that adults don't concern themselves about spacetime problems because, to them, all important issues were resolved during childhood. By contrast, Einstein says he developed so slowly that he was an adult before he was aware of such issues. This may, of course, be tongue-in-cheek hindsight, but there is no doubt that, aside from the violin and mathematics (Clark, 1984, p. 29), formal education had little impact on him.

Yet he valued education in his later life, provided that the effort was directed toward liberating the student's mind rather that coercing submission. He demonstrated this belief with such statements as, "The value of an education in a liberal arts college is not the learning of many facts but the training of the mind to think something that cannot be learned from textbooks" (Calaprice, 1996, p. 37). Certainly he completed baccalaureate study at a polytechnical institute in Zurich, although he created few currents to distinguish himself.

After graduation, he received a job in the Swiss Patent Office, which gave him valuable training in analytical processes and private time to continue his investigations in physics. His breakthrough was the publication of the paper that announced the position labeled "Special Theory of Relativity" in 1905. Later came the "General Theory" (1916). As his work became more widely recognized and its implications discussed, there was a need to interpret the theories to the general public. This he did in an article published in the London *Times* in 1919 (Einstein, 1963, pp. 227–232). He began by noting that there are two types of theory: One he labels constructive and describes data in terms of completeness, adaptability, and clearness; the other is based on a principle, depending on logical perfection and security for its acceptance. The theory of relativity is in the latter category, using research and deduction to suggest alternative explanations for natural phenomena. The special theory applies to all physical phenomena except gravitation, whereas the general theory describes the law of gravitation and how it relates to other forces in nature. From the development and expansion of these deductions came a new view of the universe.

Relativity changed the view of the nature of the universe, providing a more fundamental knowledge of why and how phenomena behave. But it was not a final answer; in fact, during Einstein's lifetime there were discoveries that challenged elements of relativity. One such source was the quantum theory of Max Planck. This idea was employed by Niels Bohr in 1913 to show that the structure of the atom could not be explained by Newtonian physics (Brennan, 1997, p. 132). This led to Bohr's award of a Nobel Prize in 1922. It also permitted research leading to splitting the atom, with all the marvelous and horrifying outcomes associated with it. Bohr and Einstein disagreed on a principle advocated by Bohr: that a physical phenomenon could be described by two different explanations, apparently incompatible but both necessary. This is the principle of complementarity. Later, Werner Karl Heisenberg, a student and colleague of Bohr's, expanded the idea with the "uncertainty principle." Hawking (1996, p. 243) defines this principle as the idea that one may not be absolutely sure of both the position and the velocity of a particle. Accuracy of knowledge about one reduces the accuracy one may know about the other. With such discrepancies, today's physicists are not able to make absolute statements about many phenomena. Indeed, new theories are being devised and tested at the present time; a good example is "string theory" (Greene, 1999).

As Brennan (1997, p. 243) has said, "Today physics has moved into a world governed entirely by mathematical and highly speculative theorizing, little of which can be empirically verified as yet." Where, then, do we stand in our knowledge of time and its role in our lives? One way to answer this question is to investigate the current theories that are being advocated and that direct research into the nature of the universe. As with any area of investigation, the history of the discipline helps define the directions considered. Using what is known to deduce what the meaning and future import of that discipline should be is a common procedure. As such, different authorities will have at least somewhat different concepts. To review all such possibilities is a task not possible in this book, so an admitted selection is the basis for what follows.

Stephen Hawking is certainly a foremost physicist today, respected not only for the quality of his science but also for his ability to interpret and communicate with laypersons who lack the sophistication to follow the intricacies of the science. He has accomplished what may be considered an unusual feat in the sciences: he has written a best-seller (Hawking, 1996) that is accurate and comprehensible.

There are several assumptions that must be made and accepted before getting to the heart of Hawking's proposals. One concerns the nature of time itself: What is time? Hawking accepts the idea that the concept of time is meaningless unless the universe had some beginning point, whether by "big bang" or creationism or whatever (p. 13). There had to be an event that established the conditions for a universe to exist and for the elements that control its progression to evolve. One of these elements is time, a construct that describes a dimension necessary for certain other events to occur. Given the fact that we observe ourselves in a seemingly obvious state of space and time, it is possible to theorize about the reasons. And theorize humankind has for thousands of years, with some gradual progression that helps make sense of a puzzling set of circumstances.

There is more necessary to determining accurately what answers should be accepted and what should be rejected than just the intellect necessary to wonder in the first place. Whatever theories are proposed must meet some basic guidelines. Hawking states two conditions for a theory to be useful in investigation: (1) comprehensive with but few arbitrary elements so that it covers the maximum sources for applications and (2) permitting predictions of future observations of the phenomena involved (p. 15). He has used this definition as the basis for considering the nature of our universe.

Current scientific thought considers the universe in terms of two theories. Calling them "basic partial theories" (p. 18), Hawking considers them the great scientific intellectual achievements of the first half of the twentieth century. One is the general theory of relativity (Einstein), and the other is quantum mechanics (Planck). Relativity deals with gravity and its function in a huge universe, whereas quantum mechanics may be used to explain phenomena on an extremely small scale. The difficulty is that the two are not congruent so that both cannot be correct. It may not even prove possible to be able to disprove one so that the other seems more likely valid.

The resolution that is under way today is to find some third theory that will combine the two, saving the best of both and eliminating the weaknesses of either.

With this background, Hawking discusses space and time in contemporary theory (pp. 22–45). Newtonian theory had proposed that both space and time were absolute and independent. While instances that conflicted with this view were recognized (even by Newton), a resolution was found by proposing an element (called "ether") that permits acceptance of the inconsistencies. The ideas seemed so reasonable and logical, and proved so practical, that physics was comfortable for about 200 years. In point of fact, Newtonian physics is still used by nearly all of us today because it "works" for our purposes.

Einstein, however, challenged the comfort and proposed an alternative with the "Special Theory" in 1905 and the "General Theory" in 1916. His essential point was that time was not absolute and that any element such as "ether" was an unnecessary construct. The exceptions to Newton's laws that had been found increasingly in research needed to be explained by a broader (that is, covering more instances) and simpler (that is, not requiring a special condition like ether) theory. Einstein believed relativity might meet that test, but he realized that only more research would offer the necessary evidence. A major feature of this proof would involve the speed of light as the basic measure of time.

As agreement was reached on this matter, it seemed evident that time was not absolute (nor for that matter was space). Although this made little difference in daily life, it was tremendously important in understanding the universe. Physicists realized that ever more accurate measures of time were necessary in order to obtain agreement among observers (in research on space, for example). Precision has increased so that such a measure as the meter is now defined as the distance traveled by light in 0.000000003335640952 seconds (Hawking, 1996, p. 33) measured by a cesium clock. This permits all researchers to use the same measures. There is no need for an "ether" that cannot be measured. But time and space are no longer independent and absolute, so the term *spacetime* was coined to indicate their true relationship.

What does it matter to those of us who are not physicists? Isn't it just an exercise that is esoteric at best and silly at worst? Certainly we can get along in life without being concerned, but there are some forces already impinging on us that make a difference—and there are others in the offing that are going to be ever more important. Consider the functional nature of space travel. Not only is it possible to send an unmanned rocket into space and control its trajectory, but we have placed men on the moon and should establish a base there in the near future. Mars has been explored by robot, and there will be a manned mission some day. These things didn't happen with measures of absolute time and space. Indeed, any such project would have ended up who knows where. Maybe that would be just as exciting to the casual observer on earth but less acceptable to the astronaut involved. And think what a heyday the Congress would have had about the money thrown away on silly projects!

There is even a corollary that is closer to home. Thorne (1994, pp. 73–79) and Hawking (1996, pp. 43–44) have both provided examples that are related to "earth time." The latter, for example, reports an experiment that was done in 1962. Two very accurate clocks (a necessary condition) were mounted, one at the top of a water tower and the other at the bottom. Relativity predicts that the clock closer to the earth (where mass is greater) would record time more slowly than the clock at a higher elevation. The results were conclusive, favoring the relativity theory, even though the differences in time were extremely small. Perhaps you still wonder if there's much point to this since you are not likely to spend your time going up and down water towers. So let me try a different tack.

If you have ever engaged in an athletic event, or if you are a parent with a child who does so, it is possible that time is a crucial element in who wins and who loses (if that's of any significance). Let's consider a track event. Your child is running in competition with five others in a 100-meter dash. Unless this is a very sophisticated event (such as the Olympics), timing will probably be made by several judges, each holding a watch that is started when the starter's gun is seen to eject smoke. The clocks run until each child crosses the finish line. Every measurement is independent of every other measure, depending on visual cues (the gun's smoke), physical reactions (the starting and stopping of the stopwatch), and the angle of the judge's vision of the finish line. It is probable that some control will be exercised over this last by having the judges stand on steps so that each has an unimpeded view. Suppose your child gets a judge who has poor vision and slow reaction time and is on the top step? Well, it's good for you and your child to learn how to lose gracefully anyway.

With relativity, one can approach an event with a system that is unaffected by individual differences in such factors as those described above. Hawking (1996, p. 34) describes an "event" as something that happens at a particular point in space at a particular time. Space is conventionally conceived of in terms of three coordinates; for example, height, length, and width. Time can be measured in different ways and when applied to this definition becomes a fourth dimension. We now have height, length, width, and time. In combination, this four-dimensional concept is spacetime. Einstein suggested that gravity is present because spacetime is not flat (as we may try to see it) but curved (warped) by its own mass and energy. Thus, gravity is not the cause of the curved orbit of a planet; instead, the orbit is the effort by the planet to maintain a straight line in curved space. This trajectory is called a "geodesic" (p. 40).

Each of us has our own personal measure of time that depends on where we are (space) and how we move (force). Space and time are dynamic quantities, not absolute ones. There is a mutual interaction between spacetime and the universe so that each affects and is affected by the other.

The concept of an "arrow of time," denoting its passage forward from one point to another, is not a new concept. Whitrow (1991, p. 157) describes an example from the discovery of radioactivity in the late nineteenth century, noting, "It is a purely nuclear phenomenon that is independent of external influences. . . . Consequently, radioactivity not only indicates time's arrow but can also be used as a means of measuring time."

Hawking (1996, pp. 184–186) uses the term in a more general sense and expands on types of arrows. There are at least three arrows, according to Hawking, based upon direction (and thus not only forward, as believed in the past). First, there is a thermodynamic arrow, which indicates direction of time brought about by entropy (disorder). Second, there is a psychological arrow, reflected in our personal ability to remember the past but not the future. This arrow points only in a backward direction. Third, there is the cosmological arrow, wherein the universe is expanding and not contracting. The direction here is forward.

Entropy in the universe increases with time, giving direction and providing a distinction between the past and the future. In fact, this arrow determines the psychological one and so precludes the possibility that, in fact, our feeling about time is different from the true path time takes. The two arrows point in the same direction, then. The cosmological arrow may not have conformed in direction to the thermodynamic one at some point in the history of the universe, but currently it does. All three arrows must point in the same direction, Hawking believes, because that is the only way intelligent beings could have evolved. Under conditions where there is only a present sense of time, which is momentary and is not related to past or future, humans would be only animal in their response to and understanding of the universe. If there were a true psychological arrow that points to the past and where humans had no concept of a future or a present, one could only react to whatever experiences had accumulated—but be unable to relate them to what is current and would be unable to visualize what might be. In turn, if only the cosmological arrow existed, a person would not benefit from past experiences and unable to respond to current events. There would be a constant search for a future that has not yet come to pass.

In this context, it seems reasonable that all arrows of time must point in the same direction for individual differences in the effects of time to be recognized, appreciated, and resolved. Meanwhile, the search for a unified theory continues. Seemingly there are three possibilities. First, a unified theory exists but has not yet been discovered by scientists. Second, no such unified theory exists. This would mean that many equally plausible theories must be used to describe our universe in the most accurate manner. Third, no theory of any type is plausible for explaining the universe. This would mean that events are random and arbitrary and can be predicted accurately only to a limited extent. The second option fits experience so far. However, Hawking (p. 225) is an optimist, tinged with realism, so that he prefers the first. Only the third is rejected by him since it would violate the basic function of science: the formulation of a set of laws that permits prediction of events up to the point when Heisenberg's "uncertainty principle" would effectively reduce the accuracy to zero.

A final comment by Hawking seems well worth noting.

Up to now, most scientists have been too occupied with the development of new theories that describe *what* the universe is to ask the question *why*. On the other hand, the people whose business it is to ask *why* . . . have not been able to keep up with the advance of scientific theories. (p. 233)

Perhaps one of the roles of psychologists is to admit their responsibility to provide an answer to *why*, not in a philosophical/religious sense but in the behavioral sense. The remainder of this book will review, first, some of the research by psychologists about time. Following that, an application to a condition (dementia) where there is obvious deviance in time orientation will be examined.

PART II

The Riddle of Time

Time slips away rapidly and has passed before we are aware.

—Ovid

CHAPTER 3

Defining Time Orientation

The difficulty in defining time was noted in Chapter 1, although a working definition was given for purposes of this book. Most often, time is defined in terms of specific components—and thus represents a circular method. For example, "reaction time" is "the time, usually measured in milliseconds, between a stimulus and the person's reaction to it" (Sutherland, 1989, p. 366). We may understand what is meant by the statement, yet it is clear that the measurement is based upon an instrument that is assumed to measure time without disclosing its (time's) nature. We are left with the disturbing possibility that time is what is measured using a watch, a circularity at best and a default at worst.

The problem is compounded by the fact that different psychologists apply the term (time) to various facets of behavior. Examples range from the clinical setting (Arlow, 1992) to memory data (Wearden, 1993) to developmental phenomena (Gutwinski-Jeggle, 1992) to psychometrics (Tismer, 1991). Whether the term *time* refers to the same dimension in every case is unclear because no definition is offered. What does seem clear is that time is viewed in the absolute sense described by Newton, although its direction is not always forward. Gutwinski-Jeggle, for example, notes that we experience time as an arrow irreversibly pointed to the future. Yet she also says that time is not linear in its progress since the past is incorporated in new experience by "cyclical rhythms embedded in physical-psychic reality." Such a statement returns us to a concept of time that repeats itself over and over (cycles of time like that of the Maya, for example) during our personal lifetimes brought about by psychological factors. Such notions are difficult to understand and to apply to everyday experience.

These proposals also confuse the meaning and role of orientation as a daily phenomenon. There have been attempts to clear up some confusion by the proposal of models, most of which are restricted in the behaviors included but which may help develop a more general model. Hawking (1996, p. 15) explained that a good theory accurately describes a large class of observations with a model that contains few arbitrary elements. In addition, it should permit definite predictions about the results of future observations. Using such a position as a basis, we can see more clearly why many psychological theories and models are difficult to comprehend and to use.

MODELS OF TIME ORIENTATION

Scientists differ in their areas of interest and research, but they share a common goal of determining laws that will explain events in as parsimonious a manner as possible. There are not different laws for various subdisciplines in physics, for example, since "truth" must apply to all the universe, not just selected portions of it. Psychologists, by contrast, tend to be compartmentalized: clinicians, experimentalists, educationalists, developmentalists, and so on. There are some efforts to show how the findings in one may relate to the findings in others, but they are not very systematic. There is even the view that one's own subdiscipline is superior to others and that there should be no miscegenation of data. Vocabulary shares commonalities but also introduces differences. And so models tend to reflect the "truth" of the subdiscipline and not for psychology as a whole. The survey that follows will illustrate this fact more amply than is desirable, but it may also disclose similarities not often realized.

Lehmann (1967) has described time as "the one-dimensional continuum of all psychic phenomena." Under this broad umbrella, he then proposes that time has two elements. One is external in nature and should be viewed as objective, universal, and absolute. This is clearly recognizable as Newtonian in focus. The measure of such time is the mechanical or, currently, atomic devices that have been invented to represent the passage of the "continuum" during which psychic phenomena occur. The psychological processes of cognition and psychophysical experience are the means used to calculate this external time. This definition gives a relatively clear exposition of Lehmann's position.

The second element, internal time, involves less physical and measurable processes. Internal time is "subjective, individual, and relative." There is no longer calculation as such so that Lehmann speaks of estimation, awareness, and perspective. These apparently are not discrete and unrelated, however, because he speaks of overlapping processes being involved. Internal time estimation uses cognition and perception as the source; awareness involves perception and emotional (affective) processes; and perspective uses the properties of the affective and existential. Further, "the essential processes involved in the experiences become increasingly complex and subjective, in a progression from pointer-reading and counting when measuring universal time, at one extreme, to emotional and transcendental experiences in one's attitude toward the personal past, present and future at the other extreme" (p. 799). Each of these ideas is developed more completely in the remainder of the article, the emphasis being placed on psychopathological conditions.

Lehmann concludes (pp. 816–819) by offering a model of time and its role in human behavior. He points out that measurement is dependent either on some accepted standard (without regard to its truth) or on a count of discontinuous elements in the phenomenon being measured. The former is impossible for psychological time since totality is lacking. Thus, the latter measure is the one that must be used. To do this, psychological time must be described in terms of the succession of discontinuous units. This leads him to the position that consciousness, which serves as a medium of perception and cognition, cannot be viewed as a continuum but as a set of discontinuous time and space events instead. Such experiences will differ between persons and even within the same person under different conditions.

Conscious discontinuity might seem to be equivalent to the quanta of physics, but Lehmann sees a difference. Mental events do not follow the laws of physical energy but proceed in a structure that consists of a succession of bits of experience. These bits he labels *oligons*—and they constitute the elements that constitute emotions, mental activity, and even personality.

Hawking (1996, p. 184) noted that entropy (disorder in a physical system) increases with time. Psychologically, Lehmann believes, the opposite condition occurs: entropy decreases as the individual experiences and orders new stimulation. Thus, humans have the ability to reduce randomness of information storage as time goes on and more experiences are stored. There is a resultant differential between the rate of stimulation input and the entropy resulting. If information input exceeds entropy, Lehmann proposes the possibility of psychosis and disintegration of personality. This leads then to errors in the sense of time and orderly memory. The utility of this model is pointed to the field of clinical psychology. Whether it has relationships to other subdisciplines is yet to be illustrated.

Lehmann makes no pretense that his model fits a general pattern, even for psychology at large. His interest and focus concern psychopathological conditions: aberrant and nonnormative. As a result, he attempts to explain the relationships of time and schizophrenia, anxiety, Korsakoff's syndrome, and the like. The premise is the existence of such conditions, and his model must fit with that premise. It is not unreasonable that he finds little relationship to external time and much to internal time, as he defines the term. The question becomes whether such ideas are pertinent to the one subdivision of psychology. If so, the model is helpful; if not, the effort has little utility.

In another direction, that of geriatric rehabilitation, somewhat different vocabulary about time orientation leads to another model. Gadow (1986) essentially used the present-past-future concept of time as the basis for describing clinical manifestations affecting some elderly persons who need rehabilitation. *Limbo* is the term she uses for the individual who is trapped psychologically in a present that has no direction (either backward or future) and no visible termination to the momentary. The principal feature is suffering that is so self-centered that it permits no external intrusion. Rehabilitation as a result has no real role to play in the perpetual immediacy of experience.

Linear time is proposed by Gadow as the most extreme departure from Limbo. Here, there is only a series of moments that have no relationship to purpose, as there is constant movement to a new moment. Neither contiguity nor continuity can be found as the person moves through succeeding moments. No moment has any relevance in its own right; there is only the past and future. Gadow refers to this condition as an impersonal functioning, living only in what she calls "public time. It can be quantified, regulated, expressed abstractly" (p. 3). There is no human individuality. It applies to many events in life that are commonly recognized and accepted as socially appropriate: chronological age expressions and timed therapy sessions are two examples listed by her.

The final symbol of time in Gadow's scheme is called *Ritual*. Now time serves the individual as the source of experience. Objectivity and realism are present as the elderly person devises new patterns of life, revising and elaborating as it becomes necessary to do so. These patterns are the ceremony that recognizes, accepts, and adapts to the strengths and weaknesses of an aging body. Rehabilitation is now possible in a way not permitted by Limbo or Linear Time. In fact, Ritual contains elements of both immediacy (Limbo) and linearity (Linear Time) but in a new combining mode so that they are no longer opposites. Dominance by the body in such a way that sensation alone is the focus of life no longer rules, nor does its opposite, the instrumentality of a succession of moments unrelated to any outcome but existence for the future. Low (1987) reviewed research in geriatric rehabilitation that provided evidence about the utility of the model, concluding that Gadow was correct in pointing to the need for predictability and meaning in the lives of elderly rehabilitation patients.

This model is focused on a specialized group with unique needs: elderly persons who are physically incapacitated in some way and who need special intervention that may be resisted or rejected or accepted, depending upon the impact of time on psychological perspective. One might say, then, that it has little relevance to most of society. Gadow has made no claim to any applications except the specific ones described. However, there are intriguing elements to the model. First, are there persons who are most influenced by a time orientation that is centered in the present or the past or the future? If so, what effects, beneficial or detrimental, does that attitude have on the behavior of the individual? Certainly the literature contains examples of such potentials, the best known of which is the stereotype that older persons are afraid of the future, are unable to cope with the present, and turn to the past as the least-threatening aspect of life. (This stereotype has its opponents as well as proponents and has not been shown to be a generalizable description.) At the same time, middle-aged persons have been portrayed as present oriented, desirous of success and acquisition, whereas young adults are described as future oriented, filled with expectations and hopes. If such descriptions prove to be valid, can Gadow's model assume the generality that would help bring understanding?

The field of personality measurement would seem ripe for relating to time orientation models, although this book is not the forum for such applications. The point is, time orientation has been largely ignored, or applied to discrete populations, when it might serve as a general housing under which diverse proposals and discrete applications could be viewed as a step in bringing greater order.

An attempt to describe a more general model of time orientation has been presented by Boris (1994). His effort, as with that of Lehmann, is based in psychiatry and behavioral manifestations in that discipline. The examples used express this bias but are not necessarily limited to them. And the general nature of his model offers the opportunity for wider application. An abstraction of the basic premises of Boris's model will help define what components are necessary to a workable paradigm.

Essential to this model is the idea that time is not a dimension but only a theory, a position that avoids encountering its nature. Boris defends this position by stating that if time, in actual fact, existed, it might move in various directions (and thus represent multiple arrows that diverge from each other in unpredictable ways). Yet time does accompany experience, even in its diverse forms such as "ever or never," "quick or slow," or "soon or now or later." Further, there is no real attempt by anyone seeking solutions to behavioral problems through analytic techniques to explore and understand either the past or future. Instead, there are anticipations about a future based upon some sense that the past and present can be extrapolated to predict a future. "They do not come [into analysis], that is, to cry over spilt milk (though, in time, they may). They come because the past never seems to get over and done with: old whines in new bottles" (p. 302). In this sense the past is continuous and tends to repeat itself into the future. Where life is uncomfortable or threatening, one may seek help to find some solutions. And time is as much a part of this healing process as it is of behavioral maladjustment.

Boris believes that we are born without any awareness of time. There must be experiences that establish markers in time to lead to understanding and application. The sources of such experiences are many and relatively uncontrolled so that the individual is changed by the environment at the same time that the obverse occurs. The key for the person lies in the notion that experience needs realization, achieved through what Boris calls "aha" events. He uses analytic examples, but they provide the grounds for a generalization that experience is the basis for realization, that awareness and understanding define the "aha" element.

Experience, then, is a party to time but is not the expression of it. For a child, Boris believes, this realization is difficult to achieve. The concept of time as an arrow, which serves the adult well, is not within the cognitive awareness of the child. With time, the past allows applications to the present, but the past contains truths that could not be realized until the present. Developmental theory has emphasized the concept of stages, containing regularity and improvement as experience continues. Time acts as a means by which the individual views personal development, leading to concepts as applied to past and future.

Analogies are conceived by Boris as portrayers of experience, symbols not only of value in lending interpretation to the experiencer but also in serving as signals. Applied to the past, the signals are useful only to a limited degree because they focus only on limited aspects of experience, implying that there is nothing else of value to consider. The memory elicited is emblematic, not representational. Applied to the future, abstractions make poor symbols primarily because the future cannot be remembered. What is created in the process will not be encountered in fact in the future since that future cannot eventuate.

Time itself cannot be equated with the measurement of time, Boris tells us, primarily because the measures are subject to error. Instead, time is judged in terms of the limits imposed by the means used. Ubiquitous as it is, we are never sure whether time flows or if we are the flowing source. In any event, time serves as an extreme provenance of negative influences on life: Depression and persecution are examples that Boris gives. "Concerning time, some people feel the first thing to do is act as if it didn't exist; the second, be late for it; the third, anticipate it and end it before it ends you" (p. 310). In the process of experience with time over the centuries, certain images have become prevalent: Father Time with his scythe is a good example. The multitude of such icons, Boris notes, are without exception negative in their meaning and import.

Finally, there is the matter of the relationship between time and experience. Earlier, Boris told us, "In any experience, time is therefore a party" (p. 301). Toward the end of his article, he repeats the idea that experience can only be acquired with the assistance of time (p. 312). Then he further delineates the relationship with the notion that "time has to be held as a kind of constant, a pulsed container, if spatial configurations are to be noted" (p. 313). He means this for application to certain conceptualizations relevant to psychoanalysis. In the general sense, if one is to apply the model beyond the specific, this must mean that Boris sees time as a controlled vessel for space. This implies the spacetime dimension in a psychological sense.

The major tenets of this model would seem to contain these elements:

1. Time and experience bear an essential relationship that permits development of concepts, generalizations, and applications to life, whether for the better or worse interests of the person. Neither element is controlled by nor controls the individual ultimately. This opens the possibility that the psychology of behavior is the key to understanding personal actions.

2. There is currently no way to determine how the understanding of a sense of time evolves. One "knows" that it does, whether patient or therapist, but one does not know how. Time must be conceived then as omnipresent without a clear explication of why. In the general sense, time is a pervasive and seminal dimension of too much importance to ignore but too little understanding to control.

3. This must mean that time cannot be conceptualized in a real sense. Boris explains it as a theory and thereby avoids an encounter with its nature. He justifies this by pointing out that the concept of an arrow of time is inadequate because time may move in any direction, not just forward. The absolute nature of time is thus denied without an adequate substitution. For a general model this position is unsatisfactory.

4. The time and space continuum exists and represents the "vessel" in which experience can be deposited for use in development. *How* these experiences are used is individual, so that they may result in constructs that are beneficial to the person (and lead to social adjustment) or to misapplications (which produce maladjustment). The variety may be too great to allow prediction. What must be done, pragmatically, is to wait until the behavioral manifestations are present, realized by the individual, and used to promote further adjustment, maladjustment, or a search for help (therapy). Such a view may be explained as reactive, and certainly it cannot be proactive. The issue becomes, with such a state of affairs, can anything other than modest success (and often failure) result behaviorally? Alternatively, of course, there is an issue about the possibility of a model that will redirect awareness of the time and space dimension so that success will be the norm.

Qualitative Models and Studies

There have been attempts to relate the findings from qualitative models and studies (phenomenological) with those from quantitative (experimental) approaches. An example of this is found in a paper by Kuhs (1991).

Time, Kuhs says, is a dimension that serves a bifurcated purpose: First, it is objectively expressed and observed as a physical phenomenon; second, it may be experienced subjectively as a process that can be investigated phenomenologically. "The polar structure of time can accordingly be summarized roughly as follows: Time is on the one hand a constantly and continuously flowing homogeneous cosmic and universal time, but on the other hand unevenly progressing personal and individual time subject to stagnation and acceleration" (p. 325). This statement accords with positions cited previously, at least by implication. It also permits viewing time in the absolute sense of a forward-pointing arrow that shows neither beginning nor end, whether quantitative or qualitative.

Based upon a description of Lehmann (1967), Kuhs has developed modes for experiencing time. The investigative modes (quantitative and qualitative) and their related concepts (external and internal) are expressed in terms of experience. Kuhs specifies calculation, estimation, awareness, and perspective as the types of time experiences available to humans. The first of these, calculation, he posits as applying only to objective time. This is absolute in its expression, found in experimental work where time is a control variable, no matter how measured.

The remaining experiences, however, are not so neatly classified. Time estimation, for example, has been the source of a number of experiments, with some mixed results (see Shaw and Aggleton, 1994, to be discussed below). To Kuhs, this experience is a mix of the external (objective) and internal (subjective), although it may be quantitatively determined. It represents some "intermediate position," what Kuhs calls the interface between the phenomenological and experimental experience. Since it is available to objective measurement, it presents an intriguing element in trying to resolve issues of time's nature and role in human behavior. (Kuhs applies each of his concepts to melancholia, which emphasizes again the special case and not the general one.)

Completely subjective in meaning and expression, time awareness deals with an impression as to the rapidity or slowness with which time passes (also widely investigated), while perspective is reflected in a general orientation to the personal past, present, and future perceived by the individual. As such, they are qualitative, involving the need for special techniques (analysis and therapy) in order to clarify their meaning for the person.

The apparent clarity of Kuhs's model illustrates the difficulties with representations that deal with those psychological phenomena closely related to mental events (emotions, motives, desires, and the like). This does not reduce their importance—they are, after all, fundamental elements of human behavior—but it does increase the complexity needed in a model as contents move beyond time measurement as such. Clinical disciplines must be concerned with time because of its apparent relation to the manifestations present and subject to intervention. Any model of time orientation cannot avoid grappling with the difficulties raised in the process.

This argument achieves some validity from studies such as one published by Shaw and Aggleton (1994). Their experimental task was to make time estimations (that is, to judge elapsed time) using Korsakoff's and postencephalitic patients as their subjects. Acting as a control was a group of alcoholics who showed no signs of brain damage of a similar type. There were two experiments: The first involved reproducing and estimating intervals of 3 to 96 seconds; the second used fixed intervals of 15 and 30 seconds. The problem for both Korsakoff's and postencephalitic patients was that memory function was disturbed. "What effect would this have on time estimation abilities?" Shaw and Aggleton asked.

The answer they found was "none." Intact memory did not need to be present in order for the individuals to be able to make estimates as accurate as those of their controls. Where estimation scores were impaired, in fact, the cause seemed not to be an impaired memory as such. They concluded, "The findings do not support models of time estimation that depend upon memory for events within the duration, but favour 'internal clock' models that propose an independent interval timing mechanism that is responsive to cognitive factors and external events but is not dependent upon them" (p. 871). The results also indicated that frontal lobe function may be an influence in the accuracy of time estimations.

This study, at least within the limits of its subjects and measures, offers evidence that time and space dimensions are related to factors not associated directly with clinical conditions as such. The reference in the quote above is a point in fact. Travis (1996) has reported evidence that interval timing is one of the "clocks" available to animals and humans. Crucial to learning and memory, the interval timing mechanism can be actively controlled as long as there is no damage to the substantia nigra in the basal ganglia. The culprit when damage has occurred is the loss of dopamine production. Under normal conditions the substantia nigra sends regular doses of dopamine to the striatum (which consists of the caudate nucleus and putamen). Without dopamine, the interval function is not complete. Subsequent accurate interval estimation will be in error. Travis echoes the opinion of Shaw and Aggleton that the frontal lobe is the eventual activating mechanism.

The importance of an intact frontal lobe has been cited by Hambrecht (1987) as well. Surveying the few controlled experiments done with patients with frontal lobe lesions, Hambrecht reports that evidence is available that damage to the dorsolateral region of the frontal lobe results in errors in memorization and recall of time sequences. This loss in accuracy prevents patients from being able to apply strategies and follow rules adequately. To Hambrecht, this reflects the fact that patients cannot distinguish relevant from interfering stimuli, and so they react to interference and produce inaccurate responses.

This brings us to the evidence relating to frontal lobe function as it affects memory for temporal and spatial information in the general population.

The issue has been studied for a normally aging group (mean age = 83.1) who were compared with a group of controls (mean age = 20.95) in the final of three experiments (Parkin, Walter, and Hunkin, 1995). The authors report a significant decline in memory for temporal context related to age in all three experiments. However, memory for spatial information was not adversely affected, although they report that other studies with different tasks do not obtain the same result. This suggests that experimentation that clearly delineates the differences between temporal and spatial memory, if any, needs to be reported. Should there be consistent differences, the findings would prove significant for our understanding of the relationship of memory to time and space expressions in their absolute forms.

As an aside, I and others working with Alzheimer's patients notice greater difficulties in recall of temporal events than of spatial ones. Alzheimer's patients, for example, are sometimes able to remain more cognizant of the location of rooms in their homes (space) than they are of the time of events in their lives. Such observations are no more than suggestive of the need for research to verify or reject such differences. Where found, a more intensive study of the extent and meaning of such comparisons could be undertaken.

In any event, Parkin and colleagues have shown that memory for temporal context declines markedly even for normally aging adults, whereas spatial memory remains relatively more intact. Those who have begun to reach old age can attest to such a finding and certainly not be surprised that it is reported. How much more significant may be the losses in those with dementia? The greatest differences were found for tasks that required discriminating position of objects in space relative to each other rather than relative to the observer.

Parkin, Walter, and Hunkin believe that different processes are involved in making temporal and spatial discriminations. The frontal lobe, and its integrity, appears to be the primary element in temporal discrimination, a suggestion that accords with research already reported. Where there is a loss in spatial memory following damage to the frontal lobe, the authors state that qualitatively there are different kinds of lesion than for temporal memory. "Therefore, it is reasonable to suppose that the impairment of temporal order memory and its association with frontal dysfunction represent more anterior damage to this [limbic] pathway and/or its target areas in the frontal cortex" (p. 310).

There is clear evidence of decline of temporal memory with age and possible differential degrees when compared to spatial memory. This serves to highlight the role of the frontal lobe, with its degree of integrity over time, as a center for allowing realistic functional awareness of time and space events. With evidence of specific outcomes on temporal demands for everyday life, a normative pattern can be established against which departures can be compared for conditions that bring varying degrees of temporal malfunction. Simply saying that older persons show a normal decline in temporal memory is insufficient. How much, when, and under what circumstances are issues needing to be resolved before we can know the importance of the losses.

Models of Time in Daily Life

Models of time have been described in fields that are practical in their import and applications. One is the field of economics, particularly as time is an influence in deciding and dealing with resources. A paper by Owen (1991) will serve as an example of this context.

Owen's interest is primarily in the family and optimum use of resources available. This concern is placed within the context of time orientation as a resource in its own right. She tells us that, in the field of economics, "time is viewed as a resource to be treated as any other scarce commodity" (p. 346). The use of the word "scarce" is interesting since time is neither scant nor abundant. To describe it as insufficient must mean that economists are concerned for the demands on and for the individual or for business and industry. To the former, demands would be greater than can be accomplished within a period of a day or week, whereas for the latter, there are strictures that prevent greater production within the same periods. If this is so, both parties will experience conflict, the resolution of which will not be accommodated easily or completely.

Still, Owen may be correct in her consideration of time as an issue in the way families accomplish goals and realize desires. She further develops her concept by saying that time "is saved, spent, and allocated in a manner consistent with the use of money" (p. 346). This would seem an extravagant interpretation even though it may be commonly accepted in economics and family resource management. It implies control in a way that may be viewed as more factitious than real. People make decisions in their own behalf and that of others within the dimension that time permits. Time, however, cannot be parceled and invested in and of itself. This model, then, seems lacking in utility.

Owen does include other conceptions of time that need to be recognized and analyzed. Interesting in this regard is what she attributes to the discipline of anthropology. There are three modes of the time model in that field, according to her. The first is labeled *linear-separable* and accords with the arrow of time as it moves from past to present to future in a linear expression. She states that such a view allows us to envision a future that may be influenced by the present. Thus, experience now becomes the basis for extrapolating to the future. It seems more likely that past experiences are the basis for such extrapolation, but that is no more than a minor quarrel. More important, she maintains that the arrow model allows us to separate time into discrete compartments (as with calendars) and then quantify them for comparison with other quantifiable units, such as money. Thereby we "save" today in order to "have" tomorrow. This is the predominant mode of cultures based on values of western Europe, she believes.

A second anthropological model is labeled *circular-traditional* and represents the cyclic notion of several past civilizations: history is cyclical, so all events will be repeated in the future. The Maya culture is a good example of this view. To Owen, outside factors such as weather have their influence on the cycle, whereas personal forces such as physical state and function do as well. This model has little utility for most social needs, as she makes clear in her discussion.

Finally, anthropologists speak of the *procedural-traditional* model of time. Here, Owen says, the critical element is the activity being carried out regardless of time itself. Ritual is the significant procedure, leading to reverence for the past and the heritage sanctioned by the leaders and/or priests who are responsible for recognizing and explaining rituals. She compares this to the attempt by modern families to preserve as much "quality time" as possible.

Overall, these models do not offer new ideas that we may apply to a generalized model of time orientation. This does not imply that they are unimportant or that Owen has raised objectionable issues. She does go on to detail some seven concepts related to time that she feels help understanding of time itself. Five of these (periodicity, tempo, duration, synchronization, and sequence) are aspects of an absolute view of time, ways of measuring what time's arrow allows. Two (orientation and perspective) she describes as psychological expressions of time and thus personal in nature. Of most interest to this book is her view of orientation, also called temporal valuing, which she says reflects the emphasis on past, present, or future chosen by the individual. This idea has been expressed by others so that stereotypes have been commonly accepted: Old people have difficulty in the present, fear the future, and therefore prefer to live in the past; young adults struggle with the present, while their efforts are directed to the future; and so on. This issue will be reviewed more completely in a later chapter.

ORIENTATION AND BRAIN FUNCTION

If orientation is a function principally of the frontal lobe, and consequently a product of the use of experience by the intellect, how may the function be established in the brain? This question, important as it is, has had little research directed to answer it. There are studies, in some quantity, devoted to the mechanisms of cell storage, although only tangentially related to the topic here. For example, Block (1974) proposed that the experience of time duration is cognitive in nature and based on the storage size of the duration interval. This storage size, he believes, must increase as the number of retained units increases. Several factors must influence this outcome, only a few of which (the organization of long-term memory, for example) had been explicated at the time of his series of studies. Judging how much time has elapsed must be as experiential as memory storage itself.

On another tack, Zakay (1993a) has proposed a dual-process contingency model in making judgments about time duration (at least for shorter time periods). One part of this model consists of a "timer" that employs cognition to track units of time. As other events distract the person, this timer is less efficient in the sense of recording fewer units. The result is the production of lower time judgments than would occur without distraction. The mind, then, will judge units as shorter in duration than they actually are. There are two other factors specified by Zakay that affect the timing process: knowing in advance that judgments will have to be made and knowing where absolute (and not relative) judgments must be made. The timer, then, is most effective with advance knowledge of the process to be used and with focus on absolute times, without distractors.

The other process comes into play when retrospective and relative judgments are to be made. Now the duration is judged in terms of the number of high-priority events that occur during the interval. The more high-priority events, the greater the time judgments made. Each of the processes plays its role according to the circumstances to be considered mentally, indicating a complex situation relying more on environmental events than on the time interval to be judged. Such a model tells us more of mental phenomena involved than it does of time orientation. It seems obvious, as well, that attention is a crucial factor in making time estimates, an issue that Zakay and others have investigated in some depth and to which we shall return later in this chapter.

There are still other factors that have been proposed as explanatory for time awareness. Emirbayer and Mische (1998) use the term "agency" in its sociological sense, allying it with social engagement. The agency noted here has its roots in the past (habits) and the future (projection of alternatives). At the same time, the present performs the task of evaluation, blending habits with potentials as permitted by momentary contingencies.

The influence of daily experience has been probed also by Ryff and Heidrich (1997) who found that young adults perceive time in terms of current life activities. Middle-aged persons put greater emphasis in their expression of time through their relationships with family and friends; older adults find greater well-being in contemplating previous work and educational experiences.

In fact, Larsen, Thompson, and Hansen (1996) maintain that personal (autobiographical) experience is "unthinkable without reference to time." This leads to a statement of areas needing research. First, how accurate are memories of events when they are to be ordered in time? Second, what is the process involved in placing events in time? Third, what information is employed as one goes through the process of dating events? Answers to these questions must be sought through experimentation with time estimation, including evidence about duration and perspective. Even limiting the discussion to these few variables must involve selectivity from the abundance of studies that have been conducted and published.

Time Estimation

Humans are unique in their awareness of time outside the present. Animals seemingly lack the ability to benefit from past experience to as great an extent, and so far, no data have been presented that they anticipate the future. The lives of animals are committed to an eternal present to which they must adapt or suffer the consequences. Since humans are capable of awareness of past and anticipation of future, the concept of time estimation is relevant. It is necessary, then, to show its applications and analyze its dimensions. Experimental psychology has been helpful in realizing this goal.

Zakay and Block (1997) have described the parameters involved. The fundamental function served by time estimation is to represent the environment, exemplified in many ordinary activities. Questions such as, "How long must I allow to get to the store, shop and return home?" are not merely personal; they are also practical. Studying such issues requires control of conditions in order to ensure that valid conclusions are drawn. As a result, psychologists control for task content, difficulty, and instructions. Subjects then perform and are asked to estimate the time needed or taken. Such estimations may be expressed verbally ("I will need two minutes" or "I took two minutes"), reproducing the interval experienced by delimiting a following time period or declaring when a specific time period has been completed. Additionally, participants may be asked to estimate the time needed prior to or following the experience.

There have been hundreds of such studies conducted to the present, and some conclusions have been demonstrated to be valid. Time estimates of shorter duration are reproduced more accurately than those of long time periods; there are consistent underestimates of longer time periods. There are also influences from the amount of information involved; difficulty of task to be performed; even the number of meaningful events involved, whether internal or external. Not unexpectedly, the research results have been far from unambiguous. Contradictions are found and must be explained. As a result, models that will accommodate as many disparate findings as possible have been proposed, each having its adherents, and put to the test to define validity.

Zakay and Block propose that the most crucial factor is prospective or retrospective methods of duration judgment, both in the laboratory and in real life. Each of these calls into play different cognitive processes, and so different models are required. One of these they designate the "attentional-gate model," demonstrated in the activity of the individual dividing attention between external events of importance at the moment and heeding the time element concurrently. This model is most helpful in explaining prospective time estimation. The other principal model is called the "contextual-change model," explaining retrospective time judgments and depending chiefly on retrieval from memory. As they note, "In short, prospective and retrospective duration judgments (or experienced and remembered duration) differ primarily in that the former depend mainly on the encoding of temporal information whereas the latter depend mainly on the encoding of nontemporal information" (p. 15).

This broad explanation by Zakay and Block is helpful in detailing some of the factors involved in time estimation and the conclusions that may be drawn. They need fleshing out, however, in order to judge more precisely their utility to time orientation.

One step in this direction was taken in a study by Zakay (1993b) designed to test specifically the validity of the attentional model of prospective time estimation. The basic element involved is a presumed "cognitive timer," nonbiological in nature, which serves to count subjective time units. An individual estimates the time to be needed based upon the number of units that are accumulated in a target interval. This is a highly functional construct, frequently employed in our daily lives: "It takes me 10 minutes to drive to the store. I must buy seven items, but I know the store layout well, and it shouldn't take more than five minutes. Service is quick at this time of day, three minutes; then 10 minutes back home. I'll need a half hour." By attending to the thought process, it is apparent that the time estimation is a result of the attention focused on the task and assigned to the timer. Of course, in the laboratory, conditions are arranged that are not so orderly and preselected; more precise analysis of the influence of manipulated factors can be undertaken as a result.

Zakay notes a number of instances where studies have supported such an attentional model. The present study was designed to refine the model. Two dimensions were investigated: the validity of the model when applied to prospective judgments and how sensitive time estimations are in terms of the particular methods of estimation used in the study. Data supported the effort but also indicated that context is an important influence in results. As has been stated so often, "Further study is needed." Support, nevertheless, for Zakay's findings about the sensitivity of estimations to the methods employed has been reported by Chastain and Ferraro (1997).

The matter of temporal sensitivity has been investigated by Brown, Newcomb, and Kahrl (1995) as well. Using a methodology of signal detection with visual stimuli, they found that sensitivity was an element in detection at two different time periods. This indicated to them that individual differences in timing are stable. Regardless of task, they conclude that high or low sensitivity was consistent across tasks. As they state it, "As long as the intensity of the stimulus signal remains constant and the perceptual-processing mechanisms within the observer are not altered in some fashion, then the observer's level of sensitivity remains the same" (p. 535). Where there is over- or underestimation, they believe that factors like boredom, fatigue, and impatience are responsible. This raises the issue of sources of variance that are uncontrolled, and ignored, in experimental psychology. Experimentalists must look to the influences of personal states to explain the differences so frequently found in time estimation studies.

Other experiments have offered supportive evidence for the Zakay model at the same time that the influence of context must be better understood. One such is a study by Sawyer, Meyers, and Huser (1994). "Within the scope of the contextual model of temporal experience, it seems reasonable that a person's efforts to reproduce a task interval would be affected not only by the activities in which she or he was engaged during the target interval, but also by contextual features that existed during the production" (p. 656). They speak directly to such instances as emotional states and experience. By contrast, Bueno Martinez (1994) has suggested the importance of cognitive change in judgments of subjective time estimation and reports data that indicate inadequacy of the attentional model but support for the contextual model. Predebon (1996) agrees that mental processing (active and passive) is an important element in estimating absolute time limits for longer intervals. Content was a more important element in retrospective time estimates, whereas prospective judgments were influenced differentially. There was a negative relation with stimulus quantity when active processing was employed. When the processing was passive, the relationship was either unrelated or negatively related. Prediction then was more consistently influenced (for better or worse) by active mental involvement than by passive.

The complexity of the encoding process is reflected in the fact that there may be many ways to encode information and several strategies employed to determine frequency judgments. Norman Brown (1997) has analyzed the present state of affairs, noting that attention to these matters is a recent phenomenon in psychology. The research done thus far indicates that the factors involved in the encoding process influence the manner in which information about event frequency is examined by the person. The particular strategy that the individual decides to use is restricted to memory content relevant to the task. In fact, the strategies chosen to estimate time have distinct behavioral consequences. Brown's own work has disclosed the import of such factors as study time, target-context relations, and instructions given during the study phase. Such matters affect context memory, which in turn has its effects on response time. One of his telling points is that "perceived accuracy and convenience may be evaluated when an estimation strategy is selected, with accuracy given more weight when one source of information is clearly more credible and convenience given more weight when competing sources are considered equally credible, or when the more credible strategy is deemed to be too demanding" (p. 911). Estimation strategies may vary depending on available information, so there are no necessarily better strategies in general than others. Each is selected by the respondent's analysis of the task, its content, and context.

Such intellectual components in time estimation have been echoed by Burt and Kemp (1994) as well. Using prospective estimates, they conclude that strategies are generated in a constructive manner and probably in a similar way for retrospective estimates. Their participants gave evidence that they used knowledge about the probable duration from past experiences; wild guesses about time needed certainly was not the rule. Indeed, they believe that even when there is little retention interval, retrospective estimates are constructed as competently as possible. The behavioral meaning of such a position is illustrated by the fact that prospective overestimation of time needed is common and "may be used as a means of controlling time and avoiding stress" (p. 166). Personal factors once again emerge as significant in whatever findings may result in the laboratory.

While it is true that experimental psychology has not yet provided significant evidence about the nature of time orientation, the work conducted has helped to clarify variables that must be considered for a general model. Continued research will also bring further clarification of roles and meanings of factors often left uncontrolled because they are not seen as crucial to the experimental paradigm used.

One element in the puzzle that could be helpful to determining the exact nature of time orientation is the brain. What neuronal components are involved in time orientation? Are neurotransmitters important, and if so, which ones? Is there some "rhythm" or "clock" that controls efforts to deal with time? It would be unreasonable with our present knowledge of brain function to expect concrete answers. It is reasonable, however, to ask, What is the direction of research on such matters?

There has been accumulating evidence that the prefrontal area of the brain is strongly implicated in orientation, suggesting the role of intellectual factors as a major one (Casini and Macar, 1993; Rammsayer, 1997a, for longer time intervals; Block, 1996; Fuster, 1995). However, there are some distinctions to be made as well as implications from the notation of frontal lobe control. Casini and Macar (1993), for example, speak of the assumption of specific chronometric mechanisms in an attentional model. Rammsayer (1997a) found evidence of dopaminergic activity in the basal ganglia when temporal processing was done in milliseconds and thereby introduces the role of neurotransmitters. On the other hand, he speculated that longer intervals were processed through cognitive mediation. Fuster (1995) pinpoints the associative areas of the frontal lobe as being indispensable for temporal organization to occur. There are two functions involved that he feels are complementary. One utilizes recent memory and its representations; the other concerns planning as it implies action at some future time.

Rammsayer's work (1997a) examined the relation of body core temperature and dopamine in tasks involving timing processes. Higher body temperatures were not related to time judgments, and so he rejected the possibility that certain physiological changes had their effects on time orientation. But he makes the more than interesting point that a timing device that is influenced in its operation by temperature change would be unreliable. Possibly, then, his results were influenced by an internal clock that was adjusted by physical mechanisms in order to protect against variability. By contrast, any internal clock may be more adversely affected when neurotransmitters are inoperative to some degree. His findings signify that, indeed, the basal ganglia must have integrity if any internal timing mechanism is to function properly. The effect of importance here is that in extremely short time period processing dopamine availability is essential. With longer time intervals, processing occurs at higher levels of the nervous system than for short time intervals.

Other possibilities for explaining time performance can be found in the literature. Treisman (1993), for example, has suggested that humans may have some form of temporal sensory system that is used in temporal performance. Usher and Zakay (1993) have proposed a multi-attribute-decision processes model to explain differences in performance on short and long time duration predictions. Jones and Yee (1997), using an auditory stimulus (music), concluded that their data "appear most consistent with views that emphasize the listener's attending as sequences unfold in real time" (p. 707). This returns us to the attention model as perhaps the most basic, if not inclusive, model.

ORIENTATION AND PERSONAL VARIABLES

If studies that control for task dimensions yield insufficient answers and lead to suggestions that contextual and personal variables must be assessed, a review of some of the literature in that domain should aid the search for a stronger model. A starting point comes from the work of Rammsayer. He has pointed out (1994) that time estimates reflect cognitive functioning. If that functioning is disturbed, as when pharmacological treatment is used, the impairment to memory that results will produce deficits in performance on time estimation tasks. As for personality traits, he (1997b) could find no relationship between a measure of neuroticism and performance on a time estimation task. However, introversion more typically led to more accurate time judgments as compared with extraversion. Those persons in his sample who scored higher on psychoticism did not show as much overestimation and reproduced time periods more accurately than those with lower psychoticism scores. Such findings provide a link between mental conditions and orientation, although they provide no rationale for the connection.

Locus of control is another of those personality variables that has been investigated often. Koivula (1996) applied the technique to time estimation, using mental arithmetic as the task. She reports clear differences, with the internal locus individuals showing superior performance. Both types underestimated the short time intervals, indicating that locus of control may not be a significant factor throughout time orientation performance. In another vein, Beiser and Hyman (1997) studied Southeast Asian refugees in Canada and compared them with longtime residents. One of the tasks was a measure of past, present, and future orientation. They found that the refugees tended to separate the past from the present and future, a trait they label "temporal atomism." By doing so and by avoiding nostalgia, the authors feel that the refugees were less apt to suffer depression. This becomes a means of adaptation so that the person may deal more effectively with the demands of the present.

Physiological factors have been examined in some studies as well. Osato, Ogawa, and Takaoka (1995) used a digit memory task covaried with heart rate to study accuracy of time estimation. Method became a significant factor in their results, with the reproduction method leading to underestimation of time and verbal estimation to overestimation. They concluded that "the influences of initial heart rate and instruction on the time estimation vary according to the methods of time judgment and the time intervals" (p. 840). Yet there was stability in the fact that low heart rate produced greater discrepancies between reproduction and verbal estimation, a finding that they relate to the possibility of stress. One of their conclusions brings us back to the complexity of understanding time orientation: "[T]here are some overlapping relations among arousal, immediate memory, and psychological time, and the relations are influenced by the type of instructions used as the social situations" (p. 841).

The effects of pain on time estimations were investigated by Thorn and Hansell (1993). They note that research available indicates that headache attenuates retrospective time estimates. They used a cold pressor test to induce pain equivalent to that of a headache. Their results compared favorably with those of other studies. However, the distortion in time estimates was reduced if participants were given a specific time goal for coping with the discomfort they suffered. Their estimations were for longer durations but were also more accurate.

Finally, Buehler, Griffin, and Ross (1994) tackled the problem of the "planning fallacy," the consistent finding that people tend to underestimate the time needed to complete a task. Specifically, they found, with a sample of 465 participants, that less than half completed tasks within the time period they predicted. Their tasks involved time periods from days to weeks and therefore bear some resemblance to everyday life. Buehler et al. concluded that their subjects would construct narratives of what would happen in the future and include detailed plans for task completion that were extended to related future tasks. Yet they ignored their past experiences with such tasks in making these plans. Participants focused on the details of the task at hand, dismissing past errors in prediction even where those were relevant. They explained away references to past prediction failures by asserting that the experiences were unique and unrelated to the present. The element of risk becomes important: What is the price to be paid by under- or overestimation? For those who wish accuracy in prediction, relevant information will be used, whereas those who desire to finish a given task as promptly as possible will ignore other instances. Thus, "time estimates may have a variety of functions and consequences" (p. 380). This implies some affective element that enters into the decision process.

Overall, this sample of studies provides suggestions that personal variables are certainly involved in time estimation performance. More definitive relationships, with particular emphasis on causal factors, must be established before understanding can occur.

Chronological Age

More absolute variables may provide greater knowledge. Chief among these would be chronological age, measured in calendar years, and gender, based upon biological characteristics. There have been extensive studies on age that will be reported in Chapters 4 through 6. Gender has been less extensively surveyed and usually as one of several variables.

This condition, for example, is found in a study by Laszlo (1995) that examined affective and emotional processes in reading materials. Several narratives were read by both males and females; some of the material was action oriented, and some of it was experience oriented. Actual reading time was compared with prospective time estimates. The action-based stories required less reading time and shorter time estimates because of structural effects, the authors believe. The experiential material was read more slowly and extended time estimates because of affective and emotional content. Differences between the sexes were explained on the basis of the reading approaches that males and females used.

For a study of time intervals measured by the production method, Hancock, Arthur, Chrysler, and Lee (1994) found that sex of the participants was significant for mean time estimates. An interaction was reported between sex and illumination condition, shown through less variability among women than men in unlighted as compared with lighted conditions. Both age and sex were variables (along with Type A and B behavior) studied in subjective time scaling by Eisler and Eisler (1994). Older persons had longer reproduction time periods than young, and males took less time for reproduction than females. Interestingly, Type A or B behavior seemed not to have any effect on results.

Different results were obtained by Fingerman and Perlmutter (1995) in a study of future time perspective with young and old men and women. Locus of control was also included as a variable. Participants were asked whether they thought more about the immediate future (a few days, several months from now, the distant future). The authors found neither age nor gender differences among these time periods. The most often reported period of musing was the next few months. There was also evidence (though not significant) that younger persons tended to think more about the distant future than older ones.

A sample of young, middle-aged, and older adults was asked to describe their personalities at three time periods: 20 to 25 years old, the present, and when they would be 65 to 70 (Fleeson and Heckhausen, 1997). The actual age range was 24 to 64, a feature that may have obfuscated the results. Nevertheless, only moderate changes in personality were anticipated or viewed retrospectively. Older persons perceived more losses than gains, but in general all looked on the positive side. Young adults tended to dwell on exploration in life now and into the future. Middle-aged persons concentrated on productivity and rewards, and older persons were more concerned for security and comfort. Generally, all age groups were idealistic in their view of life currently and to come.

Time perspective has even been studied in relation to driving behaviors (Zimbardo, Keough, and Boyd, 1997). A sample of almost 3,000 persons produced evidence that present time perspective is a reliable predictor of risk-taking while behind the wheel of an automobile. Males take more risks than females, the latter also being more future oriented and the former more present oriented. Even such factors as aggression and impulsivity did not show the predictive ability for risk-taking that present time orientation did.

Marmaras, Vassilakis, and Dounias (1995) tested accuracy of time estimation for different time durations and with various strategies. Gender differences were not found, but accuracy was affected by length of intervals and by variation of concurrent tasks. The strategies used (mental counting, using an orienting feature such as "one camel, two camels, etc.," and establishing a mental image of a familiar clock) were only partially influential. Thus, task variation and time interval were the major contributors to the results. Marmaras et al. were most interested in the effects for the workplace where accurate time estimation is a necessary feature. Their remarks in this regard are apt for our attention to time orientation. One they label epistemological, reflecting the manner in which psychological problems are considered and consequently designed experimentally. The consequence is results not directly related to the needs of ergonomists. The other comment deals with pragmatism. In the workplace, availability of and use of time-pieces by workers are essential. Psychologists avoid them for subjects in measuring time intervals in the laboratory (pp. 1054–1055).

Differences (inconsistencies?) in methodology certainly constitute a major reason why it is difficult to find congruency and comparability among studies in psychology even about the same phenomenon. When that is combined with the inconsistencies of humans in responding to tasks (because of context and personal variables), a model of behavior that can be reliable is apt to become difficult to achieve indeed.

Intellect

One of the variables that must have a marked effect is that of intellect. Several studies have examined the influence exerted on results with time estimation. Grskovich, Zentall, and Stormont-Spurgin (1995), for example, examined children, adolescents, and young adults either with or without disabilities for the relationship between time estimation and planning abilities. There were differences between the groups but—important to the issue under discussion here—control for IQ (intelligence quotient) removed their significance. They advocate the need for control of ability when groups are to be compared on such variables as time orientation. Whether or not some measure that produces an intelligence quotient is the best procedure to use, their argument that intellect may be a significant factor in results should not be ignored.

How intellect may work is not reflected in such a statement, no matter how accurate in the long run. The difficulties involved can be demonstrated from the results of a study by Josephs and Hahn (1995). The task was to estimate the time needed for various academic tasks, such as writing a paper or reading an assigned story. The interesting outcome was that their subjects showed a marked tendency to sacrifice accuracy in the estimate in favor of minimizing the cognitive effort that they must make in selecting strategies to use. As a result, the participants tended to make underestimates of the time needed for the task. This raises the interesting possibility that the amount of intellect may not be so much the problem as the motivation to use the competencies present. In such a case, IQ may be less favorable for control for some more global assessment of the intellectual-motivational balance. Dare I to mention that it would be well to find some index of the "laziness factor"?

Another example where intellect may be inferred was found in a study (Glicksohn and Ron-Avni, 1997) where a measure of "originality" was used. The outcome produced a preference for dynamic images of time, leading to longer duration predictions. The authors conclude that perception and the conception of time are related. In a similar vein, Boltz (1993) found that expectancies were a major determinant of performance on time estimation. Where the participants found their expectations were fairly confirmed, their estimations tended to be very accurate. But when they required more trials or waited for a longer time than expected, their predictions became overestimates. In turn, if the trials or wait were lower than expected, their predictions were underestimates. Even information about expectations follows the pattern (Burt and Popple, 1996). After observing a staged event, participants were given information that implied either slower or faster action than actually occurred. Apparently, the subjects encoded the instructions well, for their estimates of duration were affected accordingly. Or perhaps they simply tried to give back to the informant what they conceived as the preference of that authority figure.

There would seem to be a variety of components that are influenced and that influence cognitive approaches to task completion. Byram (1997) studied performance using a suggested strategy that complex tasks must be broken into segments that can then be combined for making a more accurate prediction. As she says, "The implicit assumption is that people's limited cognitive abilities are too strained to process large, complex projects" (p. 235). There should even be efforts to revise predictions when surprises occur and to evaluate multiple scenarios (such as optimistic and best guess). Byram tried manipulating all such suggestions. Her findings (a tribute to the good sense of human cognition) indicate that *none* of the manipulations had significant effects on predictions.

This does not mean that predictions were unaffected by context and conditions. On the contrary, she found evidence of the "planning fallacy," reflected in the shorter predictions than actually occurred when information available to the participants was used to make predictions based on expectations of success. She also found that optimism about performance was exaggerated when external incentives were present. Her results offer implications for the reason for misestimation of time. First, "People seemed to use all the information externally available to them (i.e., instructions) but no more and no less" (p. 236). This speaks well for applying one's competencies and experiences. Second, "Time misestimations may occur when people are motivated, either internally or externally, to give longer or shorter predictions" (p. 236). She interprets this to mean that underestimation especially occurs when the motivation (from any source) focuses on plans for success. Most significant is her statement, "The current research demonstrated that, like other judgments, time predictions are susceptible to bias" (p. 237). There was no evidence that any specific cognitive bias occurred, and Byram stresses the need to assess the explicit motivations present in and to a participant.

A study mentioned when surveying gender effects (Marmaras, Vassilakis, and Dounias, 1995) also included elements of intellectual factors. They asked for estimations on tasks of different cognitive difficulty and requiring different cognitive functions. The authors found that time was overestimated when concurrent tasks were performed, and increasingly so as the difficulty level of tasks increased. Distraction from an immediate task by intellectual demands has some direct effect on the effort of performance by increasing the time estimated to be needed.

Intellect has been shown to be a significant variable in time orientation tasks. Precise roles have yet to be uncovered, but to ignore this variable will yield results that may be misleading.

Many personal, external variables have been investigated in the experimental search for an understanding of time relationships. The corpus is too large to give more than a passing review—and frankly because the meaning of outcomes is not clear. Such factors as long-standing pain (Hellström and Carlsson, 1996), juvenile delinquency (Carrillo de la Peña and Luengo, 1994), and preferences in music (MacNay, 1995) indicate the interest that has been generated in the subject.

One such study (Burt, 1993) clearly indicates the complexity of time estimation as it is applied to daily life. Burt had undergraduate students estimate retrospectively the duration of public events. He concluded that the type and degree of error made in estimation where there is a longer retention interval are determined by how typical the actual event duration was (p. 71). As the duration became more atypical, there was an increase in estimation error. If the actual duration differs from the typical by being shorter, there will be underestimation; longer atypicality leads to overestimation.

This conclusion has meaning for such daily activities as eyewitness reports in courts. Burt suggests that for atypical events the court must evaluate the effect on testimony and warn jurors of the effect this might have on a witness's estimate of the duration of the event. Otherwise, injustice may occur instead of the justice desired.

More important, Burt tells us that "a theory of duration estimation may need to consider perceptual input, retention interval, the existence of abstract event knowledge, and the extent to which the interval or event in question can be defined as an event" (p. 72).

CYCLICAL TIME DIMENSIONS: DAY, WEEK, MONTH

So far, no mention has been made of applications of the experimental method to commonly accepted time dimensions: day of the week, weeks, even years. These are cyclical in their nature; research should offer an understanding of how these arbitrary cyclic intervals are adapted to by persons in their time orientation. For example, Larsen and Thompson (1995) had participants recall the days of the week when personal and public events occurred that they had recorded in diaries. As might be expected, personal events were more accurately recalled (for the day on which they occurred) than public ones. However, accuracy did not decrease as retention time increased. It seemed that the personal meaning of *both* event types was more important for accuracy of the day on which they occurred than was the memory of the essence of the event itself. The authors conclude that memory for day of the week is largely reconstructed and based on the cyclical nature of the week in personal experience. Thus, one may recall that a given event occurred on a Wednesday because of certain precursors (or successors) on other days of the same week.

As for the month, Valax, Tremblay, and Sarocchi (1996) questioned a large sample as to the current, past, or future month. They then had their subjects tell them what processes they used in answering. In the majority, answers were chosen in terms of the present. (This is March; therefore, last month must have been February; and so on.) Where future orientation was used, there was a regular increase peaking at the end of the month. Response times varied according to the orientation used by the participant and with the context of the question asked. Generally, those who used a future orientation had a quicker response time.

A series of studies concerning the systems used to account for cyclical time has been published by Huttenlocher et al. (Huttenlocher, Hedges, and Bradburn, 1990; Huttenlocher, Hedges and Duncan, 1991; Huttenlocher, Hedges, and Prohaska, 1988, 1992). The 1992 study is the focus of discussion here, primarily because it examines schemas for keeping track of time in the seven-day period. It also has distinct parts: the five days of the traditional "workweek" (although formerly this unit was six days) and the two days of the "weekend." These units have different meanings to the individual because they provide the context for different kinds of activities (or inactivities). Huttenlocher et al. were able to examine the two units for differences in schemas that might be applied to memory for events.

The authors looked at days of the week for memory of events that could have happened on any of the seven days. They propose, "The usefulness of a scheme [to remember the day of an event] clearly depends on the elapsed time since an event occurs" (1992, p. 313). Although certainly true for many events, there are clear exceptions that occur because of the strength of one event as compared to another. One may well remember the exact day many years earlier when the honeymoon began and yet forget which day last week the bill for the utilities was paid. In any event, we must accept the ground rules used by the authors in order to appreciate their findings. In this case, "memory for the day of the week of events that could happen on any day might not be long lasting" (pp. 313–314).

Huttenlocher et al. propose that there are at least two ways that temporal information may be organized. First, there is the possibility of a timeline, events ordered as one would keep a diary. Second, there may be multiple-entry organization where an event assumes a place depending on its value in a particular scheme. Their data support the latter, not the former. Their procedure called for persons to recall the day of the week when a relatively unique event (an interview) was held. The delay ran from 1 week to 10 for a sample of over 800 participants. In line with their premise about elapsed time, the percentages of those who remembered correctly showed a decreasing number from week 1 through week 10, with a high of 59% and a low of 37%. However, the percentage drop was small and regular through week 5, becoming larger and quite irregular beginning with week 6. The lowest actual number was after week 8, indicating a potential difference in samples. It is also true, however, that there were 143 participants (of 814) who refused to respond to the follow-up. The pattern of the numbers of such persons was somewhat irregular as well. Statistical analysis showed that day of the week and the reported time that had elapsed since the interview were independent after the second week. Overall, then, there was evidence to support their hierarchical model for weekday periods. (Their follow-up included a question on the time during the day of the interview.)

Their findings allow for two conclusions. First, temporal memory in their study conformed more to a multiple-entry representation rather than a timeline representation. This has implications for the meaning of orientation in daily life: Time's arrow is not forward and unbroken in every instance. There are various temporal schemes that people may use. This aligns with the contextual and personal variables that have played a fairly prominent role in the results of the studies presented previously. There was the finding also that error in remembering the day of the interview tended to move to the middle of the week and not to the extremes. This, again, may represent an organizational safeguard for the lapsing memory.

The second finding reflects the organization of the week: The five workdays are not apt to be confused with the weekend. To them, the weekdays are a temporal unit, whereas the weekends are not. There is the possibility that this statement should be modified to indicate that humans can construct and deal with temporal units of different types. In any event, their conclusion from the series of studies is that there is a basic form of coding, event sequences, that forms the basis for time representation in memory.

Any strong conclusion must be held in some reserve, however. That there may be other possible explanations for other temporal events has been illustrated by Betz and Skowronski (1997). They and other associates also have conducted a series of investigations on temporal dating and event memory (Skowronski, Betz, Thompson, and Larsen, 1995; Thompson, Skowronski, and Betz, 1993; Thompson, Skowronski, Larsen, and Betz, 1996). They used autobiographical events, part of which were related to personal activities and part related to friends or family members. Earlier research had indicated to them that there is seldom direct retrieval of the actual date of an event from memory. Instead, the usual process is to reconstruct the date of an event, using multiple sources. Where the accuracy of the sources is limited, the amount of error in dating the event is higher. The authors had found three reconstruction strategies used by participants in prior research.

First, a known event often acts as an "anchor" permitting judgment of other events' relevance. This is the often-noted reconstruction: "My little brother was born a month after my birthday." Second, memory is searched by the person for any content that will help decide the date of an event: "I graduated in the spring, so this incident must have occurred in the fall." Some greater error may be introduced using this anchor than the first one. Third, one may use knowledge of a more general type to serve as the anchor: "We had a dance every Friday night, and this incident happened at a dance, so it must have been a Friday." Obviously, even more error may occur in using this anchor, particularly when searching for a date as well as a day.

The study discussed here uses the same investigative procedures of the others but extends the method in order to describe more discretely the strategies used. Their outcomes included the following: (1) Self-events were recalled better than nonpersonal ones. (2) Charged events were better remembered than those that were less extreme. (3) Frequently rehearsed events were more easily recalled than those less well rehearsed. (4) Events that involved atypical personal information were recalled better than those that were neutral or typical. (5) The rehearsal variable extended to the recall of positive and negative events as well: others' negative events were more often rehearsed and remembered at the same time that the participant's own negative events were given greater rehearsal. This finding is at variance with their preceding results (where personal positive events were more rehearsed). They explain this on the basis that differential rehearsal is an insufficient answer: there must be some initial mental involvement that influences how enhanced the memory of positive self-events may be. This issue they leave open to further investigation. Overall, their data imply that individuals are aware of cognitive processes that can be useful in reconstructing events, apply these processes, and can explain them.

Sandifer (1997) reports an interesting variation on daily schedules. He logged behavior of families in visitations to a science museum and found that agendas in this setting depended on the reason for visiting the museum as well as attendance (crowding) on weekends as compared to weekdays.

Simultaneity and Duration

There have been limited (almost nonexistent) efforts to coopt spacetime logic into the psychology of time orientation. A notable example, although challenging to understand, has been published by Kadlub (1996). He begins by citing a definition proposed by others for physical time as a continuum of an abstract nature that contains the possibility for measurement, is homogeneous, and is divisible into equal units. Simultaneity is possible in this definition but contains only one dimension, that of duration, which proceeds irreversibly in the direction of a past to future path (p. 903). He makes the point next that time has been viewed only in the sense of "duration," based upon our experience with the instruments that have been developed to measure on that dimension alone. Time is not defined at all by such a view. A definition of time to Kadlub must involve energy as a component.

Next he offers a definition that includes both concepts: duration and energy. In this view time is defined as energy output for each durational unit, or for some total power output. The definition above then must be amended so that the second sentence does not include the concept of simultaneity. There can be no "simultaneity" since space and energy are both equally involved. And this leaves us with the relativity relationship that our clocks measure duration only but do not assure that we are all experiencing time in equal measure. Each system has its own past, present, and future so that each system exists within its own spacetime and at its own rate. Duration lacks an absolute spatial direction, with the direction of past, present, or future being dependent upon the system involved. Our clocks, after all, are not synchronous regardless of our attempts to make them as much so as possible. It is true that we are much closer to having such clocks today. Most of us, however, are still using instruments that are subject to factors (like temperature) that make them less than accurate to some degree. For all practical purposes, error may be so small as to be considered unimportant. However, that does not mean that we may then declare our measured time as absolute and equally experienced.

Kadlub quotes Lecomte du Noüy, a French biologist, as proposing that each of us has an inner physiological time with a unit of its own. One outcome of this state is that the psychological awareness of time is related to the metabolic rate, Kadlub proposes. The effect is that an increase in metabolic rate will increase interpretation of subjective time, whereas a lower metabolic rate decreases it. He presents data that he feels support the position that our awareness of duration is a function of the present metabolic rate. The point is cleverly made:

Our inherited definition and measure of time has for centuries kept us searching for substance in an arbitrarily created monodimensional durational unit based on periodic motion. *Our search for that substance has been the equivalent of staring at a meter stick in hopes of gaining insight into the nature of space.* (p. 911, italics added)

Regardless of one's acceptance of Kadlub's position, he has faced a dilemma for psychology that has been largely ignored, and he has succeeded in challenging our comfortable beliefs.

This brings us last to a psychologist who has made major contributions to our understanding of the psychology of time (Fraisse, 1963, 1981). In a discussion of orientation in time (1963, pp. 40–48), he describes adaptation of organisms, including humans, to periodic changes that occur—both internal and external. There are rhythms brought about by the environment that have psychological consequences for the individual: the provision of an internal clock. We take such factors so much for granted that we overlook their importance to our daily functioning.

Such rhythms have been augmented by the increasingly precise instruments used to measure time. They help us to organize both work and leisure, including coordination with the activities of others. But we possess an awareness of time that is independent of objective measures. Fraisse quotes an example from William James of the person who lacked intellectual capacity for many daily routines, including telling time, yet was always aware when it was time for the bowl of soup that made a meal. Only when dementia has progressed to a devastating level is there such temporal disorientation that precludes a sense of time and time relationships. This topic is so important that it will be part of the last section of this book.

Fraisse concludes then that humans are capable of adapting to cyclic changes (such as day and night) in order to accommodate to biological needs. Such physiological features are psychologically important as well. Such adaptations he classifies as classical conditioning, because the stimuli become the signals for certain behavior. An unconditioned stimulus from an external source is associated with an internal stimulus, determined by the temporal relationship. Literally, conditioning to time has occurred and determines behavioral responses.

In another section, Fraisse (1963, p. 285) discusses the notion of time, based upon the person's attempt to reconstruct changes in his life so that he can adapt successfully to such changes. The most useful tool for this purpose appears to the individual to be the absolute nature of time described by Newton. The role of time orientation in behavior is described and is shown to be most consistent with Newtonian physics with its absolute notions of time and space. But Fraisse does not leave the issue at this level. Einstein's theory of relativity required a new consideration of time and space. Although not impinging directly on practical issues of behavior, Fraisse does point out that the concept represents a new attempt at adapting knowledge to reality at the same time that it does not affect everyday psychological life. This permits many investigations of time orientation that focus on the absolute and attempt to devise laws that will explain relationships. Fraisse says, "We therefore think that the time of relativity brings us beyond the bounds of the psychological problem of temporally organized behavior" (p. 287). Such a viewpoint has been widely accepted in psychology since 1963 but may be limited to the normative sense. Today we are cognizant of behavioral conditions that do not fit the normative and are of such profound importance that some more relative view must be attempted.

Since this is true, time's value must be examined where these conditions are present, where the absolute model will not adequately describe nor explain the deviance from the norm. A good example of this is the dementias, perhaps best recognized in Alzheimer's disease but by no means restricted to that condition. In 1963, Fraisse saw these as exceptional experiences, in the general category of our attempts to escape time's pressures through such devices as daydreams or mystical episodes. He maintains that security is not found in liberation from time since our personalities are formed and organized within such pressures. If there is no pressure, there is disorientation: activities are random rather than sequenced; there is isolation rather than community. This is an excellent illustration of the behavioral effects of dementia.

Man's chief defense against time, Fraisse believes, is the memory, the function that allows us to retain the past for application to the present. What might be a fairer statement would be to say that whatever memory is available becomes the basis for applications. This means that dementia does not destroy all memory and that what is left is useful to the person even if it is inconsistent with the social order.

Being able to include the past and future along with the present does not restrict the person from organizing change. Memory is assisted by thought, after all, and this permits seeing relationships between sequences of events. We can move from a moment of order to one of duration, from what was before to what is afterward, and its reverse. As we accomplish these tasks, Fraisse believes we hold control over time and change (pp. 291–292). One task, then, in examining time orientation in dementia is to identify the process that has such clear social impress in the behaviors of the dementia patient. Fraisse states that the psychologist attempts to understand the experience of time from its motivational standpoint but declines to give opinions on the value of time. So far as this is true, it is a thesis of this book that the effort needs to be expanded so that the value of time is made explicit psychologically.

Fraisse's 1981 work expands on key concepts and refines the discussion somewhat without presenting ideas at variance with his thinking in 1963. He does take a more relative position by pointing out that each of us has a unique experience of time, reflected in a difference between the time of the universe and the time each of us comprehends. Historically, there has been progress from a reality-based conception to the modern one that time is the cognition that occurs in our organization of the changes we encounter daily. The result has been the development of a psychology of time where time is not merely a stimulus impinging on us but a medium that we realize through experience in encountering, recognizing, and organizing changes.

Today there are two modes of acknowledging time: its perception and its representation. The former lasts only a few seconds before becoming the latter, a symbolic construction (if it is retained) that is the servant of our experience and not a reflection of reality. To understand how orientation in time operates, we must study not only its perceptual qualities but its representational one as well. That task may be better accomplished as we examine the developmental characteristics of an awareness of time.

The review of this chapter seems chaotic, in large measure because no model is available to generate hypotheses related to a general thesis. In fact, however, there is a gain to be had from so much idiosyncratic investigation. That gain is the fact that many variables, researched in isolation, can be judged for inclusion in a theory that uses the minimum components to yield a comprehensive model. Resulting from that, testable predictions may follow. At present no one seems to be attempting the labor of consolidating the large number of data in order to derive the theory. That is a task that eventually will challenge some, and it is hoped young, psychologists with excellent computer skills.

CHAPTER 4

Developing Time Concepts

Earlier in the twentieth century, Albert Einstein and Jean Piaget appeared together at a series of lectures on philosophy and psychology. Einstein asked Piaget about the source of time orientation: is it an innate function, or is it learned? He also wanted to know the relationship with a child's development of an understanding of velocity. Over a period of years Piaget conducted experimentation in his idiosyncratic approach in an effort to find an answer to the issues raised by Einstein (Piaget, 1969). The problem turned out to be more complex than one might first guess, involving analysis of concepts of simultaneity and duration (see Bergson, 1965, as applied to the theory of relativity) as well as developmental progress both in physical and psychological time.

Einstein's question implied even more basic matters, of course. There has been agreement that animals tend to live in an eternal present, unable to comprehend the relationships that form past and, particularly, future. Evolution has provided humankind with a brain capable of permitting comprehension of both past and present and even speculation beyond personal time experiences. Yet humans also have a basic brain structure like that of other animals and so may also operate in certain instances on the same level. This is reflected in the literature on biological rhythms, for example.

The most often cited example of cyclic rhythms is the daily one, related to the 24-hour period that encompasses day and night. Actually, the circadian rhythm is 25.3 hours (Herrera, 1990, p. 136), but we make adjustments to compensate for the difference by using external time cues. When these cues are not present, there is a gradual lengthening of the sleep-wake cycle to the true time period. There are also more rhythms than the circadian one: an ultradian rhythm that is more frequent than the daily one, displayed in such behaviors as the REM/NREM (rapid or nonrapid) eye movements during sleep periods, and infradian ones that exceed the daily one, as in menstrual cycles. These patterns are controlled by two pacemakers, located in or around the suprachiasmatic nucleus (SCN) of the hypothalamus. Each sends aberrant signals to the areas that control rhythms (Herrera, 1990, p. 136). Although not of major interest to our understanding of psychological elements in time orientation, there is a case to be made that very basic processes may be innate and important to our functioning.

Animal studies have shown that disruption in the area of the SCN will lead to a loss of synchrony with one another and the 24-hour day, and synchrony may even fail completely (Dworetsky, 1991, p. 160). Unfortunately, there is no recorded history to tell us about the behaviors of earliest humans nor about the changes that occurred as evolution brought greater and greater competencies. Adaptation in order to survive was certainly present from early prehistory and increased significantly as social order became the norm. Time orientation was a part of that adaptation even though it only slowly became a major factor in control of the lives of people. With written history, it was clear that time influenced roles and behavior to a significant degree.

The relationship between findings on animals and their implications for humans has been a more recent phenomenon (Hayflick, 1994, pp. 303–307). Biologists today are accepting and studying the role of biological rhythms as humans age. The aging process itself may be related to such rhythms. There have been many instances where the relation between time awareness and age has been expressed (e.g., Hayflick, 1994, p. 304). Most such expressions view time as moving slowly when one is young, becoming rapid in old age. At the same time the case may be made that time moves too rapidly for youth, becoming burdensome as one ages. In either event, time perception is an important component in our adaptation to daily life and its varied demands. There is a belief that youth look to the future, whereas aged persons look more to the past. Hayflick believes this may be a symptom of the fact that we encounter fewer novel experiences to record as we age, accompanied by some reduced openness to mental stimulation.

Biological rhythms do not possess the precision of modern-day instruments to measure time, although we do not really know how the biological rhythms are controlled and so may misinterpret what we see. Certainly Hayflick makes a strong case for the fact that evolution has placed such contingencies on the patterns of rhythms that they can and are used by us as "clocks." The identification of the SCN has helped specify some locations, but there may be several others not yet specified that are synchronized with all other internal clocks at the same time that they are discrete in their functions (see Travis, 1996, for example).

TIME ORIENTATION IN CHILDHOOD

The research on rhythms points to the future understanding of time orientation. In the meantime there has been a corpus of literature collecting on the development of time awareness that begins with early life and experiences. Much of these data focus on the increasing ability to use the past for operations in the present. At the same time, there has been an increasing interest and study of future time orientation as it grows in children and affects their behavior. Thomae (1981) concludes that this function must be combined with cognitive-motivational processes in an interactive model that gives a fuller picture of human behavior than can be found in present-past relationships. So a survey of developmental features in time orientation must be inclusive of all three time periods.

The interest in the study of time orientation in children has shown a wide involvement. With 3-year-olds, Droit (1994) demonstrated the effectiveness of an external clock on spacing responses of a specific duration and producing a response of a set duration. Controls were not as effective in performance on either task, showing that even very young children are adapted to using mechanical means of time identification. In a study of four- to seven-year-olds in France (Pouthas, Paindorge, and Jacquet, 1995), duration was judged using either an hour glass, metronome, or counting as an indicator. A different approach, using autobiographical material, was employed in Germany by Strube and Weber (1988). The subjects were five- to 10-year-olds who were asked about personal events that they then had to order either with or without prompts. They were also tested on their understanding of age concepts and mastery of conventional timing systems.

Even tests devised to measure, in part, time and space orientation have been reported (for example, Lepage, 1979). There have been review articles, pulling together findings from worldwide sources (see Montangero, 1993, as an example). All such reports add to the literature and more frequently reinforce rather than dispute. This must mean that the phenomenon of time orientation, while it may be culture dependent to some degree, has a similar role to play in children's development wherever they may live. This point is supported by studies such as those by Fang, Feng, Jiang, and Fang (1993) and Fang, Feng, Fang, and Jiang (1994). The problems investigated were time measurement strategies in the first and time duration estimate strategies in the second. Materials were appropriate to the culture of the five- and six-year-olds living in China, but the results could be compared with those from Western cultures.

Such studies are common but lack the direction given by a model of time orientation that delimits arbitrary elements. As Hawking (1996, p. 15) has noted:

A theory is a good theory if it satisfies two requirements. It must accurately describe a large class of observations on the basis of a model that contains only a few arbitrary elements, and it must make definite predictions about the results of future observations.

Psychologists tend to emphasize method over model in many fields, with the clinical areas being the greater exception. As a result, we find controls imposed without a relationship between paradigms being discussed in more than a discrete manner. We have learned much about human behavior with this approach, but we have not gained much knowledge into the reason for such behavior. Since clinical areas are most concerned about the practical implications of behavior and treatment for divergences, perhaps this explains the more common presence of models. Even these efforts do not meet the limits imposed by Hawking, however.

Piaget on Children's Time Awareness

In any event, the work of Jean Piaget in child development has enjoyed some of its acceptance by the fact that it does build on elements central to the problems investigated. This is buttressed by the attempt to demonstrate predictability of the findings, at least on a verbal level. Piaget, of course, sacrificed method for attention to problem, opening himself to criticism about the reliability of prediction from his results. Yet he has given us food for much thought in the developmental characteristics of intellectual growth and various offshoots, including time orientation.

How much influence Einstein's suggestion about researching the development of time awareness in children had on Piaget's work in the area is not clear. It fits in the general scheme of Piagetian research and may well have occurred anyway. In its own right, then, Piaget's volume describing studies on children's conceptions of time is worthy of review and assessment.

Piaget (1969) tells us in the foreword that time awareness is more a practical than an esoteric issue. This has been demonstrated by the fact that teachers and psychologists have reported many instances where schoolchildren were unable to comprehend the idea of time. This suggested to him that there should be study of the processes involved in the fundamental processes of temporal order, simultaneity, and equality and combining of durations. There are premises that he states at the outset: Time's arrow moves in a forward direction ("time is conceived as a moving film consisting of stills that follow one another in quick succession" [p. 1]) and achieves early awareness in the stage of concrete operations, gradually developing to maturity in formal operations. This must be interpreted in spacetime terms: Together space and time represent the totality of the relationships among objects.

Time is the context of causality and can be understood only as the child establishes chains between cause and effect, explaining the latter in terms of the former. Sequencing is little comprehended by children before the age of seven or so but has become habitual in almost all eight-year-olds. This limits reasoning by young children about several possibilities at any one time; they are restricted to the sequence that is exposed to them first. Operational reversibility is doubtful before age eight, after which the child can effectively reconstruct the actual and unchangeable order of events. Piaget opts to avoid complex causal series in the study of time since it is necessary to discover the development of coordination among durations. By studying isolated instances of motion in space, both issues may be resolved.

With the children in his sample, Piaget was able to formulate certain questions about order of events and estimating duration at different ages. His results disclosed some three mental stages of development for the issue of order. In the earliest stage, children are unable to demonstrate competence in ordering. This is followed by a second stage that permits ordering under limited conditions, restricted to whole patterns and not partial ones. The final stage overcomes this deficiency, and the children order events quickly and accurately. What is mentally involved in the progression represents the development of an ability to produce corresponding series operationally; children become capable of anticipating correspondence between individual items in a series and thereby construct time concepts. It is not innate, nor is it intuitive; it is developmental.

The issue of durations reflects the ability of the child to appreciate the order of events. Order implies an understanding of succession and the meaning of simultaneity, to Piaget not operationally possible until the child has constructed a system of combined durations. There is the mirror-image that durations are not appreciated operationally until they are meshed with a system of successions and simultaneities. Again, he found the progression to be in developmental stages. In Stage I, there is much imprecision in a child's grasp of time durations. Stage II permits a realization that time intervals may be separated from speed and distance, but with the necessary coordination still lacking. Stage III has occurred when the child can correlate durations with the correct order of events.

Ultimately, Piaget explains, time derives an order of succession from causality, the relationship now understood by the child that cause must precede effect. In turn, causality itself is expressed by duration because duration is the ratio of distance to velocity, the basic reflection of operations in space and time. In the practical sense, Stage I is a period where distance is not differentiated from successions and durations. In the second stage there begins the differentiation or articulation needed because the child can now perceive "before" and "after" in space and time or because simultaneity is seen as independent of positions and velocities. There will be differences from child to child in the point when adequate articulation occurs in intuition. Even as this occurs there is still not an immediate articulation to all temporal relations. The process may, then, be sporadic and discontinuous. As the child achieves Stage III developmentally, however, there is the perception that operations may be applied to all groupings, leading to a mature and complete system that includes both durations and successions. Piaget has defined processes involved in the child's comprehension of time orientation along with the stages (and their approximate mental ages of occurrence) to the point of a mature grasp of the meanings. The necessary element is mental; in fact, the child cannot grow on an intuitive basis alone. Just how this evolution develops is not clear at this point.

Piaget applied the same mode of study to clarify the understanding by the child of simultaneity. Here, also, the three distinct stages leading from error and inconsistency to eventual maturity in comprehension were found. Just so with succession as well. Initially, children look on "before" and "after" in time as representations of spatial order. This essentially preserves the perceptual, sensory-motor, practical method of observing events. Only as there is gradual realization that elements that are not immediately spatial are essential to operations with time does the child move to the maturity needed.

The measurement of time, according to Piaget, is based on isochronism: motions that take the same duration to occur under the same conditions. This creates a "vicious circle" since the isochronism of one motion is dependent on that of other motions. That drawback is resolved as the "circle" widens when the child begins to realize that there is a principle of conservation of velocities that allows the construction of groups of transformations. Hence, the child must realize that all timepieces are isochronistic and conform to the principle of conservation of velocities.

The journey to this outcome involves the same stages that Piaget had identified for other elements in understanding time. Eventually, the child develops a time scale that has homogeneity and uniformity. Now units of distance that travel at a given and constant velocity are transformed into units of time. The quantity yielded by this realization represents an operational synthesis of the blending of durations and the equalization of successive durations; the former is synchronism and the latter is isochronism.

From the several studies with their results, Piaget draws conclusions and implications that answer Einstein's general question and also provide the components leading to predictability. There is, first, the issue of a child's grasp of time relationships: Is this an innate ability, or must it be learned? His results lead Piaget to conclude that the child operates on an egocentric level at first, "explaining" physical time as though it were congruent with the actions that must be timed. There is no homogeneous time that applies to all phenomena; what one sees is the only equivalency needed. This could lead one to speculate that the child at this stage realizes "pure" time that has no relation to physical time, which is spatial in its expression. However, Piaget rejects this notion that psychological time and physical time are separate. Indeed, each is based on the other. Accurate orientation in time appreciates the differèntiation of the two and uses the operations that bring their correlation.

With this position as background, Piaget then discusses the concept of age and how it relates to stages of development. He poses three questions: Does the child see aging as a continuous process in time? Is this time the same for all individuals? Can the child associate age differences with the order of births? Initially, children see age as independent of birth order so that differences in age are modified over time. Then children move on to maintain that age does depend on birth order, even though age differences are not maintained throughout life, or that age differences are maintained but are not dependent on birth order. Finally, because they are now able to coordinate duration and succession, they realize that both the order of birth and age differences are important elements to a coherent system of aging. This means that the conception of age follows the same pattern as that of physical time, requiring coordination of motions and velocities.

Psychological time follows the same pattern as physical time and age awareness. By 11 years or so, the child has matured to the level that psychological time is realized as a particular case of the coordination of motions and velocities.

In summary, the child's conception of time depends upon the developmental stage the child has reached mentally. During the sensory-motor period, there is awareness only of the present, each action has its own time, and there are as many temporal schemes as there are experiences. The acquisition of language (due to the experience and mental growth permitting it) moves the child to Stage I, beginning about 2 years of age and continuing in some forms to about age 8. During this stage, time is localized in two ways: It varies with the motion involved and is confused with spatial order. Stage II brings articulated intuitions, and the period from 8 to 11 years refines relationships and leads to operations (in Stage III) so that the child of 11 years has achieved orientation in time that is congruent with the adult. The answer to Einstein's question about velocity is that relativistic time is an extension in velocities to the ultimate speed of light.

Exceptions to Piaget's Model. More recent studies have offered a somewhat different analysis of time relations in young children than seemed plausible to Piaget. Lewkowicz (1989), for example, has observed that infants show behaviors in accord with some awareness of time and that they can respond to temporally based stimuli very early in their development. He does not describe the basis of such behaviors, stating that there needs to be intensive study of intrinsic biobehavioral rhythms and how they interact with identifiable time-related processing capacities. He posits that there may be some kind of neural timekeeper that is responsible but that this is by no means the only possible explanation. As a result, he admits that too little hard evidence is available as yet.

Weist (1989) has pointed to a further gap in the developmental model of Piaget with his attempts to trace the orientation to time that occurs between ages two and five. The focus of investigations has been on language usage by children from which inferences can be made about temporal awareness and accommodation. Weist presents evidence that past can be distinguished by the child from nonpast by the age of two years. The time established for some event (called "event time") can be related to the time current in the perceptual environment ("speech time") in such children, and Weist infers that they can not only recall some prior experience but also realize its properties. By two years, six months there is evidence that the child can contrast past locations in time.

From this point on, complex language forms (such as adverbs) are used by children to indicate the flow of time, although not always in the strict meaning of the adverb to an adult. Now the child can take a reference that is prior to, congruent with, or subsequent to speech time. Weist gives the example that "yesterday" means at some past time rather than specifically the day before. By age three to three years, five months, Weist reports that children can sequence events effectively enough that they perceive event time, speech time, and reference time as unique time intervals. The progress in time orientation from one year and six months on is apparently more complete and can be specified more exactly than Piaget deduced from his data.

Children learn to tell time by direct experience and instruction. At the same time, they develop strategies that may be varied according to the demands noted by the child at the moment. The strategies that may be employed have been identified and described by Siegler and McGilly (1989). Not only will different children use different strategies in time-telling, but the individual child will vary the procedure within or between tasks. There are five commonly employed strategies, according to Siegler and McGilly, in place by age eight or nine, when the transition between unskilled and skilled time-telling is taking place. The procedure seemed to be that children first located the number on which the hour hand had just passed, thereby indicating the hour. That was followed by one of the five strategies that would be most helpful in specifying the minutes after or before that hour.

First, on half the attempts, the authors report that children used a retrieval strategy, immediately telling the time without seeming effort and explaining their skill as "just knowing by looking at the clock." On about one-sixth of the trials, there was a counting from the hour by five-minute intervals, by one minute from the intervals, or by five- and one-minute intervals. One-fourth of the time the children counted forward from an earlier five-minute mark. In a few cases, less than 10%, the children used a backward counting procedure.

A major distinction in time orientation involves realization of the relationships between distance, duration, and speed. Acredolo (1989) offers some support for the notion that even in early childhood such relationships are partially realized. Principally, this involves the correlation between distance and duration, and between speed and duration. There is even some awareness that a relationship exists between distance and speed. The overall correlation, however, develops only during middle and later childhood. Acredolo is unable as yet to specify precisely when such mature judgment has developed. But since the total awareness is absent, younger children rely on either speed or distance cues when they must give an estimate of the time taken by two observed objects. This leads to an inadequate attempt to equate duration with distance and/or speed. Mature development allows them to evaluate time cues in terms of starting and stopping.

Specific cyclical time periods (days of the week and months) have been studied by several psychologists, and Friedman (1989) has reviewed his own and others' research on this topic. Several models could be used to encompass knowledge of the systems of understanding days of the week and months of the year. He concludes, however, that the most trustworthy models are of two types: *serial order*, where each element is linked to the next (Tuesday follows Monday, June follows May, etc.), leading to a sequential realization and explication, and *imaging*, where information in a position format can be mentally encoded directly. This allows perception of the relative closeness of elements.

Friedman tells us that the verbal list system is effective in permitting coding between each day or month and its successor(s). With the image system, one may build mental models of relative times when different elements occurred in time. The two should differ in the fact that backward order judgments are more difficult in using a verbal list system but more accessible with imaging and in the fact that judging the relationship between two elements is slower with the verbal listing procedure as the number of events intervening is greater. Such factors imply that different systems will be used for different types of tasks, especially with adults who use both systems on a regular and accurate basis. The most efficient will be chosen, almost automatically, by the person who has reached maturity in functioning in time.

There is a developmental aspect to awareness and use of the systems advocated by Friedman, beginning in childhood and reaching maturity usually in adulthood. But the development is not automatic or consistent only with age achieved. Children show skill at different ages, without any real disclosure (to date at least) of the processes involved. Friedman proposes that three factors influence development of the representations used in a domain. First, there is the formal structure of the content for that domain. Second, there are constraints on what may be called the "natural" representation and processing of the content. Third, the experience that the individual brings to the task in terms of operations already tried and found useful is important. The first, then, restricts the information available to the individual to perform adequately. The second is restricted by the ways in which information can be processed by individuals. And the third is a reflection of the mental development and use of experience at particular points of individual development. Whatever the exceptions, Friedman contends that, by adolescence, the abilities needed for imaging as well as serial ordering have developed.

CONTEMPORARY STUDIES OF CHILDREN'S TIME AWARENESS

In recent years the study of time orientation has continued to focus on developmental features with particular emphasis on cognitive factors. A recent review (Bates, Elman, and Li, 1994) on language learning highlights the pervasive presence of time in human behavior, at the same time that the authors point out that "it is particularly curious that most theories of human behavior completely neglect time" (p. 294). Perhaps it is because we are so involved with time from early in life that it is taken for granted. Among the few theories that recognize the importance of time, the authors describe connectionist models that posit neural networks, employed in time dimensions as a feature of prediction by children. Information on past and present events has been found to be a tool of the networks in estimating linguistic elements. Temporal constraints frequently are part of the mental behavior of children in the studies surveyed, affecting comprehension and production. The results of the studies surveyed by Bates et al. lead them to suggest caution in assuming that prior innate knowledge must be involved to a significant degree in language acquisition.

They also see a key role for anticipation that the world will change over time as a background for induction by children. Prediction (and thus some future time orientation) may be a powerful means by which children bring some order to their worlds. Further, by such induction they establish the basis for further learning. From the neural networks established in time, the child can achieve original ways of considering the rules of language usage. They begin to understand that rules are nothing more than the elements in mental space that assist communication. There follows a comprehension of language and how to produce it at the proper moment, on time. After that, the child learns to talk about time.

More in line with the work of Piaget, Montangero (1993) examined reasoning in children as it related to events in time. He proposes a "prelogic" of time that is based on dyads that are of unequal importance. Children develop increasing competence in judging durations using one of several systems of relationships. One of the outcomes was a linguistic perspective that achieved rapid development around age 10.

The developmental pattern in children's ability to put events in their proper sequence has been described in a study by Fivush and Mandler (1985). It is also a good example of the concept of the absolute expression of time's arrow in a forward direction. Children of ages four, five, and six composed the sample, arranging pictures in both a forward and backward sequence without having seen the correct order. Not surprisingly, the easiest events to sequence were familiar ones in forward order. The authors explain this expected finding on the basis that performance is best when a child has a well-organized representation to use. This does not mean that the child understands the basis of this organization; the fact that the task is temporally organized permits the child to retrieve information in a sequential form.

Unfamiliar events in a forward order were somewhat more difficult for the subjects to sequence. Retrieval from a prior-established organization is not so applicable to this task. What is now required is an understanding of the logical relations that link actions. Children of the age group used had not reached a developmental level that allowed them to understand the relations, or even if they had, they were not necessarily capable of making inferences about them.

As for sequencing of events backward, even familiarity is not a sufficient basis for correct behavior. Now there is a need to organize the events temporally into a new organization; retrieving the material in the sequence presented is no longer feasible. The reason for this is unknown at present, the authors state. But it is apparent that some manipulation of the material is required in order to give a correct reverse sequence. Familiar material is more apt to be dealt with correctly eventually, whereas unfamiliar material may be totally deficient. Other research seems to duplicate the overall findings of this study. Even adults require more effort and time in reconstructing events in a backward order than in a forward one, and especially when the events are unique and unfamiliar.

This brings the issue of what it is that is developed in dealing with time orientation of the type studied here. The authors conclude: "The recurring pattern suggests that it is not so much sequencing ability per se that is developing: rather, what develops are organized event representations and the ability to manipulate these representations in increasingly flexible ways" (p. 1445). This emphasizes the roles of intellectual maturity and experience in dealing effectively with such time dimensions.

Friedman has examined the nature of temporal structure in children through a series of studies. In 1986 he reported results of three experiments that traced the development of understanding of the structure of days of the week and months. Friedman concluded that a two-stage model about information storage offers the best explanation. First comes the order of storage, following the pattern of verbal list learning, which is then followed by the use of an image system for processing. The development is protracted, beginning about the third grade, when children learn to recite the days of the week and the months in order but evolving into adult-level competence only in early to middle adolescence.

Explanations for the extended period needed are not clear. First, Friedman points to the difficulty younger children have in dealing with retention of the list of days and months, particularly in the middle of the list (Wednesday and Thursday or July and August, for example). This seems to reflect a deficiency in coping with the structure of the list. Since performance is achieved only after several years of practice, it would seem that a second possibility is the absence of the mental operations necessary to reach the second level of his two-stage model. This would reflect a developmental cognitive factor over time. But more appealing to Friedman is an explanation that is more specific to the contents of the temporal structure that must be understood by the child.

This leads him to the conclusion that three kinds of factors are involved in developing representations of a particular content. First, there is the formal structure of the domain to be represented, involving properties of material such as forward order and the relative time at which nonadjacent elements occurred. Second, one must consider constraints imposed by pertinent representational and processing procedures. These would include cognitive systems that are responsible for the operations that are used in working memory, ways of extracting structural information. Finally, there is the history of operations that the child uses to perform on the task. Only this could account for the representations chosen and the processes used during the development of the child.

Experience must play its role as well. Friedman points out that small children encounter day and month representations only in terms of simple events of personal importance, like a birthday, until formal instruction begins on teaching the successions of days and months as series of inherently rigid construction. Rehearsal then occurs until the verbal list quality is established, usually about second or third grade. This system tends to remain in place, without other representations being practiced.

However, there is a second stage, imaging techniques, that becomes available by adolescence and is common (along with the verbal list technique) during adulthood. These occur, Friedman tells us, because of a patterning sequence. Through much of childhood, the operation used with days and months is recitation that satisfies the educational criterion that the child "knows" the names and order of days of the weeks and months of the year. With adolescence, solution of real-life problems achieves increasing importance. There must be planning for the future in many ways other than the personal ones like birthdays, responsibilities (such as work require-ments) that require planning within an order of events as well. So children begin to combine the verbal list approach with an imaging system in order to bring problem solving. Friedman uses a school example to demonstrate this process. Thus, the child uses a verbal list system to order the days when assignments are due. At the same time, an imaging occurs whereby working memory records the relative times when different assignments are due (p. 1399). Success with this method leads to an increasing facility and dependence for its use in more and more complex problem-solving situa-tions. Times of occurrence become increasingly relative in the mental life of the adolescent, a factor present throughout adulthood. Precision leads to image construction imposed on particular tasks. Friedman acknowledges that questions were left unanswered by this explanation, and there was no empirical body of data to answer them.

The development of time memory has been an area of interest to Fried-man as well. In a study published in 1991, he examined the memory for events in terms of relative recency of two instances (called "distance") and for the time of day during which an event occurred (called "locations"). Using children of four, six, and eight years of age, he also looked for the developmental pattern that might be present. Children were used since there would not be the confusion of processes found in adults.

Friedman found that children of four were capable of discriminating the relative recency of the two events he used for study. However, they were not able to specify the time of day on which each event occurred with consistent accuracy if the time scale exceeded one day. Since six- and eight-year-olds could do so, Friedman concluded that there must be separate processes that operate independently on different time scales. This means that there are two ways to know the time of events: first as the distance from the present and second as the location within time patterns.

By four years of age, children share with adults similarities in the proc-esses used to remember when past events occurred. They also share the ability to judge the relative recency of events. However, it is only by age six that they share with adults the ability to reason about locations in the past over long time periods (more than one day). One possible explanation for the incremental gains in six-year-olds is that children may develop in-creasingly elaborate representations of the meanings of conventional time patterns. A second possibility is that the older child may have discovered flexibility in ways to represent the order of components in a time pattern. It is even possible, Friedman maintains, that the early stages of imaging for days of the week and months that he has found present in adolescents and adults have begun their expression.

Friedman tells us that a reconstructive model implies that two different kinds of information are needed to locate past events in time. First, it is necessary to recall elements that have temporal value; second, there must be present a general time knowledge that includes a representation of the time pattern within which the event is to be located along with sufficient knowledge of the attributes of times so that the event can be recalled. Four-year-olds are as accurate as six- and eight-year-olds on recalling and recognizing information about target events. But general time knowledge increases with age: The four-year-old knows time patterns only for a given day; the six- and especially eight-year-olds also have knowledge about days of the week, months, and even seasons. The distinguishing characteristic must be knowledge about particular time scales. Friedman concludes:

Not only do children need to know about the seasons, months, and days of the week to master time as presented in the school curriculum, they also must grasp temporal patterns to orient to the present and achieve a sense of a chronological past. (1991, p. 154)

This idea was taken a further step in a study by Friedman published in 1992. Here he gathered data in an attempt to answer several basic questions about the ability of children to link memories to long-scale temporal locations. (The events used were real-life in source, including yesterday, last weekend, last summer, and a few holidays from the past year.) The first issue was the age at which children were able to retrieve differentiated memories from conventional time locations of the type used. He found that even four- and five-year-olds could recall events from such past locations.

Second, he asked whether such memories are updated from time to time. Again, his data led him to conclude that many children, even in the youngest group (four- and five-year-olds) were able to retain events that were specific to the most recent occurrence of the stimulus location. Question three asked: Does the ability of children to recall events from locations imply knowledge of the relative order of these locations? Here, with these young children, the answer was no. Even nine-year-olds were unable to determine which of a pair of locations from the previous year had happened in the more distant past. Finally, the study was designed to determine whether the ability to produce a correct ordering of a set of locations was developmentally distinct from the ability to judge which of two locations was more distant from the present. There was some evidence that the answer might be yes, although that must be tempered by the fact that some young children who were more accurate on one sort of task were also more accurate on the other.

It would seem, then, that in young children locations are largely a matter of isolated islands of time without an integrated view of the relative times of occurrence of these islands. Gradually, these isolations are overcome, and the adolescent begins to show the competencies found in adults.

Personal Variables in Children's Time Awareness

To this point, the research surveyed has focused on intellectual variables relevant to childhood development of time orientation. There has been some study of other personal variables as well. Gjesme (1975), for example, looked at motivational characteristics that are involved in future time orientation. With 12-year-olds, he found that those youngsters who held high motivation for success but low motivation to avoid failure (called "approach oriented") showed increases in performance on a distant achievement task as time passed. Those who were motivated to avoid failure also showed a greater slope on the plot of a negative goal gradient on future time orientation than those who had high motivation to approach success. Partial support was found for the position that avoidance-oriented youngsters would show decreases in performance as a distant goal was approached, along with a steeper gradient toward a positive goal for those who were lower in future time orientation. In practical terms, then, children with high future time orientation perceive an event as far off as a year in the future as nearer in time than those who have low future time orientation.

A follow-up study (Gjesme, 1981) examined the prediction that "the higher instrumentality of activity and goal importance the lower the perceived temporal distance to the goal" (p. 176). Using German students in grades seven, eight, and nine, Gjesme asked questions (p. 178) concerned with a practical task (taking a test) but involving a time dimension as perceived by the student. The tests were to be taken in one month or one year. Gjesme varied his queries in terms of importance of the test. For example, he asked his subjects to state their perceptions of time distance for a test in one year, an important test in one year, and an unimportant test in one year. For a week or month, the question inquired only about time perception for a test, without regard to importance. Ratings were possible from very brief to intermediate to far away on a nine-point scale.

Gjesme concludes that time itself (one week, month, year) is the most significant determinant of perceived goal distance, followed closely by the importance of the goal in its own right. It would seem that how the student perceives a goal in terms of its distance in time affects the importance of positive or negative motivation. "That is, high orientation toward future time, high instrumentality of activity, and the particular importance of the future goal may augment positive motivation for success-oriented individuals. In contrast, low orientation toward the future, low instrumentality of activity, and especially the *unimportance* of an anticipated goal may minimize negative motivation especially for failure-oriented (high anxious) individuals" (p. 181).

The meaning of future time orientation for adults may not be consistent with the findings of Gjesme, particularly with older persons. There have been a number of studies that suggest that the present and past become increasingly prominent in the lives of middle-aged and older individuals. Future time orientation may be less comfortable, and more avoided, as time passes even for those who once had a strong orientation to the future. Thomae (1981, pp. 271–272) offers several hypotheses about this possibility, including the position that humankind must anticipate a future. As one ages, this anticipation becomes more difficult and even a threat. So there is a greater concentration on the present. The past and future consequently become personally infinite, bringing restructure by the older person of a time perspective.

This restructuration offers the illusion of an unlimited range of future and past time perspective, laying the dark around the bright center of the present and some spots in the nearest future. Therefore anticipations seem possible everywhere, even if they are not made unless to the nearest future. (p. 271)

Thomae believes that balance of time relationships is a basic process in motivation by the aging. This balance becomes more disturbed as restructing of time relationships occurs. So the individual adapts, using many variations that bring a developmental peak to motivational processes. This does not reduce the importance of any approach such as Gjesme's. It does indicate that development of *future* time orientation may mean very different things at different periods of one's life. This issue will be more deeply probed in later chapters.

DEVELOPING DIACHRONIC THINKING

The literature surveyed indicates that children develop time orientation as some correlate of their experiences and mental capacities. Some of the studies focus on a limited point in time, as at age 4 or 9; others examine behavior over a period of several years, as from age 6 to age 16, in order to describe the developmental nature of a behavior. Neither of these, however, gives us information on the processes involved at any of the levels or developmental periods. In fact, there is a disturbing tendency to reflect the Newtonian absolute in time's arrow, without regard to the roles of past, present, and future for the child in any behavior or from one time to another. This deficiency has been recognized by Montangero (1996) and dealt with in part in a series of studies of diachronic thinking and its development in children.

In fact, although he reports the results of these researches, he makes it clear that his purpose for the book is something quite different. Montangero places his emphasis for time on a perspective of knowledge rather than content of knowledge. Here, the person uses a perspective of time to frame reality and to analyze the realities for understanding once they are formed (p. 1). Montangero is interested in much more than the demonstration of children's acquisition of time-telling or even perception of time awareness. He wishes to determine the processes involved in moving from present time to an awareness of the past events leading to the present event and the succession that this allows into the future. To him, children use temporal knowledge to better understand the environment.

Montangero credits Piaget with bringing such a scientific method to the study of children's development. The work was diachronic because it explained knowledge in terms of its genesis and the processes that fostered it. More recent research bears the same stamp in some cases, although that is the exception rather than the rule. Too often, developmental psychologists have shown the presence of a skill in a child of a certain age but without relating that to its evolutionary history or its future maturity. Montangero considers this an observation, not an explanation.

The diachronic method is worthy of investigation because it is conducive to problem solution. If one approaches a problem with an intent to determine the origins and the conditions that have led to the present state, the possibility for future development is increased. A solution to the problem that may be more fruitful and avoid recurrence is enhanced.

Montangero used children of ages 8 to 12 in the studies cited here but maintains that the movement from the present-only orientation of the infant begins in early childhood, evident through the behaviors of anticipation and reconstruction. By age two, memory can be used to evoke relationships of the past to the present, and diachronic perspective is under way. As children become increasingly curious about the environment and their relations to it (ages three to five), they enquire about the origins of persons and events, further enlarging the corpus of knowledge that can be used diachronically. Already, the child will have realized the unidirectionality of time's arrow, which Montangero maintains is shown by an awareness of the irreversibility of certain events. By age five, then, children have the basic capabilities needed for expression of diachronic thinking. Montangero admits, however, that there can be disagreement over the issue of diachronic thinking as a true mode of thought. To him, it is certainly a way of understanding and appreciating reality; that, however, could be argued as a manifestation of some other competence. Within such constraints, he conducted experiments and draws conclusions about their importance in the development of time orientation in children.

From the practical standpoint, Montangero has only limited evidence of the nature of knowledge perspective. He does propose that cognitive functioning has some reference to the past since anything new must be accommodated to what is already known. There is even some element of anticipation because activity is normally related to some goal, no matter how poorly conceptualized. In the main, however, it is probably true that we usually consider events as they present themselves and try to deal effectively with them under those circumstances. Our responses are situationally attempted. However, if we have the opportunity (and particularly after the situation has been dealt with), we may begin to use the diachronic perspective. What led to this situation? Was it "caused" by some action that is under our control? Do we need to be concerned that we may be creating problems for ourselves because we do not recognize relationships between past and present? And what does all this mean for the future? Are there things that we should do to avoid repetition or recurrence of the problem? Can we ensure stability by being more alert to this situation in reference to its past and probable future? Montangero proposes that such mental behaviors represent our intention to understand the dynamics of a situation and to permit control. This knowledge perspective is diachronic since it gives us a view of life in temporal terms. The flow of time is filled with experience that is relevant to the present, maximized when the past and future are allowed to enlarge our perspective. In sum, *"the representation of the past stages and origins of an event make it possible to enrich one's knowledge of its present and predict its future"* (1996, p. 165, italics in original).

Montangero believes that the strongest argument that diachronic thinking exists as a true mode is supported by the fact that with age and cognitive processes there develop evolutions containing different knowledge contents. Once the child can think, diachronic expressions of cognition are possible. Although his experiments in this case ended with age 12, diachronic thought was incomplete in many respects so that further development was both possible and needed. Indeed, one might wonder how many mature adults consistently and completely use such a panorama of present-past-future analyses. One effect that he did observe experimentally was dramatic change in the quality of diachronic thinking about the age of 10 or 11. In fact, this finding compares with those of other developmental psychologists who have reported marked changes in cognitive abilities at this same age.

There is an essential interaction of diachronic thinking with age, environment (experience), and personal tendencies and interests. Some persons may live in the present only, the here and now absorbing most or all of their efforts. Others may expand to enrich their cognition with the suffusion of past experience with the present, and still others may go the added step to a future implications mode. Consideration must also be given (at least in research on this topic) to personal variables such as emotional states and psychological stability. In old age there needs to be consideration of the quality of brain function, including those conditions that produce dementia.

Montangero stresses that understanding the world and adapting to it require an ability to think in time. Many phenomena can be understood only when diachronic thinking has reached a sophisticated level of development. Complex problems may be more completely understood and solved with a diachronic perspective. As the history of a current situation is clarified, the proposal of alternative means to improve conditions will be amplified and increasingly realistic.

The study of time orientation in children has been sparser than one might anticipate. Before the efforts of Piaget prior to World War II, there was little or no interest in the subject. Einstein's challenge to Piaget to bring psychological study to the issue led to several publications that indicated the affinity of the stage model to children's awareness of time and adeptness in dealing with it. The great influence of Piaget's acceptance among psychologists undoubtedly led to the many other studies that presented normative data related to time-telling and time awareness. Such data have been essential and helpful—but are also limited. There was no real attempt to explore processes that subserved skills and gave meaning to thinking in time until the past two or three decades. That work is still in its infancy, and there are too few psychologists who see the issues as crucial and worthy of a career-encompassing effort.

Our knowledge of the mechanics of time, time in the absolute sense, time as a forward-pointing arrow that moves inexorably, has certainly been served by the research of the past and present. As important as that may be, we are woefully lacking in our knowledge of the meaning of time and the use of time in cognition by our children. True, change is under way and more satisfactory answers to questions of time orientation in children may be a major product of the twenty-first century.

CHAPTER 5

Defining Time Concepts

Limited as it may be, there does seem to be a case that can be made that infants begin to respond to internal and external temporal signals. Such responses may be explained as conditioned by a reinforcement system, but the alternative should be entertained that time awareness is present from early in life. When the hungry child stops crying as the door to its room is opened, the explanation is certainly not clear. If it is conditioning, there has been an impressive generalization by the infant. If it is temporal, it implies that the child has already begun to structure its present on past events and future consequences, limited as the connections may be.

Certainly there is an increasing ability to respond to temporal cues as the infant continues to develop. There is not yet time orientation that comprehends the relationships of duration and succession, nor can the baby demonstrate the role of speed in a relative sense. By age two or so, that process has begun to express itself in its primitive stages, to be refined and expanded as experience and mental capacity increase. The skill of time-telling is taught successfully to almost all children during the school years even as the meaning of time scales remains idiosyncratic. Late childhood seems to be a watershed developmentally if the research done to date has meaningful implications. By early adolescence the person realizes the import of duration, succession, and speed in a variety of ways.

VARIABLES IN ADOLESCENT TEMPORAL DEVELOPMENT

The direction and the dispatch with which the adolescent achieves the maturity to function in an adult temporal world now depend on personal variables to a significant degree. There are individual needs, goals, and

desires that are based on social class experiences. There are also the demands of social forces such as schools, parents, and peers. Diversity is the
rule and leads to the wide individual differences that make prediction a
risky game. But there is an increasing accommodation toward adult meanings of time and adjustment of life's routines to those meanings.

In adulthood societal demands predominate and help direct the expression and meaning of time orientation. There are the adjustment variables
that include one's mate, family, and group contacts. Modern societies also
impress time demands and adaptations through the workplace and work
roles. The workweek may be discriminated greatly from the weekend, with
divergent roles that seem antithetical to one another. The general expectation is that the mature adult will accommodate to societal values both
for personal and for social benefits. Time is a major factor in this structure
and must be appreciated in its explicit and implicit meanings.

Variables, both experimental and control, used in the process of such
study become a major concern. In adults one must consider more than the
mechanical aspects of time expression and accommodation, in many ways
the limiting point of study with children. There must be, instead, a regard
for the adult's conception of the relationships between past, present, and
future along with the applications to present behavior. Indeed, the picture
must ultimately include as well the understanding by the adult of the temporal perception of others who impinge within the environment. Such issues have not been traditionally the context of psychological research,
although we are seeing an increasing awareness and attempted application
in certain ways.

Measures of Temporal Effects

Measurement is a central feature for psychologists and must be considered in the developing context of studying temporal effects on behavior.
An example is found in a study of Gjesme (1983) focused on future time
orientation (FTO). He points out that results from a variety of studies show
contradictory results as FTO is considered in relation to other variables.
He believes that the measures used may be a significant contributor to the
discrepancies found and proposes that experimental conditions must be
differentiated from personal traits. As he states it, when the person deals
with the environment there is commonly a component toward something
new, something that is ahead, and so with FTO. But all individuals do not
conceive of "future" in the same respect. Some are more affected by goals
far in the future, whereas others concentrate only on the near future. One
of the factors that leads to such differences and that would produce differences in results in experimental studies lies in different time orientations.
He advocates differentiation between (1) FTO (with its various subdimen-
sions) that is conceived as a latent capacity to anticipate, structure, and be

involved in the future and (2) the arousal and manipulation of such capacities in the specific tasks and activities used in an experiment. This again opens the door to consideration of the personal traits that are so often ignored by the laboratory technician. As important, it details the need for time orientation to be considered more broadly than has been true in the past—resulting from a complex of personal and environmental conditions and events interacting with problems requiring solution either in life or the laboratory.

This viewpoint is buttressed in other studies as well. Rammsayer (1994) conducted research that produced results emphasizing the need for intact cognitive functioning in time estimation tasks. Specifically he affected, and altered, the cognitive competencies of his subjects by use of pharmacological agents that impaired memory and subsequently produced decrements in performance. Memory was highlighted as a considerable agent in certain time orientation tasks in agreement with other studies already cited. A physical component is thus added to the complex, requiring the experimentalist to control more precisely than is usually found.

Complicating the situation is a study by Dube and Schmitt (1996). They proposed that unfilled intervals during a social episode (thus, in-process) would be perceived by the person to last longer than similar unfilled intervals before (preprocess) and after (postprocess) the social episode. The unfilled intervals lasted for 10 minutes and were placed early in the episode, in the middle, or near the end. Their assumption was upheld: those individuals who had an unfilled period somewhere around the middle of the event perceived them as lasting longer than when the unfilled period was either early or late. The outcome held whether the estimation was made immediately after the episode or after a delay. Overestimation was greater when there was a delay than when it was immediate, however. Dube and Schmitt take the position that memory traces during an episode have a different character than those traces at other points in the process. They speculate that the specific information derived and used by participants is greater while the episode is ongoing rather than before and after. What might lead to such differences is unknown, but it is possible that a memory trace is not a memory trace in the same sense, depending upon the conditions and perhaps even the interpretation of the person.

The concept of gender and its effects has been studied in future time perspective as well. As one example, the work of Bouffard, Bastin, and Lapierre (1996) can be cited. They propose that future time perspective may well show transformations during adulthood in women according to such factors as chronological age and social roles. They used students, homemakers, and career women between the ages of 20 and 64, asking them about their aspirations. They analyzed the responses on the basis of implied time extension and motivational content. They found that there are a variety of changes that occurred during the years examined, although the fact that this was a cross-sectional view must be kept in mind. Both age and social role were associated with the aspirations expressed, influencing strongly the motives ascribed.

EFFECTS OF ADVERSE CONDITIONS

Perhaps this brief survey makes the point that understanding time orientation in adult behavior is far more complicated than has been generally realized. As a result, some more direct attention to research that specifies details will be helpful.

For this purpose, let's examine first some research focused on time orientation as it is influenced by adverse conditions. One reflection of such a condition is organic memory disorder. This condition was studied, with its effects on time estimation, by Williams, Medwedeff, and Haban (1989). A case study, there are the usual limitations in generalization, but that fact may be assuaged somewhat by the ability to examine effects more precisely.

Williams et al. used a 55-year-old woman who suffered with severe amnesia, comparing her competencies with 10 other nonimpaired women who averaged 58 years of age. All were asked to estimate time intervals using standard and accepted procedures. The authors point out that one of the prominent features of memory disorder is the broad, general inability to remember *and monitor* autobiographical experiences. (This despite the commonly held notion that memory of the remote past is better in dementia patients than is recent memory.) This generalized disability leads to a clinical disorientation to time and place. It is expressed in one behavior by the inability to order events in time accurately, even when they are personal (autobiographical).

This patient had damage near the third ventricle, a disorder that affects the medial-temporal lobe structure with particularly adverse effects on the limbic/hippocampal memory system. The patient and the controls compared closely in age and educational level (13 years for her and 12 years on average for the others). Both reproduction and verbal estimation methods were used as measures. The former required the person to go through a period of a certain duration and then reproduce it as accurately as possible. The latter was to experience the interval, then tell how long it was. Distractors were employed during the interval.

It is important to note that the patient was considered to have an excellent memory for events before the brain damage occurred. She had surgery for a brain mass 10 months prior to the experiment, consistently showing misjudgment of the current year after the operation and unable to remember the current day or month. In fact, she was uncertain about the details of her life after the operation. As expected, both time estimation and reproduction were significantly poorer than that of the controls.

Williams et al. conclude, "These findings are strong evidence that estimation of longer time intervals is a cognitive construction which is strongly dependent upon memory for temporal cues." In addition, "time construction relies on memory for such cues and the association of autobiographical content with specific time cues" (p. 722). These include everyday events, from telling time with a watch to assessing the room temperature to judging light levels.

There is a tendency to criticize the utility of such studies because they deal with the "abnormal" rather than the usual. However, there is clear evidence of this patient's functional abilities before her operation, the nature of her physical disorder was known and corrected, and the effects following the treatment were observed frequently. In some ways, this gives us a better basis for judging physical and subsequent mental disorders than could otherwise be possible. It also permits us to realize the basis for accurate autobiographical time orientation. Perhaps most of all it provides us with some basis for defining the essential elements for a scientific model of temporal behavior than is otherwise possible.

Socially Catastrophic Events

But we do not have to depend solely on physical disorders of a specified nature to give us inferential (at least) data on time estimation. There have been socially catastrophic events that influence behavior to extreme degrees, undoubtedly including time orientation. Such an example is the Holocaust, culminating in the deaths of millions and continuing to influence the lives of the survivors even today. Of course, much of the information available is anecdotal (see Hilberg, 1992), but other is documentary (see Hackett, 1995). Both represent rich sources that can be gleaned for variables of import to the effect of adversity on mental and physical functioning. There are such notable outcomes from severe trauma that immediate effects are often reported. Read and Fisher (1992, p. 347) in reporting on the final days of World War II in Berlin tell us that the severe artillery shelling by the Russians, without warning or alert, produced physical and mental hardships such that "[m]ost Berliners lost all sense of time. Days and nights merged into one dark, stinking nightmare as they waited helplessly for the end." Such reports can help us isolate the precursors, influences, and outcomes of events that bear on orientation and disorientation.

There have been a few studies of such conditions. Lomranz, Shmotkin, Zechovoy, and Rosenberg (1985) looked at past and future orientation among Holocaust survivors and compared them with an age-matched sample of Jewish non-Holocaust victims. Time orientation is defined as "temporal organization of experience usually conceived in terms of past, present, and future, which are often endowed with different weights, degrees of attentiveness, and cognitive or emotional investments" (p. 230). This definition was applied to measures used with some 44 Nazi concentration camp survivors and compared with 31 controls (Jews who had not been in camps). At the time of the study all subjects were between ages 50 and 60. The authors thus had data permitting an assessment of long-term effects of extreme trauma on time orientation.

Hypotheses were of four types. First, Lomranz et al. proposed that survivors would attach a greater significance in time orientation to the Holocaust period than controls. Second, these survivors should also place a greater emphasis on the past than their controls. Third, there would be evidence of less future orientation than for those never having been in concentration camps. Fourth, camp survivors would have a more pessimistic attitude toward life in general. The first hypothesis was strongly supported, whereas the second was given some support. However, hypothesis three was, if anything, reversed from what was expected. In part, the survivors showed some higher future orientation than the controls, although this is tempered by the fact that only one-third of the survivors mentioned a future event, while about half of the controls did. Hypothesis four also received confirmation.

Socially Minor Stressors

There seems no doubt that, in this study at least, a traumatic event can have adverse effects on time orientation even at some future point in time. The role of personal factors, in this case highly stressful and destructive, affects time orientation well beyond the period of the event. It would not seem untoward to consider that even lesser stressors and catastrophes must have their effects as well. Perhaps some of the observations about withdrawal as people grow older may be explained in part by the effects on time orientation by past and present circumstances. Lomranz et al. suggest that their results raise questions about how time orientation should be conceived in general. The *meaning* in past, present, and future needs more stringent demarcation and measurement than has been true in studies to this time. And, as inferred in comments above, less devastating events in life than the Holocaust should be investigated for their current and long-term effects on the time awareness and adaptations of adults.

A partial answer to such issues is reflected in the results of a study conducted by Shmotkin (1991). He examined life satisfaction from an evaluation by subjects of their pasts, presents, and anticipated futures (using 5-year periods). Almost 6,000 adults of age 18 and older participated in the survey. As expected by Shmotkin and in agreement with other findings, there was an increasing satisfaction with the past as people were older, *although the actual level did not increase with age.* The latter point is an important one when considering the common stereotype about the elderly and their emphasis on past memories. In any event, elders did attach increasing satisfaction to the past as compared to their assessment of the present and future and as compared to younger adults. There were two points in life where the change appeared most pertinent: age 51 and over, where the past begins to surpass the present, and age 66 and over, where the past surpasses the future. Shmotkin proposes that these represent developmental transitions of middle age and retirement.

A more exacting look at life satisfaction in his sample led Shmotkin to declare that from age 23 on the importance of the past was increased in perspective linearly. At the same time, the present always has greater import, regardless of age. Interestingly, he found that past and future have equal salience in old age. (His sample lived in Israel, and there may be sociocultural factors that produce somewhat different results in other countries.) Whatever the condition, present time has the greatest impact on life satisfaction generally through length of life. There is some decline in future orientation with old age, but the relative importance of the future on life satisfaction is not significantly reduced.

In fact, Shmotkin reports that the relative salience of the future on life satisfaction peaks in old age, not earlier. He posits three possible reasons for this fact. One, elderly persons realistically see that the future is short and potentially dangerous. Yet they also realize that their attitudes have some effect on what happens in that time period. Two, older persons are less apt to differentiate between the factors making up life satisfaction in general. Everything is important, not just selected elements. Three, the final years of one's life may be a time when there is an attempt to integrate experience into a meaningful whole. One's mortality is apparent, and there can be an attempt at least to conclude life with as optimistic an evaluation as possible. Shmotkin realizes that this is no more than a beginning in the study of life satisfaction and temporal orientation, with other subjective measures yet to be considered and the influence of such personal features as self-image and values evaluated.

MEMORY IN TIME PERSPECTIVE

Overemphasis should not be placed on personal variables, given our absence of comprehensive model building. As already indicated in this survey of literature, the role of memory in time perspective must be recognized. Memory is a function, of course, that has different meanings and influences on many facets of behavior at different ages. A model of time perception that includes both memory and chronological age could be helpful in delimiting the absolute variables and their roles necessary to a comprehensive theory. For this purpose, the social psychological model of time proposed by Flaherty and Meer (1994) seems pertinent. As they point out, there has been considerable research on the social imperatives imposed by measurement devices such as clocks, calendars, and schedules. These are, by and large, objective in their intent and usage and so lead to objective findings of the social organization of time in life. But Flaherty and Meer also believe that the objective must be balanced by the subjective, and their purpose here is to attend to that deficiency. So they have formulated a general theory of time as it is lived.

They remind us first that there are variations in how time is experienced. Those variations are not due to differences in people so much as they are due to differences in circumstances in which people find themselves. This simply means that the experience of time is a function of the culture in which the person lives. Each of us, regardless of culture, may experience time in three ways: first, in the way that our time is synchronized with the flow established by temporal units, such as days and months; second, an appearance of extended duration where time seems longer than it actually is as measured; finally, an appearance of compression where time seems much shorter than it actually is. The difference among the three is due to density of experiences within a time unit, although this is influenced by subjective factors as well.

Time seems longer when situations contain high or low levels of activity. A situation that has sparse *or* excessive experiences will seem interminable. Flaherty and Meer specify five sequential elements that produce feelings that time is passing slowly. Immediate circumstances are over- or under-loaded with events, first. Second, the person is involved emotionally in the context and adequate dealing with its elements. Third, there is the possibility that there is greater mental involvement with the situation than is normal or useful. Fourth, complexity is enhanced by greater attention to the stimuli. Finally, the outcome is the sensation of intensified density of experience for each temporal unit. All of these emphasize that the perception of protracted duration is the result of subjective factors operating within an unusual circumstance.

Synchronicity is the norm of time perception, with experience in harmony with time units so that effort and time passage are in balance. As with protraction, the five elements described above are also at work, only with a different focus. The situation contains no disturbing problems, there is moderate and appropriate emotional involvement, the mind is working in harmony with the self and situation, stimulus complexity seems appropriate and governable, and experiential density for each time unit is routine. The person is in harmony with life and time, and experience seems in accord with time.

Temporal compression is the only one of the three reactions that is associated with the past. (The others, Flaherty and Meer say, are present-time oriented.) This compression of time is the result of less experience within each temporal unit. Either habitual conduct or loss of memory would account for the result. The former contributes to automaticity of processing but may require greater attentional control if circumstances are unusual. This possibility has not been investigated to date, according to the authors. Events of the immediate past, and thus short-term memory, are often concerned in compression associated with habitual and automatic processing.

By contrast, memory loss in longer time intervals (essentially from one day backward) is common in the history of the individual. The past is remembered as having passed quickly, relatively and increasingly as we think back into our pasts. Memory loss reduces the fund of experiences available to us so that the past contracts, speeding its effect as increasing numbers of experiences are lost. Again, the sequential factors applied to protraction and synchronicity fit here. The person seeks and uses habitual conduct, with little emotional concern about the situation, little cognitive emphasis with self or event, and very low complexity since there is no need to attend to self, bringing as a consequence less-than-normal density of experience for each time unit.

Given this model, Flaherty and Meer decided to test its adequacy. Both protracted duration and synchronicity have already received study and support in other research. The emphasis here, then, was on time compression, with two hypotheses about memory as it may be involved in compression. Hypothesis 1 was stated as the perception that time will be perceived as having passed more quickly the further in the past that the experience occurred. Hypothesis 2 proposed that participants would not report a feeling of protracted duration if asked how they perceived time to have passed the day before, the last month, and the last year.

Three different "age groups" were located and tested, all students in a university: one traditional (mean age 19.8), one nontraditional (mean age 38.4), and one in the Elderhostel program on campus (mean age 71.2). All were volunteers, and sample sizes were equal. Perception of time was measured for "yesterday," "last month," and "last year." Both hypotheses were supported (age and memory), but no interaction was found for age x memory. The participants as a group reported that the further back in time, the quicker the perception of the time involved, each group showing the same order. However, the magnitude of the means differed, with the nontraditional students (middle-aged) showing the higher time compression scores. Interestingly, young and elderly means did not differ. "In sum, the effects of memory on the perception of time seem to be more general than do the effects of age. While age generates temporal compression only among the middle-aged, memory generates temporal compression among all age groups" (p. 715).

Flaherty and Meer evaluate the model by saying that it emphasizes the density of experience as a seminal factor in the perception of the passage of time. How one directs attention to any situation depends on the location of the event on a continuum from repetitive only to problematically unique. In this context each time unit contains experiences in some density; this density (either high, low, or normal) determines how time will be perceived.

The role of age in time orientation has been studied by Marcus (1978) in a somewhat different paradigm but similar context. The group studied were participants in adult education. They further compared to Flaherty and Meer's sample in the sense that they too were middle-aged (mean = 43.19 years compared to 38.4 years). Marcus, however, considered immediate and deferred need gratification, defined as the way these adults perceived an opportunity to satisfy their practical needs (sources of tension such as low income, poor health, discontentment with life) and practical goals (expressing a motivation for growth through educational achievement). Data indicated that the participants made a distinction between the two, and their perceptions helped them to decide what they considered instrumental (needs) or expressive (goals). They subsequently decided whether they would continue the educational process or drop out, presumably to direct efforts toward meeting needs more directly.

A clear result of the study was that adult education does not meet the instrumental needs of those who are aging. In fact, even when taking courses that are instrumental in direction and content, the participants here tended to perceive them more as expressively than as instrumentally useful. The role of age was central, as indicated in Marcus's summary of his findings. Marcus also found interactions among the variables, demonstrating the complexity of behavior in participation in educational settings. He found as well that the number of life interests decline with age, suggesting to him that older persons focus their interests more than younger ones do.

There are, of course, such differences between the two studies (Flaherty and Meer versus Marcus) that direct comparisons are unfair and unwise. There are some hints of differences in findings that may be more critical, however. Memory, rather than age, was the significant determiner of perception of time's passage in the first study. There were no memory measures as such in the second, but age displayed the critical feature of differences between needs and goals. Indeed, in Flaherty and Meer there was no evidence of an interaction between memory and age. Perhaps this may be explained by the fact that Flaherty and Meer looked to past events (at least one day), whereas Marcus concentrates his efforts on the present with its problems and rewards. Whatever may be the eventual resolution, it is apparent that time perception, however divided and defined, has far too many facets and implications to be understood in single, limited-focus studies. If nothing else, the very differences introduced experimentally create confusion as to the meaning of similar, or even the same, variables.

Internal Tempo

Boltz (1994) has attempted to reconcile differences between areas of research, in this case dealing with time estimation. To do so, she investigated how differences in internal tempo may influence both learning and retention of the duration of events. (She makes the pertinent point that the effort is incomplete "because there are various other topics in both the cognitive and clinical realms that have not been addressed" [p. 1169]. At the same time she does propose that eventually there is the possibility of integration among different areas of the time estimation literature into a unified structure for application to everyday behavior. That outcome will depend on psychologists making efforts that are, at present, little under way.)

From the clinical standpoint, a concept that each of us possesses and reacts to an internal tempo that mediates certain behavioral effects is not uncommon. Boltz mentions effects of aging, induced stress, or psychoactive drugs as examples. In fact, time distortion is seen in a number of mental illnesses as well as brain disorders and can have adverse influences on perception of clock time. Boltz concludes that when internal tempo is changed (either increased or decreased), there will be a systematic effect on the perceived duration of an event as either longer or shorter than the actual duration. This suggests that the person brings some form of internal timing mechanism that, when aroused, may produce differential responses to the temporal nature of environmental events. The effect is an influence on encoding and processing of environmental events.

Boltz believes that there must be some reciprocal relationship between the person and the temporal environment. Over time, and certainly by adulthood, an internal tempo has developed and become relatively stable. It is a part of the self, part of one's identity. However, special conditions (such as stress or drugs) may increase or decrease the tempo temporarily and cause distortion in the way time is perceived during that period. By contrast, relaxation may produce a similar outcome since it alters the usual balance of the individual with the environment.

Boltz also found evidence that changes that occur in internal tempo could disrupt even the most experienced and practiced perceptions of the temporal nature of events. As subjects experienced stress or relaxation, for example, they showed better performance in learning and remembering for the event rates that matched the internal tempo present. This must mean that there is some systematic bias in the perceptual recognition of information toward synchrony for optimal processing cognitively. The bias in perceptual recognition of information is explained on the basis of a change in internal tempo, being either accelerated or decelerated. There is a consequent shift mentally to a faster or lower rate in order to compensate (p. 1169).

From such results it is possible to conclude that both the person and the environment contain temporal structures that maintain a reciprocal relationship. This permits an individual to learn event durations in an incidental but significant degree that leads to retention of the event duration with considerable accuracy. If this is true, we have a mechanism that explains at least certain temporal behaviors in the adult that otherwise seem inexplicable. Further, being highly adaptable, the individual becomes increasingly attuned to environmental tempi that accord with those most rehearsed internally. There is the interesting observation that

[g]iven that this type of synchrony is also assumed to underlie the activities of attentional tracking and interpersonal interaction, the areas of clinical and cognitive research may not be as different from one another as the dichotomous nature of the literature seems to suggest. (p. 1169)

TIME PERCEPTION IN ADOLESCENCE

Adolescence has distinctive features, but the literature on time perception has portrayed it more as a transition between the building of cognitive structures in childhood and the mature development of the adult (for example, Piaget, 1969, and Friedman, 1989). This position depends in no small measure on the sparse nature of studies available (and particularly with no model of adolescent time awareness) plus the assumptions employed in designing studies.

Some of the research lumps adolescents with children, and others include the period as an early part of adulthood. The former was considered in Chapter 4; the latter is represented in such publications as one by Pandey and Agarwal (1990). Done in India, there were 50 adults (ages 19 to 23) and 50 adolescents (ages 12 to 15) who dealt with verbal tasks that reflected future time orientation and efficiency in using temporal codes. As might be expected, the adults performed better, leading Pandey and Agarwal to propose that type of material, providing situational motivation about the future utility of material, and the idiosyncratic nature of future time orientation in the individual are components in making temporal judgments. This outcome stresses once more the influential nature of personal factors of mental maturity and individual traits.

Other studies have used samples more congruent with the adolescent period itself. Carrillo de la Peña, Luengo, and Romero (1994), for example, report results for high school–level males, one group in school (mean age of 16.3 years) and the other imprisoned because of juvenile delinquency (mean age of 17.5 years). One of the variables dealt with time orientation as it related to delinquency and antisocial behavior, producing results of differences between the groups that would seem to have only limited generalizability. Indeed, the emphasis on the adequacy of standardized measures for such groups may be of greater interest than the results of the study itself.

Comparisons within an adolescent age spread were made by Mahon and Yarcheski (1994), focusing on time perspective and health practices. One group was designated "middle adolescents" and consisted of youths between the ages of 13 and 17. The other was labeled "late adolescents," and the subsample ranged from ages 18 to 21. The outcomes were not encouraging for any statements about growth with these variables. Only low correlations (though statistically significant) were obtained between length of future time perspective and use of positive health behaviors. Even less impressive results were obtained for specific health practices and future time orientation. Either there is only minor growth in employment of health practices and time awareness in adolescence or the measures employed lack significance for the adolescent period of life.

Perhaps more helpful is a study by Nurmi (1991), specifying processes that are a part of future time orientation: motivation toward the future, planning for the future, and a means to evaluate progress. Nurmi found that the goals and interests of adolescents comprise a central feature of their developmental tasks as they move to adulthood. From his results Nurmi came to five conclusions.

1. The future-oriented goals of adolescents and the temporal extension they derive from them reflect what he calls "expected life-span development."
2. Whenever the teenager acquires relevant changes in knowledge about life-span development, changes in specific goals are a natural concomitant.
3. Although adolescent interests and goals were congruent with expected life-span development, there has not been prior evidence about the extent to which contextual factors influence planning and evaluation by the adolescent.
4. There remains the viable position that the content of oriented goals is not fixed; indeed, there are likely to be changes as age-specific developmental tasks change.
5. There should be a test of the extent to which adolescent goal-setting is based on the goals, values, and standards of their parents. Further, the degree of relationship between parent awareness of different domains of life and adolescent goals needs assessment as well as the effect of parental supports on the evaluation of the future by the adolescent.

All of the above fit within the examination of time orientation in adolescence by the inclusion of predecessors and current influences on the way adolescents conceive the future.

The stereotype that adolescence is a period when the person looks more to the future than was true previously, and divides the emphases of their lives on the present and its influences on what is ahead, has long prevailed in developmental psychology. Study of future orientation and the effects of time in that process is more common, as a result, than normative research. A study done in Germany (Trommsdorff, Lamm, and Schmidt, 1979) with two measures of future orientation, one taken at ages 14 through 16 and the other done at ages 16 through 18, is an example. Half the sample was on a university-bound track, whereas the other half was preparing for entry in the job market when school years were completed. Trommsdorff et al. call the former group "high social status" and the latter "low social status."

The authors defined future orientation as the attitudes and judgments concerning one's future. This definition would seem to underlie the social status labels assigned. In addition, the cognitive and affective components involved were assessed through determining the number of events and circumstances that the adolescent hopes for and/or fears in various domains of life. There was also a measure of optimism: the hope one entertains for positive changes in one's future life. Measurement of these factors was conducted in personality and self-actualization, physical well-being and appearance, family, and occupation. There was also a measure of locus of control.

There were four hypotheses established by Trommsdorff et al., with divergent results among the two groups. The first hypothesis focused on hopes and fears. The assumption was that the older group (ages 16 to 18) would have more such events in their expectations than the younger. This was confirmed in the areas of personality and self-actualization and in occupations. Additionally, the authors predicted that working adolescents would have relatively more hopes and fears connected with their occupation than the young people still in school. This also was confirmed. Time of measurement was not a significant factor. Finally, in this sphere, the prediction was made that female adolescents would have more orientation to family than males. This was not confirmed. While there were sex differences in physical well-being and appearance, females in fact listed *fewer* events of a hopeful and fearful nature at the second measure than males.

The second hypothesis contended that older adolescents would have more extended future orientation than when they were younger and that working youngsters would have the longer orientation in respect to their occupations than would those still in school. There was only partial support, that in personality and self-actualization and only for males. Differences between those working and those in school were not found.

Third, the authors hypothesized that older adolescents would be more optimistic about the future than younger ones had been. However, only partial support was found. Trommsdorff et al. also posited that working adolescents would have more optimism about their futures in their jobs than students would. In fact, the *Gymnasium* (college-preparation) group was more optimistic about their future work, and there was actually a decrease for the *Hauptschule* (work-training) sample in personality and self-actualization and in physical well-being.

The locus of control measure was used to test the hypothesis that working adolescents would evaluate the future as more in their own hands (internal) than subject to other factors (such as decision making by bosses). On the whole, results did not yield confirming evidence.

Time elapsed during adolescence does not seem to be a critical factor in major attitudes and expectations. Some factors conceived by Trommsdorff et al. as central to the cognitive and emotional development of adolescents, and to their view of the future, were supported, but other factors, surely as defensible, were not. The complexity of time orientation in the behavior of youngsters, even when applied directly to circumstances in current life, has yet to be clarified.

TIME ORIENTATION IN THE ADULT YEARS

Following adolescence, demarcation of age periods becomes arbitrary. There are references to young, middle, and old age, with cutoffs at 40 and 65. The increase in length of life in this century has led some authorities to cite age 75 as the beginning of old age, and there has even begun the citation of old-old age, beginning at 100. Whatever is used, the groupings are for convenience rather than demonstrated changes. Behavioral changes do occur from age 18 on, but the gradations are too gradual to pinpoint and the differences from person to person more confusing than clear. Physical changes are more demonstrable than mental ones, yet even here there can be noticeable differences within sexes at the same age. All of this merely means that chronological time is less distinguishable than desirable. Unfortunately there has not been sufficient study of other dimensions, such as time orientation, to help clarify the picture. In this book, the convenience is observed by using the term *adulthood* for the period from about age 20 to age 65 and *elderly* for persons beyond that point. No solution is implied or fostered by the decision.

If little emphasis is to be placed on chronological age, the events studied must assume greater prominence. The characteristics of time must be explicit for orientation to be implied or proposed. This means that the various studies must examine such features as past, present, and/or future for persons at various points between the youngest and oldest age limits included in the sample. At the same time there can be inclusion of other variables: schema used by the person to deal with temporal events, memory processes involved, cognitive devices, emotional features, and so on. Since there has been no model proposed, tested, and accepted for time orientation, this procedure is like the assembling of a puzzle without a template. The result is what must be expected: often competent research, the place of which in the puzzle is unknown, and less illumination of where to proceed with the effort than one would like. Nevertheless, the efforts deserve the chance to be judged and consolidated, to the degree permitted from a critic who does not know the template either.

Past Time Orientation

A study by Friedman and Wilkins (1985) illustrates the points made above. First, the sample met the chronological age limit: the subjects ranged from age 22 to 67, in two separate experiments. In the first there were 19 women subjects who ranged from 32 to 66, with a mean of 50. In the other there were 23 women and 4 men with a range from 22 to 67 and a mean of 53. Unfortunately, there is no notation of actual numbers in any age grouping.

Second, memory for the time of several (in this case, 10) news events at different times in the past (6 months to 20 years) was tested. Third, specific time scales (day of month, year, hour, etc.) were estimated by the subjects. Finally, the memory processes used were stated and used as the basis for an explanation.

Some decisions critical to the eventual findings apply in all these areas. For example, the 10 events selected by Friedman and Wilkins were real and had potential significance to the English sample used but not always to the same extent in all subjects. For example, the events chosen were:

1. John F. Kennedy is assassinated.
2. Donald Campbell is killed in a speedboat accident on Lake Windemere.
3. The first spaceman sets foot on the moon.
4. Lord Mountbatten is killed by an explosion aboard his boat.
5. Former Beatle John Lennon is shot.
6. Pope John Paul II is shot.
7. Prince Charles and Lady Diana exchange rings.
8. Egyptian president Anwar Sadat is assassinated.
9. Prince William is born.
10. The ship *Mary Rose* rises above the surface (p. 169).

There is no quarrel with the events selected, but there must be some awareness that there is no evidence that each has some equivalent importance to any of the others; indeed, the fact is that they do not. Some of us would have greater feeling about a given event than other persons would. Yet each is a fair selection for the purpose: determining the memory processes involved in how people remember the time of events from the past.

Friedman and Wilkins used conventional time periods (scales) as the basis for determining whether storage of time events is based on time ordering or on context. Estimates of the events cited above were made by participants based on the year, month, day of the month, day of the week, and hour of occurrence (Experiment 1). A variation, using generic descriptions of the events, comprised Experiment 2. The results better supported a contextual-reconstructive explanation, although there were exceptions within certain of the time scales used.

Overall, the authors conclude that the evidence indicates that it is not likely that the dating of past events is based on a direct age-of-the-memory principle. Other factors have a significant influence on how persons determine when events, significant to them, occurred in the past. The better explanation is that memory is reconstructed, using two sources of information: details associated with the event itself, and general information that helps specify the time relationship. The authors conclude that "these findings illustrate the importance of inferential processes in dating events and show that proper controls are necessary if one wishes to distinguish memory in the narrow sense from inference" (p. 174). In a more general sense, the findings also demonstrate that the study of time orientation is more complex and more difficult than has heretofore been realized or postulated. This applies not only to past event memory but to present awareness and future predictions and expectations as well.

Memory for the time of an event must depend on some temporal scale (or perhaps even several such scales) if the person is to be accurate. Aside from the personal value or strength of the event to the individual, some peg to mark the event would seem useful and perhaps necessary. Study of such pegs becomes a meaningful means of defining time orientation for past incidents. One such study, using an Israeli sample, has been reported by Koriat and Fischhoff (1974). They investigated the means used by participants to specify an answer to the question, "What day is today?" Although the answer might seem obviously easy to retrieve, the means to do so has not been clarified.

Two hypotheses were established: (1) The latency of a correct day retrieval and (2) the frequency of errors in responding both will increase as the distance of the actual day from the closest weekend (backward or forward) increases. Thus, Wednesday should take a longer time to recall and produce more errors than either Monday or Friday. The role of the weekend, and thus of the week, as a separate but helpful scale was also implied. As a secondary hypothesis, Koriat and Fischhoff proposed that past anchors are more often used in specifying temporal points than future anchors, so long as both are equidistant in time from the day. They point out that the structure of the Jewish week had a notable effect on the results, since there is a six-day workweek with Saturday representing a rest day as well as the Sabbath. Everything in Israel closes down on Friday midafternoon, further defining the meaning of week and weekend.

Their sample of 273 participants was tested over a two-week period. Both retrieval time and errors were measured in order to answer the hypotheses, which were supported both for latencies and errors. The authors speculate that a two-stage model would seem the best possible explanation for their results. This would include a preliminary orientation to the general location of a target day in the week, followed by a more definitive process using personal information.

Now the issue arises: What do we learn about the processes involved in time orientation from research on the commonly used scales such as day, week, month, and year? In Chapter 3, several studies were surveyed (Betz and Skowronski, 1997; Huttenlocher, Hedges, and Prohaska, 1992; Larsen and Thompson, 1995; Sandifer, 1997). Evidence was presented that personal factors are highly influential on dating events and that weekdays form one basis for retention and the weekend a separate one. The studies in this section reinforce these conclusions, with somewhat greater detail on the internal units in the time scales used. There is reason, as a result, to conclude that one piece of the matrix we need to complete our puzzle has been highlighted: Persons learn to use the system of time scales to help them retrieve specific memories of events, certainly for those that are perceived by the individual to be "important" and possibly also for those of lesser importance. Beyond this, there is speculation and proposal of explanations that remain to be tested.

Present and Future Time Orientation

There is an advantage to investigating time orientation in the past: events with clear time dimensions can be selected, memory processes (a recognized constituent in psychology) can be tapped, "importance" can be defined in either the public or private sense, and measurement can be relatively precise and statistically reliable. To some degree, the present may offer the same opportunities but with some reservations. The future is guesswork, anticipation, and hope rather than fact and filled with potholes of potential danger. Research efforts, as a result, have not been so extensive nor trusted as the investigation of the past. Nevertheless, there is a body of literature to consider. Some reserve is demanded, however, because much of the literature is designed within external conditions rather than events: some in clinical settings, others in social settings, still others in consumer settings. There is the danger that consideration will bow to the conventional mixing of apples and oranges.

This is demonstrated in a study by Cooke, Rousseau, and Lafferty (1988) that related time orientation, in part, with various symptoms of strain. A large sample (816 persons) who were being trained in stress management gave self-report data on their own symptoms. The outcomes were mixed. As a contrast, Verma (1992) compared time orientation and work behavior with a sample of bank executives and academicians to disclose how time was managed and how that related to managerial effectiveness. The two groups differed on two dimensions, the accuracy with which time was judged and the structure imposed. In the final analysis, the behaviors of difference involved such matters as time of arising, use of time after arising, and activities undertaken after work.

The social setting has been investigated in a study of future time orientation (Koenig, Swanson, and Harter, 1981). A measure of future orientation was compared with social class and anomia. The greater the inability to retrieve appropriate words in discourse or to understand such words in conversation was inversely related to social class but directly to future time orientation. The authors conclude that lower-class persons avoid thoughts of the future as a defense mechanism. Within a different social context, Rothspan and Read (1996) proposed an interesting hypothesis that college students would show a positive correlation between future time orientation and behaviors that lead to reduced exposure to HIV (human immunodeficiency virus). Those who practice risky sex are more apt to emphasize the present with its immediate rewards. They did indeed find that the students with greater future time orientation were less active sexually, and when they were, they were more likely to have fewer sexual partners. The hypothesis about present time orientation also held. The time perspective of choice also interacted with gender and with fear of AIDS (acquired immunodeficiency syndrome), since women and, for either sex, fear of AIDS related more strongly to time orientation. Still another investigation of future time orientation in a clinical condition has been published by Suto and Frank (1994). Schizophrenic patients living in a board and care home (ranging in age from 29 to 60) were studied to determine their ability to carry on the routine life of the home as well as function in an occupation. The authors found evidence that competence in elements of future time orientation (extension, coherence, and density) correlated with performance on goal-directed activities. The home itself, however, was somewhat a distractor to better functioning since the rules invoked and the expectations established for the patients were restrictive to future time orientation. Present time orientation was more influenced as a result.

Outside the clinical field, several studies have been reported using future time orientation as one variable. Brannigan, Shahon, and Schaller (1992) looked at gender effects with a sample of 194 undergraduates. They report that female subjects reported significantly more future-oriented daydreams than males did. Reasons for this may lie in the setting (university), life period (young adult), and social pressures (gender roles) than may be generally true of women. Content of the daydreams might give greater meaning to the finding than proposed by the authors. An interesting sidelight was results on the Rotter Internal-External Locus of Control Scale. Here, externals were more past oriented than internals, regardless of sex. Gender may interact with this variable to produce the results obtained.

Philipp (1992) examined time orientation and participation in leisure activities. Future time orientation was the most prominent time measure when such participation was determined. In other studies, consumer behavior has been studied for associations with future time orientation (Amyx and Mowen, 1995). The authors hypothesized that time orientation is an influencer of consumer decisions. They set up a situation where participants were to decide whether to delay or expedite payments on an automobile when other purchases were to be made. They found that those with a present time orientation tended to express a preference for delayed payments, whereas future-oriented individuals were more likely to state a preference for on-time payments. One drawback to generalizing is the fact that only undergraduates were used. The "reality" of the situation may be considerably less than in the general population where such decisions are more common and more meaningful.

More suitable for generalization is the study of Ganesan (1993) that compared time orientation with negotiation strategies in a business setting. Retail buyers (n = 124) in six regional department store chains made up the sample. The strategies consisted of problem-solving techniques, compromise, or aggression as means of resolving conflicts. Where future orientation was present, the author found that problem-solving was the more frequent strategy and that it led to greater conflict resolution. In such individuals, as well, passive-aggressive techniques were sometimes used successfully. But the problem-solving approach yielded higher outcomes and greater satisfaction than either compromise or aggression. This study tells us less about time orientation, of course, than it does about personal relationships. Future time orientation may be less important than the employee/customer attitude toward the negotiation strategy that may be used.

This survey of literature has not been profitable for the purpose of defining time orientation. Although experimental design, measures used, and statistical analysis are honestly presented, there are limitations that seem far too prevalent in psychological study. For example, a heavy percentage are conducted in university settings with undergraduates, understandable since the experimenter is employed in such a setting. There is not even assurance that the sample is representative of such institutions, much less that the findings may be typical of the general population. The same comments may be made about clinical conditions or business settings or whatever else may be the convenient place to do a study. This is not to accuse the experimenters of making general statements that cannot be defended. Indeed, the reporting is so confined to the local situation that the world is ignored.

Still a final effort to find some rapprochement will be attempted with publications that have proposed a model at least partially suited to our purpose. As a beginning, we can ask, "What does 'time' mean to adults?" Dapkus (1985) recognized the problems already cited and attempted to develop a theory that would be more enveloping than had been available before. She notes that "time" has been used in several ways in psychology, depending on the interests and resources of the psychologist. As a result, she proposes, "A unified conceptual framework capable of integrating these diverse aspects of the subject of time seems both absent and needed" (p. 408).

Dapkus then moves to a more fundamental form of science for such study, wherein observation is made of all that can be observed about a given phenomenon (such as time). This allows inventorying the elements of the system, leading only then to the study of parts in isolation. The relationship of parts to whole is clearer and more systematic than is allowed by the piecemeal approach so common to experimentation and as reflected in the survey of the literature in this chapter. This is not an easy goal to achieve, since "time is not uniquely associated with one thought, feeling, or behavior" (p. 409).

The format she followed emphasized the experience of time as perceived by 20 "mature, articulate adults." The information they supplied was analyzed for themes common to all experiences reported, permitting the establishment of a system that marked the first step toward a description of the experience of time. The procedure seems fair, although the sample contains elements of bias that prevent it being considered representative of all adults. For example, all were white, middle class, mostly college educated, married, with children living at home. Interviews used questions about the development of an awareness of time during their lives, their current experience of time both when alone and when with others, periods of life when time was most conscious, and so on.

What resulted, through analysis of participants' responses, were three categories of temporal experience.

1. *Change and continuity.* Change is constant and inevitable, but there is at the same time a continuity recognized through awareness of time. Involved must be the symbiosis of past, present, and future that accepts the possibility of change. Dapkus calls this the category of "becoming in time."

2. *Limits and choices.* Here, time helps determine and govern the experiences that people have and the choices they must make selectively. Part of the result is a feeling of worth of time, depending on whether effort was successful or a failure. Dapkus labels this the category of "doing in time."

3. *Tempo.* Within time intervals there is a perception of speed and/or pattern of movement. One may feel rushed or held back—or something in between. Called "pacing in time" by Dapkus, this category reflects the subjective reaction to the demands of tasks within a dimension that always proceeds at the same speed.

The analysis by Dapkus results from an extensive detailing of the categories experientially. Because there may be overlap and duplication, the three primary categories (change and continuity, limits and choices, and tempo) are abetted by a secondary order (a combination of change and continuity with limits and choices, of change and continuity with tempo, and of limits and choices with tempo). There is even a single third-order category, where the three primary categories are combined into an interactional description. It is of more than passing interest to note that the participants reported "Limits and Choices" concerning the use of time most frequently (about 80% of the elements in interviews). "Change and Continuity" was next (63%), and "Tempo" was last (52%). The first is practical and directing, the second is uncontrollable, and the third is a personal trait under some control of the individual. All percentages reinforce her contention that these categories are prime in her sample's awareness of time. In her discussion, Dapkus defends the findings as representative despite the limitations of sample mentioned earlier.

One of the most difficult achievements in time orientation, and perhaps the proof of maturity in the individual, is the development of a future time perspective. Visualizing the future is not possible without realization about both present and past; still, having the basics does not assure the final outcome. Further, as Dapkus points out, there must be a balance among the three temporal elements so that the process of change is realized within the context of continuity. Only then can the future be achieved in the fashion desired, if it *is* to be achieved. The intellectual capacity to appreciate the means to that end is essential also. Choices and limits become important here.

Social problems, and potential ones, may be related to time orientation as well. The concern with nuclear war has been present since the 1950s, with some abatement only recently. How the attitude toward nuclear destruction may affect future time orientation was a factor in a study by Jason, Schade, Furo, Reichler, and Brickman (1989). The subjects were all women, ranging in age from 19 to 49, with a mean of 31 years. Above average in educational level and occupational status, most were single (76%) whereas 22% had been married, but only 2% were currently married.

Participants were asked to rank the time they spent thinking about the past, present, and future. In addition, they were asked to list the behaviors, customs, and traditions that they perceived to be common 20 to 30 years earlier but now considered bizarre or unusual. They then speculated on behaviors current at the time of the study that were apt to become just as bizarre in another 20 to 30 years. Finally, the subjects expressed their expectations for the quality of life in 20 to 30 years and their concern about a large-scale nuclear war within 30 years.

The results seem consistent with those of other studies, at least on basic matters. First, respondents reported that they spent about twice as much time thinking about the present and future as they did about the past. Numerically, they said that they spent most of their time in future orientation, least in past reflections. Percentagewise, the rankings favored thinking about the present, with almost as large a percentage thinking about the future (41% versus 38%). The discrepancy in the rankings under the two measurement conditions is explained by Jason et al. as a reflection that adults believe they spend most of the time contemplating the future when in fact they are more present-centered. As a result, future time orientation should be measured in more than one way, the authors contend. As for their expectations, the subjects looked for their quality of life to be slightly better in the future, while they considered a future nuclear war to be possible but neither definite nor impossible. Such undecided caution may tell us more about the inability to predict than it does about future time orientation and what the future may bring.

Jason et al. report that educational level was inversely related to expectations about quality of life in the future, and they interpret this to mean "that the more one knows, the less one expects from life in the future" (p. 1202). This may be one way of expressing the probability that the greater the education, the greater the skepticism. As for specific matters once prevalent but no longer acceptable and for those now prevalent that will be unusual in the future, most would seem somewhat distant from the daily lives of the women who made up the sample. The lists included such items as

1. *Once prevalent but now (1989) unusual*: traditional male/female values; dress and social values of the 1960s; economics and unemployment.
2. *Now prevalent but destined for rejection in future*: the "punk" movement, computers and technology, prejudices leading to victimization, Yuppies, aggressive women, current issues, terrorism and war, and drug usage.

In their conclusions, Jason et al. contend that their sample used mainly a present/future time perspective with most decisions being based on what may lie in the future. They also point to the limitations cited earlier concerning the representative nature of the group. Despite the drawbacks, Jason et al. have offered us findings that may be compared to the categories of time proposed by Dapkus. The idea of becoming (change and continuity) has been displayed effectively by the design employed by Jason et al., but the categories of doing (limits and choices) and pacing (tempo) are lacking. In that sense, one may conclude that the study does not give evidence whether the women participants had a true future time orientation since there is no measure that displays the presence or absence of the three categories in Dapkus's system. Future studies would benefit by building upon the system of Dapkus, at least until something more compelling is proposed.

In Chapter 3 there was a discussion on means to measure time estimation, from both a prospective and a retrospective orientation. The two have been defined: "In prospective time estimation, subjects are informed that they will later be asked to estimate the duration of a given interval, whereas in retrospective time estimation this information is not known in advance" (Zakay, Tsal, Moses, and Shahar, 1994, p. 344). Studies have indicated a difference in results, leading to the contention that different processes must mediate the estimates made. The experience of time awareness must be part of the process in prospective studies, whereas remembering is a greater component in retrospection.

Zakay has explained the two on the basis of cognitive competencies employed in each. When informed that the elapsed time must be estimated once a task is completed, subjects use an attentional device toward the actual time elapsed as the information is presented. Techniques to do so may vary from respondent to respondent, but most apparently have some "trick" that permits them to estimate how long or short the interval was. Where the participant is merely told to perform on a task, with no foreknowledge that elapsed time is important, a different approach is necessary. Memory competencies become the major mode that the respondent must use, based perhaps on experience with similar tasks or on a generalized knowledge of how long an event seems to take or on any of several other possibilities. In other words, the actual processes may not (perhaps cannot) be specified, but participants are still capable of giving an estimate of greater or lesser accuracy.

In the study at hand, Zakay et al. conducted five experiments to test the effects of segmentation level of an interval on how long it is perceived to last (duration). In two experiments a prospective paradigm was combined with an absolute time estimation method, in two others a retrospective paradigm was combined with comparative estimates, and in the fifth there was a combination of paradigm with estimation method and segmentation level. Zakay et al. concluded that events that hold a high priority to the participant are perceived and encoded as changes in context, and segmentation affects estimation of time through the mediation of memory processes.

Such findings help us acquire a better understanding of the processes that may underlie specific findings related to time awareness. There has been ample demonstration of the need for facility with encoded material in order to maintain time orientation of a realistic nature. Indeed, the greater the experience, usually the more accurate can be the temporal realization. In a sense this says nothing more than that memory itself is an aid to memory function. Zakay et al. have made a significant point in demonstrating how the process may work under specific imposed conditions. Beyond this the prospective/retrospective dichotomy pertains more to the environmental conditions under which time awareness is to be manipulated than it does to the nature of orientation.

Dapkus's model can be applied to the Zakay et al. study as it was to Jason et al. Now the category of major emphasis is based on limits and choices (doing in time) and tempo (pacing in time). Change and continuity (becoming in time) is not an issue in studies of the type conducted by Zakay et al. This raises a question about the possibility for all the categories derived by Dapkus being employed in a single study. If it is important to do so, and an ultimate test of the model would seem to require it, experimenters have a basis for designing such an investigation. The outcome would strengthen our understanding of space and time applications, assist modifications in the model, and open the door to possible scientific progress. Resistance, a common motive apparently among psychologists, would reinforce the long-standing and accepted procedure of investigation without regard to its relationship to completing a coherent picture. To me, there are far too many studies that exist in their own niche, published in various journals without a requirement to show what contributions to psychological science have been made. One describes and discusses a myriad of studies as though each was significant for having been done and published. While it is true that it would be better to simply ignore such conditions, there can be no progress toward improvement unless the issue is faced, stated, and challenged.

This survey of the literature on adult time orientation has enlarged awareness of the methods and motivations of research that has been conducted. It is still not possible to make definitive statements about the nature of time awareness currently. Whether this will change in future years depends upon the efforts made by those who propose models and those who test them.

CHAPTER 6

Finalizing Time Concepts

The study of human behavior by psychologists has been more a matter of digging channels and limiting the scope than of identifying and amalgamating processes. Starting with the study of memory by Ebbinghaus, there has been extensive, redundant, and exhaustive examination of retention— resulting in a clearly defined model (essentially with segments of short-term and long-term dimensions) that is still being researched. At the same time, other subdisciplines have been identified and attracted adherents. One of these is developmental, particularly with focus on children. Norms of development, both physical and mental, have been specified and applied, sometimes almost with religious fervor. Personality has become a central concept, most frequently based upon some set of "traits" that sometimes contains double-digit entries. In these areas, along with others, there has been little attempt to bring order from what otherwise appears chaotic to the noninitiated.

The most systematic explications have been with infants and children. Adolescents have received lesser but significant attention, whereas adults of all ages have been relatively ignored. Among the elderly, stereotypes have been the norm, many of which are still widely believed even though they have been questioned or even disproved. Consider the idea that as people age they tend to withdraw from social demands and contacts, a mutually satisfying outcome supposedly (called "disengagement"). There is no doubt that some elderly people may disengage extensively, although there may be a need to demonstrate that this behavior occurred only after the aging. Certainly, many older persons disengage in certain activities, probably depending more on other factors than that of becoming older. And there is abundant evidence that a significant number of older individuals remain

socially engaged, given adequate opportunity—many times creating opportunity where it is limited. The significance of all this is that our understanding of most behaviors in adulthood is limited to the historical interests of
psychological investigation. We know more about the reaction time or the
ability to learn and retain lists of verbal stimuli by older persons than we
do about the dynamics of adaptation to the forces of change. Even identifying such change forces has not been a major thrust with psychologists.

THE STUDY OF AGING

There are numerous evidences, of course, of "changes" that have been
documented with age. One of the leading examples is represented in the
Baltimore Longitudinal Study of Aging (BLSA), begun in 1958 and continuing today. Hayflick (1994, pp. 142–149) has summarized the major findings in various physical measures and, to a more limited degree, in mental
characteristics. His general conclusions are that many factors influence the
rate and amount of "slowing" as we age and are extraneous to the aging
process itself. It is apparent, as Hayflick points out, that there is no single
aging process. There are differences both between and within individuals
in when aging has occurred, how aging has occurred, and how much aging
has occurred. What should be even more sobering is the fact that most of
the data result from study of characteristics that are most amenable to
rigorous measurement devices. A psychology of aging is incomplete because
psychologists have not grappled with the more evasive qualities that make
us most human. Included in that search must be the role of time in understanding human behavior.

Aging in Context

More emphasis has been placed on changes that reflect decrements than
on those that reflect increments. This has greatly influenced our view on
what to expect as we age. There would seem to be a role for identifying
those changes that are positive (or at least not losses). Observational reports
indicate that there are certain general areas where, within age increases,
there are benefits to the individual and to society.

In context, then, aging offers many gains, only a portion of which have
yet been expressed. The next century is an opportunity for society to am-
plify and extend the worth of life in old age to the benefit of all who still
wish to grow.

Aging in Outcome

Most of the stereotypes concerning aging have emphasized losses, perhaps because they are most obvious, at least in their most severe forms.

There can be no quarrel with an objective analysis and listing of such changes, although the approach might be better accepted if more inclusive. In this regard, what may be called the most significant of changes with age is the fact that physical systems and mental processes begin to gradually but steadily *slow*. They are not so much lost as they are decreased and in a pattern that is inconsistent across and within individuals. Older persons usually remain competent to do many things that younger ones may do, but only with patience and persistence in a longer time framework.

E.L. Thorndike, Bregman, Tilton, and Woodyard (1928) studied the ability of adults to acquire materials. Their "old group" would hardly meet the definition today, although it may have been satisfactory considering the demographics of the time. In any event, the conclusion was drawn that "you can teach an old dog new tricks; it just takes longer." Somewhat surprising in its day, the validity of the concept has been illustrated widely ever since. Many older individuals, given the opportunity and motivation to do so, have returned to schools and universities and performed creditably, have developed new skills and applied them to products, and have learned techniques (such as problem solving) and applied them to existing conditions.

The physical limitations of the human body are currently the source of much investigation and effort to find solutions. How far this may go seems to depend less on the benefit to humankind than to the material gains to be made. Rifkin (1998, p. 147), for example, has described current research on genetic disorders and their correction. He notes that genetic diseases are perceived by the biologist in genetic engineering as an error in the code that should never have happened and that needs to be eliminated and deprogrammed. This may sound humane and concerned, promising the removal of sources of pain and trauma to be replaced by perfection. But if an assumption is made that the genetic code is fraught with error from its transmittal, what is the "ideal norm of perfection" to use as the ultimate criterion? We apparently all have genetic errors. Should we attempt to find perfection in human traits of all types? Diversity would become meaningless in such a case. Even more chilling is the possibility that the creative productions that evolve from diversity might be lost altogether. Rifkin seems to imply that perfection would bring robotic outcomes. If so, then who controls and directs the robots?

The slowing process has its effects more obviously in degrees of deterioration that involve daily life activities. As we grow older, we are more likely to experience major, terminal illnesses. The immune system is less competent, leaving us suspect to more deleterious effects of illness that we handled capably in our youth. We compensate by taking care, albeit with only modest success. The most frequent cause of death remains pneumonia, sometimes referred to as "the old person's friend," but we also have higher incidences of cancer, heart disease, circulatory deficiency, pulmonary infection, and on and on, even though all are not necessarily fatal.

Still, the concern about terminal illness remains more a threat than a reality for most persons. Length of life has continued to increase so that a sizable population of those over 100 years of age now exists (about 17,000 currently)—and should become an increasing proportion of the world's citizens during the twenty-first century. This puts even more emphasis on the slowing that occurs. Competencies require longer for expression even when still plausible and possible. We already know that reaction time (that area of study in psychology that has produced so many thousands of data sets) increases with age. The most important outcome of that fact may lie in the effects on short-term memory, leading to lessened ability to encode immediate stimulation so that response can be quick and efficient. This has negative effects on many daily activities and may even lead to the inability to function that we have labeled *dementia*. Even where such gross deficits are not found, learning new material (either academic or nonacademic) becomes more difficult for the elderly because the encoding process is so adversely affected in its daily operation.

The increments in length of life are certainly closely associated with the increases in changes in neuronal functioning. As we grow older we are more susceptible to alterations in brain plasticity, cell viability, and mental proficiency. At its best this amounts to little more than an inconvenient and frustrating effect on memory for minor details and efficiency in carrying out long-rehearsed skills. At its worst the consequences are grave indeed. It is now estimated that such conditions as Alzheimer's disease are found in about 5% of all persons over age 65, increasing in expression to around 40% of all those over age 85. Enough examples are available so that the fear of loss of mental competence is becoming as great as the fear of terminal illness. The consequences are so severe because people realize that reversal and cure are impossible, with no real evidence that research will soon produce a preventive and that the costs in financial and social terms become more and more prohibitive. When we realize that a 70-year-old-who develops a dementia such as Alzheimer's may live for another 20 years or so, becoming more and more dependent and less and less able to care for self or contribute to family relationships, there is more than ample need to be concerned.

The status of the elderly has varied from society to society throughout history. In some instances the roles have been significant and important, most frequently taking the form of advice and counsel on issues facing the group. More commonly, however, old persons have been looked on as a burden, in some instances being abandoned or killed, in others leaving the group in order to die out of sight and concern. Our society tends more toward the positive than the negative—but only as long as older persons retain power, most often coincident with money. Once control shifts to the child, it becomes easier to socially abandon than to care for. Witness the numbers of nursing homes (or health care centers, to use the current euphemism). Less expensive is simply to leave the elderly in their own homes (admittedly an outcome the old person truly desires) without contact or support.

Under the more adverse conditions, older people tend to express lower and lower expectations and to develop a negative self-image. Feeling useless and unwanted inclines to a belief in not being worthwhile. Not only the present and future may be questioned, but the individual may also reappraise the past, concluding that little of value has developed over a lifetime. It is then easier and easier to drop contact with others and with life, awaiting death as the only escape.

Aging in Expression

Almost everything that I have said above is based on impressions; little has been codified about aging, in this or any other society. Normative standards for children, even when as idiosyncratic as with Piaget, have been described, tested, and modified. To a lesser degree, the same may be said about adolescents. Only when we come to adulthood do we begin to express opinions as though they were facts. There simply are few norms for adults, and those reported have not been adequately tested. With an increasing population of elderly, the knowledge deficiency is even more significant.

A central focus in norms for old age must consider two dimensions: what things about aging are *age related* and what are *age caused*. Age, after all, is simply a chronological expression of time lived; it is not an explanation. We blithely report matters relating to aging as though *relationship* and *causation* were synonymous, while they may very well be independent. The examples are many: dementia is related to age, but time does not cause it; immune system deficiency results from an aging organism at the same time that it is consequently related to age; loss of status is the result of time without regard to the credentials of the individual and so bears no relationship to age as such. Distinctions such as these are not typically part of the literature of gerontology (or any other subdiscipline in psychology). Until they are resolved, there can be no normative schema that will permit interventions where needed or research paradigms where appropriate.

Aging in Time

So what role does time play as the person moves into late maturity and chronological old age? More precisely, what does time mean to an older person? The answer lies, in some part, not only in experimental data but in observational material as well. Neither of these is attainable without some direction, helped in no small measure by a model that defines the components necessary to attaining an answer and suggesting the avenues of investigation that will achieve answers. Once again, reference to Hawking's definition of a "good theory" (Hawking, 1996, p. 15) is useful, including many observations that yield a model without arbitrary elements and allowing testable predictions. To do violence to such an approach leaves an investigator in danger of producing misleading and meaningless results.

Such a danger is current in the field of biotechnology today, according to Rifkin (1998, p. 234). He points out that genetic engineering may never produce the effects hoped for because there is a difference between the current challenges of cosmology and dedication to a historical research methodology. The result is "to try to force living processes into linear contexts, believing it possible to manipulate development, gene by gene, as if an organism were merely an assemblage of the individual genes that make it up." This is the time-honored reductionist procedure found so commonly in psychology as well as other sciences. It reinforces a belief in causality that may yield useless, or at least misleading, results. Rifkin proposes that biology today requires more emphasis on process than construction, looking at the totality of gene, ecosystem, and biosphere as integrated, not easily nor usefully separated for examination and reassembly. Just so, I believe, psychologists must be willing to depart from the paradigms of the past and view human behavior as a process of many integrated, inseparable parts.

So where is the "supermodel" of behavior? We don't have one. There are some suggestions from model builders that should prove useful indicators at the same time that they are less than comprehensive. Fraser (1982) has attempted one such, based on his concept that time is the crucible of "a hierarchy of creative conflicts" (p. 153). Fraser considers nature as a series of levels, each integrated with the one that follows on a definable scale. At the base are the particles without mass that move at light speed (186,000 miles per second). The next higher level consists of particles (waves) that have mass but cannot be subdivided (elementary particles). One moves up next to the universe of matter, which has organized into masses that we call stars and galaxies. At some point there followed the evolution of life on one of the bodies near a star, and from this eventually resulted human life. Finally, there evolved what we call civilization, based upon cultures.

The model has greatest meaning for this book on the levels entitled Ponderable matter, Life, and Mind. Fraser describes the first of these (Ponderable matter) as implying the beginning of time, wherein causation is deterministic. Within this level there was no way to relate past to future, or vice versa, and "now" was a meaningless concept.

With evolution, however, a biotemporal temporality was developed so that the present became defined. Life consisted of a series of "nows," accompanied by progression to greater complexity and awareness of aging orders of life. Future and past were increasingly distinguished and polarized. Causation could then be assigned in meaningful terms. Now life could move to a level we recognize in our own existence: signs and symbols are developed, shared, and understood; personal identity, similar to others but maintaining its own character, is sharpened. Humankind's present became increasingly mental (as compared to the biotemporal present of animals) and allowed the recognition of constantly changing boundaries in time. Fraser also believes that the causality resulting must include human freedom.

The next level, not yet present but developing, Fraser designates as sociotemporal, wherein humans evolve to a global collective. The distinction between levels is more apparent than real, since there are instances where phenomena do not fit neatly but lie between or overlap adjacent levels. An instance of this is the present status of human temporal behavior. Evolution is thus not complete; its physical manifestations must be integrated with the social that represent the future well-being of humankind in time.

A retrospective on the time perspective of elderly persons has been presented by Thomae (1989) and is a second model. He examines three viewpoints of change in time awareness by aging persons, both as proposed by the model builders and as tested by research. His survey is helpful in assessing our current position relative to the understanding of time relationships in mature adults.

As a background to his assessment, Thomae discusses the difficulties involved in age and time relationships. It is necessary, first, he says, to examine (and conduct) research in a variety of fields: anatomical, biochemical, neuropsychological, psychological, and sociological, followed by an integration of the many findings resulting. Only then can there be developed a true gerontological science. Obviously, this is a state far removed from reality at present, no matter how defensible the argument.

One convenient approach has been to use chronological age as the major (even the sole) base for assessment. This has been true particularly in biological and psychological research, yielding generalizations about the magnitude of individual variability in time awareness. Such concepts as "psychological old age," "biological time mechanisms," and "functional abilities in old age" have resulted. These constructs then assume points of reference from chronological age to its effects. There is, as well, a similar data set that focuses on the social meaning of chronological age.

Within psychology Thomae speaks of a history of over a hundred years where the psychology of time has been compiled, including work in perception on sensory input and reaction. In a more comprehensive sense, he credits the work of Paul Fraisse (e.g., 1963) where time is considered as an element in all behavior as well as in such specific components as perception.

This leads to a contention that a geropsychology, if it is to be complete as a subdiscipline, must include the psychology of time. With this position Thomae moves to a consideration of the three general hypotheses concerning time perception in the elderly. First is a general discussion of the model of Raymond Kuhlen, which is proposed in terms of a presumed sensitivity to time, with its effects and meanings, as we grow older. Its expression is shown in some mental restriction of activity, a form of withdrawal that is shown with greater or lesser self-limitation. Hence, there is an adaptation by older persons reflecting a sensitivity to escape time along with changes in experience and behavior. This leads to the inference of an old age that is focused on crises.

The process began in childhood as a part of socialization learned by the child. It continues into maturity and hence into old age, one of our culturally defined reference systems leading to a particular structure of the time factor. The concept in this approach is that time perspective evolves in crisis-oriented experiences. Thomae finds the conception to be limited and unsupported by research efforts.

A corollary to this idea is found in a less commonly articulated position that changes in time perspective occur within age periods. Based upon an analysis of developmental differences in the transition from childhood to adolescence, the concept is viewed by Kurt Lewin, according to Thomae (p. 59), as a clear withdrawal of past, present, and future time perspective, whereas to others it is expressed in loss of future time orientation in old age. This leads, in this view, to increased regression into the past, a stereotype that has received much credence even though it lacks support.

The third general contention about time awareness in old age revolves around analysis of the way the elderly deal with the finiteness of life, the nature of mortality, and adjustment to the inevitability of death. This involves what Thomae calls a normative hypothesis, unsupported by facts. Generally, the finiteness of life has been explained religiously, philosophically, or psychoanalytically. Unfortunately, such prescriptive explanations must be accepted on faith, not on demonstrated data.

The remainder of the paper is a careful and detailed analysis of the research in each of these areas, leading Thomae to suggest their insufficiency and the need for other models. These should include greater divergence in their content and predictions and must of course be tested thoroughly. Overall, this article provides a clear view of the insufficiency of models of time perspective in old age as of 1989. Since then, other models (several of which have been described in this book) have been proposed. A periodic reexamination of such efforts would benefit the researcher as well as the consumer.

RECENT RESEARCH ON TIME PERSPECTIVE IN THE AGED

There has been no stint in research on time relationships with older people. Much of this has been reductionist in its focus, so it is difficult to know how to use it to complete the mosaic of lifetime time awareness. Much of the information is certainly interesting and may represent factors of importance to a complete model. St. Pierre and Dubé (1993) used a Canadian sample of persons over 65 (N = 160), comparing results on the time competence scale of the Personal Orientation Inventory and the estimate of a 40-second interval as their measures. Experimental variables included sex, age, living environment, activities, health, and socioeconomic status. The results were limited in their expression and meaning. For one thing, they decided that estimating a 40-second interval was not a good measure of time competence. As for the variables listed above, there was variation in level of time competence by age, satisfaction in the number of activities engaged in, subjective assessment of health (do you believe your health status to be excellent, good, etc.), and living environment. They conclude that *objective* health measures may be important to assessing time competence, that life environment (such as a nursing home placement) should be considered for its impact, and that health status is a factor to consider when deciding on activities.

Cross-Age Studies

A number of studies have yielded cross-age comparisons of time competence either between age groups or within an elderly sample. An example of the former was reported by Park, Morrell, Hertzog, Kidder, and Mayhorn (1997). They focused their research on prospective memory, which they define as "the memory required to carry out planned actions at the appropriate time, such as meeting a friend for lunch or taking a medication" (p. 314). Such a memory function has great importance in many daily tasks and is reflected in the most central aspects of behavioral malfunction in dementia. The authors studied this form of memory in time within a context where the person was engaged in some different kind of task than that to be remembered.

Their intent was to disclose decline or loss, if any, as people age. To do so, Park et al. established two experimental conditions. In the first they examined performance on an event-based memory task in an effort to disclose the roles of age and event density in the results. The second experiment used the same methodology but substituted time-based prospective events. There were two groups: a young adult (mean age of 19.21 and 19.59 years in the separate experiments), all undergraduates, and an older set (mean age of 69.77 and 69.8 years). The young sample met the usual requirement of fulfilling a research requirement, whereas the old was paid a fee of $20: The groups differed on self-reported health status and number of medications taken, favoring the younger ones in both instances, while the older adults outscored the younger on a vocabulary test. There were 48 subjects in each of the groups for Experiment 1 and 56 for Experiment 2.

Four hypotheses were established:

1. Age differences would be found on both event-based and time-based tasks.
2. Performance on a primary working memory task would be most adversely affected in the time-based conditions since there would be a requirement for greater self-initiated processing.
3. Older adults would do less well in time monitoring on a prospective-only control condition. This result, if found, would reflect that age effects on time-based responding is affected to some degree by a fundamental deficiency in time monitoring for the elderly.
4. Individual differences in perceptual speed and working memory should yield better predictions of time-based responding as compared with event-based responding. This too could be explained by the fact that greater processing requirements exist in time-based tasks.

Their results for the two experiments led them to declare that they had "convincing evidence that there are age differences in both event-based and time-based prospective memory, even when the retrospective load on a task is low" (p. 324). Aging, then, has its negative effects on either form of prospective memory, although that does not provide any evidence of the cause for this outcome. Park et al. suggest that these results should lead us to think of the variables that influence performance on event-based prospective memory tasks. What these variables may be was not stated.

There are several paragraphs that interpret the data in terms of the hypotheses (cited above). Each is considered as a discrete entity, and there is no attempt to judge their relational status. For example, the authors speak of the role of control conditions where only prospective responding was required, reporting that performance was poor in older adults only if the measure was time-based. They explain that introducing the working memory task, however, must have acted to reduce the probability that the task content could be maintained or could attend to event-based cues as they were presented. This, to them, means that the older subjects had difficulty in a simultaneous maintenance of task needs while attending to a cue rather than isolating their efforts in initiating a response. This seems a clear, justifiable possibility.

Another example centered on performance on the time-based task. Results were poor for older adults even when there was no associated working memory task. This outcome they explain as probably due to a failure to use clock checks regularly. This, too, is a potential explanation that merits consideration.

There may be other possibilities, however. In the first instance above, one could speculate that the results represented the increase in confusion that accompanies complexity in unfamiliar tasks as persons grow older. And in the second instance a case might be made that older persons have learned and practiced an attitude that clock-watching is not an acceptable action when there is work to be done. Of course, one might say that such explanations are hardly scientific, and perhaps so. However, it is interesting to note that in the definition of prospective memory quoted at the beginning of this discussion, there is a citation of practical matters illustrating planned actions such as meeting a friend for lunch when other activities are being carried out. For those who wonder what psychological research tells us that is relevant to life (at any age), there would seem to be a need to include both elements (scientific and behavioral) in discussing findings.

An investigation that pursued factors in time orientation in a less rigorous form has been reported by Brotchie, Brennan, and Wyke (1985). The study of Koriat and Fischhoff (1974), described in Chapter 5, spurred their interest in attempting to obtain information on the accuracy with which older persons tag time. Such matters assume importance since they are involved in assessments that relate to dementia. Those with dementia show increasing difficulty in identifying the time of day, the date, location, and so on.

Brotchie et al. established four questions for which they wished to find answers:

1. How do younger and older adults compare in number and types of errors about time orientation?

2. Within an elderly group, are there differences related to such personal items as sex, social class, and years of retirement?

3. Is there a relationship between errors and ordinal position of day of the week for older persons that assumes a curvilinear form comparable to the relationship in younger adults?

4. Is there some systematic deterioration in information about time as persons grow older?

The sample was 235 individuals visiting a patient in a hospital, so it represents an unusual population of potential subjects, although not necessarily any more so than undergraduates and paid volunteers. The age range was 50 to 84 years and consisted of more men than women (an atypical relationship with increasing age). Marriage status and socioeconomic level were assessed, along with retirement status and length of retirement, where present. Reported alcohol consumption level was also included for an unreported reason.

Time orientation was measured by interview, inquiring about such matters as: "What is the time?" "What year is it?" and the like. Errors were judged on the basis of the extent of misjudgment (one hour or more for time of day, for example). Chi-square analysis yielded significant relationships between time errors and both age and alcohol consumption. Other comparisons were nonsignificant. However, errors about the date were significant for age, with the oldest subjects (71 to 84) showing the larger number of mistakes. Aging women made more errors than did men.

The means by which members of their sample tagged the correct day were event-based, personal, and practical. There were five times as many references to a tag associated with the day before than with the day to come.

Brotchie et al. conclude that time orientation for older individuals remains reasonably intact. Remembering the month is most stable, followed by time of day, the year, and day of the week. Remembering the date showed the greatest percentage of error. As with other studies (such as Koriat and Fischhoff), midweek days were associated with more errors than the extremes.

The findings of this study accord with recent data gathered by Edwards (unpublished) for an orientation scale to be used with dementia patients. To ensure that the items in the scale were fair, a sample (n = 54) of adults attending senior centers in southwest Missouri was administered the scale in group settings. The ages ranged from 52 to 91. For the 20 items, the mean score correct was 19.15 with nonsignificant differences by age bracket (52–69, n = 14; 70–79, n = 23; 80–91, n = 17). Further standardization will be conducted so that these results cannot be considered stable at this time.

The Park et al. and Brotchie et al. studies provide us with examples from two approaches to the study of time orientation in aged persons. The first is rigorous, controlled, and laboratory based, whereas the second is fluid, loose, and practical. Neither of these really advances very far our need to understand the nature of a model of orientation. Both are essentially reductionist, differing principally in the means by which they establish and answer questions on a fairly discrete form of behavior. If the matrix of time orientation is established, it should be possible to place such studies in their appropriate slots. For the time being, that is not possible.

Within a group of aging individuals there have been studies of time perspective, particularly with attitudes toward the future. The Brandstädter and Wentura (1994) study serves as an example. Their sample consisted of 1,256 persons between the ages of 54 and 78. They were subdivided into six cohorts by three-year intervals (54–57, 58–61, and so on, to 74–78). The number in each cohort varied slightly, from 201 to 206, with parity between the sexes. Each participant was paid an honorarium of unreported amount. The authors also report the percentage married and widowed, those maintaining themselves in their own homes, economic status, and those still employed.

With this sample, they compared time and future expectations in seven areas.

1. What does the aging individual expect of the future? The central question here was the clarity and concrete images of one's future as well as the horizons of planning and expectations within a temporal structure. An example is the reaction to the statement: "I have clear goals for the future, which I work toward."

2. How open is the person toward the future? Here, the experimenters sought information on the richness and anticipatory incentives of a personal future in contrast to a lived isolation as reported in a personal biography. Example: "I believe that, in my life, I still can achieve much."

3. What affective valencies does the person have with the future? Items here probed personal optimism and pessimism regarding one's personal future. Example: "I look forward to the life that lies before me." A pessimistic statement would be: "A view of my future life fills me with concern."

4. Does the person still feel in control of life's future? Here the participants reacted to the possibilities that exist in the future. Example: "What happens to me in the future depends on me." A negative statement would be: "The pattern of the future concerns me so that I feel very limited in the possibilities."

5. What is the participant's orientation to the past? This variable reflects the comments and thoughts about the past as compared to the future. Example: "When I talk with someone else, much of the conversation refers to past experiences."

6. Does the person have a feeling of obsolescence? Included here are orientation and alienation problems that interfere with the older person because of changes in the social dynamic. Example: "I have increasingly the feeling that I missed connection in my daily life."

7. What does the participant think about mortality and life's end? The emphasis here is on emotional adjustment to the issues concerning the questions of an imminent life's end. Example: "I view the end of my life with calmness." Negative: "Thoughts about death cause me stress."

Each of these seven areas contained four to six items, selected from items used in a pilot study. Internal consistency (Cronbach's *alpha*) ranged from .61 to .83. In addition, the authors obtained data on five other areas: sense to time orientation, coping dispositions, subjective attitude to the remainder of life, life's quality to the person (including life satisfaction and depressive tendencies), and subjective reporting of health status.

With such a complex design, results may be expected to be difficult to sort out and explain. Brandstädter and Wentura elected to make comparisons between the cohorts in order to yield the most meaningful interpretation. They report that, with increasing age, perspectives about a personal future become less concrete and open and are felt to be less controllable.

This projects a general picture of loss and dependency, producing stress and insecurity. One result, they found, was that the oldest groups become more preoccupied with the past, a compensation perhaps for the feeling that life is too obscure and demanding to live even in the present, much less the future. Within the cohorts, depression and reduced life satisfaction begin to yield increasingly attitudes toward time that are like those that are more typical of even older age groups. However, there is evidence that age-specific changes in future perspective are not synonymous with feelings of helplessness or depression. What becomes important, then, is to identify adaptive processes available to the elderly (or that can be taught to them) that will assist in better adjustment and stabilization so that quality of life is maintained.

This study is one of the few that has produced a follow-up that could be used to determine the validity of the original findings (Brandstädter, Wentura, and Schmitz, 1997). As must be expected, there was considerable loss in sample size, now 896 persons (almost 30%). The results were virtually the same as had been found in 1994.

Time and Social Variables

The range of socialization factors that might be incorporated in temporal behavior and awareness is, of course, quite large. Certain ones have been studied repeatedly with various samples: engagement and disengagement, attitudes toward death and dying, and relationships with children are just a few. In some instances, the scope and meaning have been better defined, as in the case of social engagement. Others have been more confusing than helpful, as in the case of sexual adjustment and participation. Still others have been incompletely considered, as in the case of temporal awareness in a developmental sense.

One set of factors (health, income, and memory in terms of self-evaluations) has been studied by Robinson-Whelen and Kiecolt-Glaser (1997) with a sample of middle-aged and older adults. In addition, they gathered data on the hypothesis that temporal comparisons become more important in the self-evaluations of the elderly than do social comparisons. Participants were asked how they compared with others of their own age and whether or not changes had occurred within the last 5 years. There were 70 women and 21 men, with an average age of 70 (53 to 90 years). Income was modest ($20,000 to $30,000 per year). Educational level was moderately high (97% completed high school, 41% had a college degree).

Participants responded to inquiries about, say, their health as compared with others of their age and with its status five years ago. Self-evaluations were obtained on appropriate scales from the Older Americans Resources and Services (OARS) Multidimensional Functional Assessment Questionnaire. Life satisfaction was also assessed. They found that subjective ratings of health were described as good, about the same as five years earlier, and somewhat better than their age peers. Their income was felt to be sufficient, equal to five years previous, and the same as their peers. Memory, the participants said, was good, similar to their peers, and only slightly worse than five years earlier.

The hypothesis about temporal and social comparisons was problematic. Health and income sufficiency were nonsignificant, but self-rated memory was significant (with a modest $r = .39$). Social comparisons, however, were significantly related to all three. Social and temporal comparisons had no significant effect on self-evaluations across the age span used. Health and income were significantly related to life satisfaction, but memory was not.

Perhaps the most important outcome of this research effort is found in the quote that "temporal comparison processes do not appear to increase in importance with age, nor do social comparison processes appear to decrease in importance with age among relatively healthy community-residing adults" (p. 965). They conclude that a new model demonstrating changes, if any, in comparison processes with age is needed. The decision on the importance of such comparisons to temporal perspective is open to argument. Essentially, we must ask: Is this a variable that should receive major emphasis in a scientific model of time?

Two of the variables described in the introduction to this section (engagement and dealing with the inevitability of death) were considered in two studies by Johnson and Barer (1992, 1993). It is not clear that the same sample was used in both cases, but the procedures followed, the location of the sample, and the similarity in characteristics make it appear that they are the same persons. It is interesting that the first study, after pointing out the rejection of disengagement theory, nevertheless proposes that some portions of the theory have survival value and relevance to the aged. Specifically, they say, with a sample of 150 very old (85 years and older) adults there have been social losses from the deaths of family and friends coexistent with limiting physical conditions that restrict the occasion to benefit from socialization. This leads to a response that seems congruent with disengagement. As a result Johnson and Barer cite three purposes in the 1992 study: a description of the characteristics of a large, very old group (in itself a potentially useful and significant contribution), behaviors related to remaining engaged socially, and the processes that enter selective disengagement when it occurs.

The sample of 150 persons had a mean age of 89 years and, as must be expected because of realities in the population, consisted of females in almost three-quarters of the group. There was divergence in socioeconomic status. Education levels were divided into thirds for some college, high school graduation, and less than high school diploma. The participants reported a high sense of well-being, with 12% saying they are very happy and an additional 50% reporting being mostly contented. Most report being only rarely lonely, angry, depressed, bored, uneasy, or restless; in fact, one-third say they are more comfortable with themselves today than was true formerly. They acknowledge the imminence of death but without fear. Preparations have been made by them in both the practical and mental senses.

What remains, then, is an explanation for engagement or disengagement that meets the purposes stated by Johnson and Barer. Even in the face of inevitable social losses, very old persons move to a selective modification of their personal environments by accommodations in several ways. A few make new friends or become more involved as a resource for the community (as in volunteering). Others change their priorities about life and re-structure what is for them a reasonable set of social roles. Where disengagement occurs, the individual refuses to continue conformity with social norms that their physical or social capabilities no longer allow. Others redefine their time orientation, moving from a future orientation to a present one. Finally, there are those who become more oriented to interi-ority, moving from so much interest in the external world to a concentra-tion on the internal world. They justify this reaction by cognitive and emotional rationalizations to justify the new attitudes and roles. Thus, the authors present a picture of varied but pertinent validation that allows the sample to continue with their lives in a context that is rewarding and adap-tive at the same time that it is restricted.

Of most direct relevance to the focus of this book is the contention that there is a shift in emphasis from future time orientation to present as participants lost family and friends. This both agrees and disagrees with the original theory of disengagement in the sense that the shift does occur but that it is more linked to actual losses most prevalent in old age than with a midlife crisis. In contrast to the stereotype that the elderly increas-ingly live in the past, Johnson and Barer found that very few of their sam-ple had such an inclination. They say, "The awareness of finitude comes from the feeling of an absence of a future and impending death" (1992, p. 361).

The second study by these authors (Johnson and Barer, 1993) appears to use the same sample, but the analysis dealt with coping mechanisms and with feelings of control over their lives. Daily routines were assessed, in-cluding pacing of activities, handling of daily tasks, social contacts, and the kinds of events that engender feelings of well-being or lack of it. In addi-tion, participants were asked about problems and how they handled them.

As might be expected, the problems most frequently reported were im-paired functioning that complicated dealing with the environment, health problems that interfered with activity, and losses among family and friends, largely through death. Where there are others who might act as social sup-ports, functional impairment is also a problem, thus restricting the avail-ability of contacts. Yet as illustrated in the first study, there is little depression, anger, or boredom. Loss does not necessarily bring major damage to a sense of well-being. As before, older persons adapt to adverse conditions in a realistic and successful way.

One adaptation, already noted in the 1992 study, is to move from a future time orientation to a present one. More and more, these elderly persons live on a day-to-day basis. They usually mention the past only if urged to do so by an interviewer; they certainly are not living in the past. When they mention the past, it is more often of pleasurable experiences, even though this is selective to avoid reliving unpleasant events. Some think they are creatures of fate, living longer than was necessary or desirable.

The deaths among relatives and friends help these very old persons prepare themselves for their own deaths, Johnson and Barer believe. The most devastating loss has been that of a child, following which other negative events pale in significance. However it may have to be accomplished, adjustment to the reality and imminence of one's own death often is made. The degree to which this is accomplished seems to benefit facing life for what it holds and what it may be.

Johnson and Barer conclude by saying, "Over all these findings point to the importance of forms of adaptation which are not generally tapped by the many instruments used in aging research to evaluate such outcomes as well-being" (1993, p. 78). They point out that their participants considered themselves as the active agents in problem recognition and analysis and that they then acted in a fashion that gave them control over their lives. Such a positive conclusion lends credence to the position that time orientation remains a viable component of successful aging and that a model of time must allow for the entire life process.

Personal Factors in Time Perspective during Old Age

There is an assortment of studies examining details about time perspective in the later years of life. Mostly, these are unconnected to models or even to a consistent line of research so that they stand as exploratory studies—very frequently with no further exploration by anyone. Even so, sampling such disparate efforts may be beneficial to understanding the trends in psychological research about aging and time.

Since Rakowski (1979) pointed out that nearly all such research had been cross-sectional to that time (an approach that has been altered somewhat since) and that the impact of changes across age in functioning is almost absent, it is difficult to draw conclusions about such matters as future time orientation. He did report that age did seem to risk some diminishing of future time orientation. The normative data to support such a position had been largely lacking to that time; Rakowski proposed that research needed to be directed to use of time perspective as a predictor *and* outcome variable. In addition, development of a model (or models) to direct such study was essential, he stated. In the some 20 years since this proposal, there has been only minor attention to his recommendations.

There are several components involved in accomplishing advances of the general sort raised by Rakowski. Certainly one of them focuses on the attempts to assess time orientation itself. There is a tradition here, well known to professionals who must make decisions and recommendations about the ability of patients to function independently in society. In conjunction with other sources of information, of course, but with great acceptance of the utility of specific measures, the Mental Status Questionnaire (Kahn, Goldfarb, Pollack, and Peck, 1960) and the Mini-Mental State Examination (Folstein, Folstein, and McHugh, 1975) have a hoary history and are still frequently used. Their application to those with dementia has been demonstrated and tested, with primary interest on the content that relates to orientation in time and space. Factors that would adversely affect performance must be identified and controlled for (hearing loss, for example), and there has been little compelling evidence of validity of such instruments for diagnostic purposes (Edwards, 1993, pp. 98, 101, 103).

The development and use of more wide-ranging and subjective means for information gathering have been phenomena of recent times. While they may overcome some of the limitations of the older tests, they suffer from some imprecision that makes their use suspect. In any event, most use of such measures has been fostered by a desire for diagnosis and/or differentiation among conditions producing similar symptoms. Winokur and Clayton (1994, p. 11) discuss "orientation" in terms of time and place. One who is oriented in this sense has what is labeled a *clear sensorium*. They follow this with a discussion of alterations in orientation typical of various conditions (affective, schizophrenic, etc.), thereby permitting differential diagnosis (but with additional data needed). Such usage, no matter how helpful to identifying functional problems and leading to treatment for the patient, cannot help us much in a search for the nature of time perspective and awareness, unless there is some inclusion of time awareness as a specific component of study.

Nevertheless, it is easy to find examples of such an approach. An example is the study by Joslyn and Hutzell (1979), examining differences between schizophrenics and brain-damaged individuals in their temporal differentiation. One comparison was between groups being admitted (though some had previous hospitalization); the other comparison was between groups who had been hospitalized for a median length of 3.5 years. There were distinct differences, on average, in temporal orientation favoring schizophrenics over brain-damaged. In fact, the schizophrenics differed only slightly from the norms for adults.

In the groups being newly admitted, 57% of the brain-damaged had temporal orientation performances that were rated as "defective," with only 8% of the schizophrenics being so classified. For the long-term patients, two-thirds of the brain-damaged patients achieved no credits on temporal orientation at all, for whatever reasons; the schizophrenics had 43.5% who were unable to supply a creditable answer. Overall, some 80% of brain-damaged in this sample either were defective in performance or could not perform well enough to signify awareness. Almost half of the resident schizophrenics merited a similar labeling. Whether, and how much, institutionalization is responsible for such deficiencies is unknown. Whatever the reason, it appears that those with brain damage, from a variety of causes, will find it virtually impossible to maintain contact with a world that is based on time relationships.

One of the issues in research that makes comparisons among groups with varying diagnoses is the one of measures that are used. There are always the basic matters of statistical reliability and validity, usually illustrated by internal data. One may judge the adequacy of such tests for the purposes for which they were used and decide if they were sufficient to the decision-making process.

But there are other matters to consider as well. A study by Staats, Partlo, and Stubbs (1993) reflects, in part, such persistent but frequently overlooked considerations. Their concern was the generality of nonresponding in elderly subjects, with particular reference to apprehensiveness. (This fits with a considerable portion of the samples in the study above by Joslyn and Hutsell.) As Staats et al. point out, nonresponding must effect bias in data collection, regardless of the age group, with serious consequences for both the quality and meanings of the results. Additionally, being apprehensive as a basis of nonresponding has been judged to be evidence of some psychological factors such as low feelings of esteem and depression. These ideas are defended on the basis that orientation to the future, and particularly its anticipation with relish, is both psychologically healthy and typical. Staats et al. admit that other explanations are possible, but they confine themselves to nonresponding to future time orientation items as a lack of future time orientation or indication of apprehension about responding.

Their sample consisted of 251 persons older than 55 years, living at home and attending a senior citizen's center. This setting produced a group whose ages ranged from 50 to 91 (with a mean of 63.9 years). Almost three-fourths of the sample was female. Typically they were white, with about one year of education beyond high school, with income of just over $20,000, and with self-reported health status being good. All were interviewed in small groups, with responses reflecting five years in the past, the present, and five years in the future. Their results were compared to those of Shmotkin (1991), a study described in Chapter 4.

The results were mixed, especially as compared with Shmotkin's. Men had fewer nonresponses than women, but the difference did not reach statistical significance. Future orientation was not lacking in this study, showing great similarity both to present and to past responding. This places in doubt, at least for this sample, a position that elderly persons have abandoned a future orientation. However, there was notable nonresponding on one measure, where wishes and expectations were elicited. Seemingly, there is reticence in answering about one's hopes and expectations for the future, perhaps a tacit admission that older persons such as the respondents here may prefer not to commit themselves on such matters, for whatever reason.

Further analysis yielded data that the nonresponding was statistically significant only for expectations about the future. Here, age and education level accounted for most of the variance, age being positively correlated and education being negatively. Thus the older the person, the more likely a nonresponse about expectations; the less educated, the more likely. The latter may be one of the social variables deserving of greater study. Staats et al. conclude that age is essentially independent as a correlate of nonresponding. More important are factors such as health, education, and functional status. Further, they point out, "Future item nonresponse occurs (a) in a complex questionnaire, not in an interview; (b) when items are not enlarged and not presented individually; and (c) when one is presented with a difficult cognitive task (i.e., the degree of expectations of specific future events)" (p. 442). Interpretation of results about responding about issues such as the future and its meaning may need to take a closer look at structure of the measures used than has been the custom.

In a similar view, there needs to be an examination of some concepts proposed in the past and accepted as valid since. Among these are Butler's proposals (1963) about life review and reminiscence. Better stated, there needs to be consideration of the way such concepts have been used and interpreted in research on time awareness in the elderly. Butler proposed that life review is a process used by all of us in order to revive past experiences. Particularly it is employed for unresolved conflicts so that we may integrate them as a part of the self. Reminiscence is a therapeutic procedure used by professionals to assist the individual in dealing with those vulnerabilities from the past that cannot be resolved satisfactorily by the person. This includes, but is not restricted to, the acceptance of the imminence of death, a feature of life that all older persons must face and resolve in order to continue effective living. Indeed, most elderly individuals succeed in that task. Since Butler's original proposal, the ideas have been used in various and often idiosyncratic ways.

An exemplar of this statement is found in an article by Kiernat (1983) in which she reviews literature on retrospection. She maintains that the child can reminisce as soon as the past is separated from the future. To her, daydreaming and reminiscence are the same. Yet she tells us that reminiscence is not common among the elderly. Life review represents a special case, according to Kiernat. The concepts as used by Butler and Kiernat are seemingly not the same in meaning and utility. It is not necessary that either be declared right or wrong. It is, however, important that the meaning of terms used in explaining behavior, when identical, be clearly differentiated.

Such discriminations need to be made as well between instruments intended to measure the same or highly related features of temporality. Strumpf (1987) published an analysis of measures of subjective time that may be used to illustrate the point. He pointed out that measurement of subjective time presented a number of difficulties but found three that were commonly used at the time. The difficulty with each would seem to be the marked subjectivity in choice of content and presumed behavior being measured. One, for example, used "poetic descriptions of time's passage"; a second assessed attitudes about the passage of time and its consequences; the third consisted of statements that the participant was to assign to past, present, or future. The results were less than enlightening, although a case was made for the importance of temporality in successful aging. A central factor in judging *how* and *why* time is such an influence requires measures that can be demonstrated to be valid to the purpose. The current armamentarium of "tests" cannot stand much scrutiny, as witness the fact that few are ever submitted even to such a basic review as is found in the various volumes of Buros's *Mental Measurements Yearbook*.

In this regard, Cameron, Desai, Sahador, and Dremel (1978) have pointed out that there have been several theories and models proposed for the advantages and disadvantages of reminiscence in the elderly. There is the implicit acceptance in these models that reminiscence is an increasing feature in aging and that it must serve some useful (or at least important) purpose.

Before describing the advantages and/or disadvantages of reminiscence on the part of the old, it would appear reasonable to establish that, in fact, the old do reminisce more frequently. Were this confirmed, then we might profitably proceed to establish the parameters associated with the reminiscence phenomenon. (p. 246)

Such reservation might well be applied to a large number of the assumptions underlying current studies on time orientation—and consequently on their validity and generalizability.

Indeed, there is a need for much better understanding of the processes involved in how temporal information is accepted in the frontal lobe and stored in memory. Parkin, Walter, and Hunkin (1995) have presented evidence that both time and space dimensions are subject to the influences of age. What import does this hold for the relative importance of past, present, and future time orientation or for the need for psychological exercise of reminiscence or for any other complex issue?

This matter was considered by Raynor and Entin (1983) in several studies designed to measure the influence of future time orientation with cross-sectional age groups. Sentences were presented to various age groups to be scored for need for achievement, although the age differences were blurred by the types of subjects available. In any event, the authors found that stories based on future orientation referring to young adults yielded higher need achievement scores. Past orientation was more common when the sentence referred to an older person. The more extreme the age differences, the more consistent the results. This outcome would seem to support the stereotype of time perspective, but this must be modified by the possibility that the measures (the stories created) reflect an attitude *about* rather than *by* given age groups.

Nevertheless, we have a body of studies intended to help us delimit time orientation, its effects, and meanings. The survey cuts across a variety of such effects. Guy, Rittenburg, and Hawes (1994) described the ways in which the elderly perceive time as consumers in modern market economies. Effectively they desired to determine how the subjective time perceptions of the elderly affect their behaviors as consumers. Of particular import in such societies is the influence of mechanical time, defined by the authors as clock or calendar time and described as the source of social upheaval on a level of such inventions as printing or the steam engine. Most of the research they surveyed was based on this mechanical notation.

Three models are proposed. The first coincides with the frequently used differentiation of past, present, and future, being linear and separable in character. One's time becomes itself a commodity that serves as a form of investment that can yield dividends in the future. The important issue, then, is one's future, with actions judged in value for their assistance in brokering a future return. Individuals who use this perspective are ordered, scheduling their efforts in one behavior at the time. The often-cited expression "time is money" is the attitude most prevalent.

The second perspective is cyclical in its expression. Events must reoccur in some predetermined order. The present is the important element in life, with the future being merely a repetition of the past. There is no need to plan time; instead, the emphasis is upon simultaneous activities so that the present is fulfilled as completely as possible. Do what needs to be done now without regard to what the future may bring.

The third perspective is action centered, reacting to the tasks of the moment and successfully dealing behaviorally with each. Time is allotted to such a need, and time needed is not a concern. Things should be done when they are relevant and in a fashion to expedite completion. Arrangements are made for efficiency and efficacy alone. Guy et al. refer to the use of the "snake lines" now so prominent in banks, airports, and governmental offices. It is most convenient for the system to have people line up in such a pattern, then move to the first available clerk in order to conduct business properly and economically.

It is possible for each of us to adapt to any (or all) of the three models in our daily behavior. For the elderly, however, Guy et al. propose that the linear model with its continuous flow of influence from past to present and future is most typical. Unfortunately, they also identify the stereotype of social disengagement as the primary reason for this preference. Some better explanation will be needed for the position to be tenable.

The cyclical model, according to these authors, has three expressions for older persons. These are based on daily, weekly, and yearly time measures. There is, for each, an identifiable pattern that occurs on a regularity that is predictable and standard. It is the events that are important, however, not the clock time at which the repeatable events occur. And this spills over to the third model, so one activity is accomplished, regardless of time needed, before the next begins. Guy et al. speculate that gender differences must be expected, largely dependent upon social forces and learning. This inference requires some verification even as it may seem reasonable. The authors also point to the complexity of references to future and past in the perspectives of the elderly, noting that traditional assumptions about orientation have been shown to be questionable. As a result, they note, considerable further study is required of individual adaptation, suggesting that life satisfaction and time perspective probably depend more on adjustment to one's own aging and its physical and mental consequences than to predetermined patterns of time perspective with age.

In evaluating this article, it would seem that the "consumer" element is only tangentially related to the conclusions drawn. Yet the arguments presented are intriguing and worthy of further study for verification.

As with other topics where investigations have been conducted, cross-age comparisons have been popular. One can find research from other cultures (e.g., Bouffard and Bastin, 1994; Cremer, Snel, and Brouwer, 1990; Vanneste and Pouthas 1995) as well as the United States. The same paradigms are usual and so are the results. Occasionally there will be a more interesting or esoteric or challenging component to the research, however.

This is true in a study published by Powers, Wisocki, and Whitbourne (1992). They concerned themselves with the role of worrying as measured in both young adults and elderly ones. Powers et al. predicted that older persons would report fewer worries because of particular traits such as time perspective, locus of control, and feelings of well-being. Their samples consisted of 89 elderly (mean age of 77.6) and 74 undergraduates (mean age 20.4). The younger obviously had more education on average. An interesting feature is that each older person was paid $1 for participation, whereas the students received one experimental credit. There is no justification of the comparable value of each of these to the subjects.

Data were gathered with a standardized scale that assessed worry about health, finances, and social conditions; a measure of attitudes toward past, present, and future; a test of psychological well-being; and external versus internal locus of control. College students reflected more worries than the elderly in total score and on financial and social features. They did not differ significantly about health worries. Younger participants were oriented toward the future, whereas the older ones more often chose answers congruent with past and present. The younger persons were more internal in locus of control, whereas the elderly were more positive in terms of well-being.

The principal conclusion is that both age groups showed a negative effect from their worries, whatever those might be. The more external the locus of control, the greater the worry factor. Psychological well-being was more negative also when worry was a greater factor. The authors conclude that worry is not a prominent feature of an older person's life per se. What is not reflected in this study is the reality of life's factors as the basis for worry. A study that examines worry in terms of real-life features would be a valuable addition. For example, it would seem reasonable, even wise, for a person on a fixed income at age 75 to be concerned about the costs of living in a society where there are sometimes daily increases in food, medicine, and so on. Similarly, younger adults may be justified in worrying about future needs such as employment, not apt to be an issue of importance to the elderly.

This discussion could be extended greatly by the inclusion of the many studies referring to an element of time orientation as it occurs in relation to major variables (for example, Klapow, Evans, Patterson, and Heaton, 1997; Libman, Creti, Levy, Brender, and Fichten, 1997). Little light would be shed on a greater understanding of time in the life of the elderly by doing so. Where there is some more basic relation to the concept of time, the effort may prove more rewarding.

An example of this is a study published by Parnetti, Ciuffetti, Signorini and Senin (1985). Here, the relationship between short-term and long-term memory with space and time orientation was a major variable. Essentially, Parnetti et al. looked at a set of factors involved with memory impairment. For the issue of time orientation, unfortunately, a sample of 106 men and women was reduced to one of nine because of deterioration in functions controlled by the cortex or because of depression. Such a decision may have removed the more significant influences on awareness and adaptation to time by older persons. In any event, the authors report that their remaining group had a selective memory defect. They assessed the members with several scales used to test memory for recent and remote events, short- and long-term span, retention for time and space orientation, and immediate visual memory. Remeasures every two to three months over the next three years indicated drops in visual memory and in recent memory function. Time and space orientation was not significantly affected over time. Just what is to be made of this outcome is problematic. One may speculate that the eliminated subjects might have shown changes in orientation more revealing. Parnetti et al. restrict themselves to a position that any selective memory loss in the elderly does not mean that dementia is occurring in some form. They would account for such incidents as the result of brain changes with age that are specifically structural, influencing the memory system as a result.

Much more clinical in its thrust is a study by Bascue and Lawrence (1977). Death anxiety in the elderly was the focus, particularly as it might influence or be influenced by subjective time. Two questions were asked: Is death anxiety greater in those who have a future orientation than in those with a past or present orientation? What effect does the person's attitude about time have on feelings of death anxiety? Their sample consisted of 88 women over the age of 62 who were aging "normally." Most participants were between the ages of 70 and 79, fairly well educated for their cohort, and largely widowed.

The answer to the first question above was positive. The second was also positive for time anxiety, submissiveness, and possessiveness but negative for flexibility. However, all correlation coefficients were only modest. The authors conclude that there is evidence from their results to support a contention of "an intimate relationship between death and time for elderly people" (p. 86). Since only 20% of the variance in death anxiety measures was accounted for by time measures, the conclusion should not be pushed too far. Beyond the results, Bascue and Lawrence propose that older persons may turn away from a future orientation in order to protect against thoughts of imminent death. To them, this conclusion assumes greater validity from the fact that other factors such as educational level and income do not yield significant results. Yet they point out that death anxiety is "not necessarily inordinately high in normal elderly people" (p. 87).

The gradients of such studies are marked, with great variation in the variables presumed to be related to time orientation. The results are equally diverse and frequently more confusing than illustrative. Have such studies helped lift the obfuscation from the meaning of orientation in time? Is the term more clearly and objectively defined as a result of a survey of the many studies published on the topic? To answer these questions needs a more precise and definitive clarification of what is involved.

THE CONTEXT OF TIME ORIENTATION

The concept of orientation in time and space has been accepted for many years by psychologists as an important dimension in recognizing and dealing with reality. One of the components of diagnosing dementia has been the facility of the patient to supply the answers to questions that test awareness. "Where are we now?" "What is the date?" and so on, are routinely used to screen cases where there is concern that the person is no longer capable of dealing effectively with environmental demands. Other data will be incorporated into the final decision about the integrity of the mind— whether to label behavior as a result of Alzheimer's disease or multi-infarct dementia, for example—but it is unlikely that such a diagnosis will be used where the individual continues to be cognizant of relationships in time and space.

Essentially, the evaluation focuses on the orientation, accepting the nature of time and space as a given. This leaves us in the position of defining that *nature* in order to ensure that orientation is present. But psychologists have not grappled with the basic question, being satisfied in their research efforts to accept that time and space are absolutes that do not need justification or proof. For this reason, the studies examined in this Part II prove more often disappointing or irrelevant than they need to be for definitional purposes.

The idea that time is absolute, pointing always forward in direction, was made concrete by Sir Isaac Newton in the eighteenth century. The implication that there is predictable order was welcome: each of us recognizes time in the same form and degree when our clocks and watches are calibrated. Behavior *in time* was predictable psychologically once the components of reality were stated, once the normal and abnormal were differentiated. Deviation could be observed, measured, and evaluated. The prevailing model was the progression of past to present to future.

This neat arrangement, unfortunately, was strained a bit by the fact that one must be aware of stimulation in the present in order to establish a past. Experiences must be stored by some process not easily explained, and there must be some intelligence that permitted the realization of relationships to what will occur in an unknown future. Psychologists began to nibble at these problems, although there was no systematic attempt to dovetail one with any other. There was an accumulation of data leading to inferences and predictions that were singularly insular. The most frustrating element in all this was that no real relationship to time was explicated anyway. The fact that science (if psychology is one) does not provide laws that distinguish between forward and backward directions in time (Hawking, 1996, p. 194) gave no cause for concern.

In 1916, Albert Einstein published a paper that threw a monkeywrench into the orderly and visibly logical world of physics. It would take a little time, but slowly all those clocks that were calibrated to conform to actual time were found to be questionable. Mysterious new terms became part of the scientific vocabulary: *relativity, spacetime, warp*. Dimensionality was enhanced not only to include the observable but to add others. In this view, time was defined as a finite dimension with a beginning and an end. What this had to do with the practical everyday world of behavior was ignored or explained away as a nonrelevant event so far as psychology was concerned.

The history of psychological experimentation clearly discloses the Newtonian view, leading to the position that Danziger (1990) has labeled "methodolatry." Psychologists opted for a scientific posture where quantification was a requisite, developing increasingly sophisticated statistics whereby significance was equated with probability levels. The result has not always been fortuitous—and often has led to repetitious production that simulates more "reinventing the wheel" than it does progress.

The viewpoint applied to time awareness has led to the host of studies surveyed in Part II, where time serves as a dependent variable used with a variety of independent ones. This process has been clearly described in several contexts, including Garrett's (1941, pp. 372–373) explication of research on reaction time. This is not to imply that such studies are ill-conceived or unimportant. What should be inferred is that results provided from such data yield little information about the role of time in human behavior.

The devil in the machine in this case is the slavish dependence on numerical substance for data to be considered meaningful. Danziger (1990, p. 5) has pointed out that "elaborate deductive procedures" are a crucial part of procedure in natural sciences. Psychology, in contrast, has avoided such use so that "theoretical constructions have seldom been marvels of logical sophistication, and pessimism about the likelihood of reaching rational consensus on the basis of theory has long been widespread." Most published studies involving time orientation (but hardly restricted to that area) do not yield nomothetic conclusions. Such universally valid generalizations are seldom even mentioned, much less delineated from the results achieved. The result is an insular explication of individual events, idiographic in its context. What seems necessary at this point is to present alternatives in models that might generate theories and research pointed toward generalizations.

Model 1

Despite the criticisms so liberally used above, there is a continuing need for the experimental approach that has persisted since the work of Wundt and Ebbinghaus, becoming more refined as paradigms, measures, and statistical tools have become increasingly sophisticated. We have learned some basic things about human behavior by the procedure, and increasingly accurate data are possible with the mechanical devices available today. Without attempting to be "cute," one might speculate about the precision possible with the use of clocks that can measure at the level of the nanosecond. Measures to date may have disguised individual differences by their gross nature. In the same way, improvements in the precision of measurement should permit wider variety in independent variables of concern to the presence of time awareness in all age groups. Finally, including assessments or evaluations of relevant personal variables, rather than assuming them to be error sources or to cancel each other out, could yield interesting and significant outcomes. Means to ends assumes greater totality under such circumstances.

Model 2

There is a crying need to conceptualize the basic elements of psychological phenomena throughout the experimental field. This is certainly true in time orientation. The blind acceptance of Newtonian time (unidirectional and absolute) closes the door to progress. Some consideration of the behavioral relevance of concepts is currently well deserved.

For example, psychologists have accepted the idea that past, present, and future are discrete but related elements in time orientation. Implied is the position that each is measurable and that comparisons on independent variables such as age groupings are valid and useful. It may be time to reconsider this position.

Let's consider the possibility that we must analyze the nature of terms. Perhaps, like other animals, we are bound to an eternal present. What we can respond to is only in the present. It is true that the evolution of the brain has somehow permitted us to store experiences in a way that we recognize in each present that which has already occurred (or at least to a large degree). We become more proficient in responding because of practice plus the availability of identifiable past experiences. This latter skill allows us to anticipate that the present, with its past history, will reoccur. Insofar as there is a cyclic nature to experience, we can anticipate how and when a given experience may be repeated. That is as close to a future as we can ever achieve.

Outside repeatable present events, what we assume about the so-called future is fantasy. Rarely do such fantasies actually occur, and even when they do, they are only partially achieved (depending really on the part of the fantasy based in repetitious past history). In other words, there may be no such thing as a future. Using experience we try to anticipate what will happen if—. Error in the new present is recorded and used as a basis for reformulation, and so on and so on, until we may eventually achieve the result we wished for.

Conceptualizing accepted variables in such a way could be a source of more meaningful, and certainly more interesting, research.

Model 3

Psychologists should allow the light of deductive proposals for essential and testable elements of psychological phenomena. It is the way of science, and it may be the key to understanding. Certainly theory building and testing can be applied to time awareness. In some instances, efforts have been made in this direction (e.g., Rakowski, 1979). He concluded, more than 20 years ago, that more prospective efforts were needed.

To adopt the dichotomy employed earlier, there is little doubt that temporal experiences in later adulthood are significant to the person. Research, however, is still at the beginnings of creating a correspondingly meaningful area of study. (pp. 82–83)

More important, such daring holds great promise for those conditions where there is time *dis*orientation. That application we can reserve for the next part of this book.

PART III

The Impact of Time

Hypotheses are nets, and only he who throws them out catches something.

—Novalis

CHAPTER 7

Defining Time Disorientation

There are a number of medical conditions that produce disorientation in time and space. But the outcomes are more complex even than this. They also cause memory loss, particularly, and confusion. Even personality changes of some types and degrees have been noted. Given such diverse and debilitating results, there is a need to understand the responsible agents and the specifics of their consequences that describe dementia.

THE NATURE OF DEMENTIA

The case has been made (Edwards, 1993, pp. 1–2) that the term *dementia* is little more than a convenience for a sizable number of effects that share some similarities and more differences. A diagnosis of dementia thus assumes the aspects of a scrap basket: several conditions with similar outcomes in their behavioral effects. Indeed, a definition is more apt to include the effects as an indicator that the condition is present.

The imperfections do not reduce our need to confront the nature of dementia in order to communicate knowledge and survey research and its meanings. For this reason, Edwards proposes a "definition" that is disease and behavior focused, leaving us with less of an understanding of its effects than of its nature: "Dementia is defined, then, as *a result of a set of conditions, medically diagnosed, and leading to recognized and measurable behavior changes in an individual*" (p. 6, italics in original). The "set of conditions" is a list consisting of several diseases held responsible for dementia: Alzheimer's, Pick's, Creutzfeldt-Jakob, and so on. A physician provides diagnosis, at times including input from a psychologist. Either way, there is more attention paid to behavioral changes that buttress the diagnosis. These "behavioral changes" consist of a variety of recognized and accepted outcomes but particularly for memory loss. In the context of this book, disorientation in time and place will be a key feature as well.

Just as in Part II there was an attempt to define orientation in terms of the research available, so will disorientation be considered in this Part III. There is a problem, however, in the fact that orientation implies a reasonably intact and healthy brain. *Dis*orientation, in contrast, suggests that the structural integrity of the brain must have been disturbed in some ways. This leads then to the position that such disturbance must involve loss of some competencies that are important to functioning. Relative roles must be decided and described, then related to the observable evidence that the person has some degree of space and time orientation. Does the explanation involve only the integrity of the brain, or must we take some position on the presence of "mind" that operates within the context of brain but has powers of its own?

Whether all behavior can be explained in terms of the functioning of the brain depends on personal preference within the context of the limited knowledge about the cortex that exists currently. The prevailing view is that brain and mind are synonymous or corelated. Greenfield (1995, p. 2) tells us, "There is no little creature in the deepest recesses between your ears to appreciate all that is going on: There is no brain within the brain. . . . Brain electricity and brain chemistry are ultimately all there is to your mind." Dennett (1995, p. 370) agrees and gives us some notion of the complexity involved. "*Of course* our minds are our brains, and hence are ultimately just stupendously complex 'machines'; the difference between us and other animals is one of huge degree, not metaphysical kind" (italics in original). Not so adamant is Pinker (1994), since his interests center on language and its instinctual role (if any). Indeed, he tells us, "Language is the most accessible part of the mind" (p. 404), offering the position, "So the language instinct suggests a mind of adapted computational modules rather than the blank slate, lump of wax, or general-purpose computer of the Standard Social Science Model."

To extend the complexity of the relationship of brain and mind, Ferris (1992, pp. 73–74) describes a symbiotic arrangement where mind is explained as the subject of consciousness, encompassing all brain input. Consciousness, however, is only a small part of operations in the brain. Ferris sees the mind as a restricted area of the brain where unconscious processes are dealt with.

There is, of course, considerable similarity in the selected citations used here. All agree about a basic structure that is the brain and that contains the elements (neurons) that conduct, through an electrochemical process, the business of living. But there is some speculation by two of these authorities that something more may also be at work. The evolutionary process brought to humankind a cortex that is unparalleled in the marvels of its manifestations. There is something more than a machinelike organ that, when properly understood, will explain the complexity of life. What that "something more" may be is speculative and so is dismissed, or at least is ignored, by those with hard-nosed notions of reality.

Perhaps this may seem a moot point—and would be in some other treatment of time and space orientation. It is not, however, when one considers the nature and meaning of *dis*orientation. Perhaps I may be forgiven for seeing the need for something more than intact circuits or impulses to explain some of the complexity of dementia's ravages. In any event, the remainder of this book will make some case for a brain/mind relationship that exceeds its simple nature. Ferris (1992, p. 74) has echoed the same point with his comments on the "multiplicity" that "keeps peeking from behind the scrim, and what it reveals is that each of us, like the wider universe, is made of many different entities." It may be a key to moving from an absolute notion of time and space to one of relativity.

THE FACES OF DEMENTIA

Behavioral effects may be observable and measurable, but their elimination depends on treatment in some form. In order to treat, it is necessary to know a cause for the symptoms. Cure and prevention, the ultimate desired goal in the case of deleterious effects, require that the source itself (the cause) must be eliminated. In the case of dementia, the effects have been widely noted and accepted (although the quantity of descriptors may vary from one authority to another): often cited are such symptoms as memory loss, particularly in short-term loadings, confusion, disorientation in time and place, and personality alterations. Unfortunately, such effects may result from a variety of causes, some of which are treatable and others that are not. Depression is a good example of the former; Alzheimer's of the latter. In this book, the treatable conditions, which should yield excellent results when addressed, are not considered. Depressed patients rarely show evidence of disorientation in time, even without treatment. Instead, the descriptions that follow are for conditions that are untreatable, at least at present, for the condition itself (although some symptoms may be partially treatable for some patients some of the time). The list should be considered representative, not all-inclusive.

Alzheimer's Disease

Alzheimer's disease (AD) is a recent phenomenon in the sense that its description and diagnosis first occurred about 100 years ago. It seems reasonable, however, that it must have been present for centuries before. Two events led to its present status as a "diagnosis of choice." First, the publication of Alois Alzheimer's article describing a case of a strange illness (*eigenartige Erkrankung*) in a woman patient, appearing in 1907. Second, the increase in the number of survivors in old age during the twentieth century, with length of life currently about 75 years and a population of centenarians approaching 20,000 today. The longer the individual lives, the greater the opportunity for illness to occur. Longevity brings losses, as already referred to in this book. There are at least 2, and possibly 4, million persons showing the symptoms associated with Alzheimer's, most of them elderly. The problem will not go away since there is no definitive diagnosis and no treatment because of the unknown cause.

The report by Alzheimer represents one of those events of critical importance in medical history. The woman was 51 years old at the time she was referred to him by the director of the asylum in Frankfurt am Main. She had come to the institution with an unusual complex of symptoms: suspiciousness of her husband (presumably unjustified), increasing memory loss, inability to orient herself in her own home, and abject and unreasonable fear of other people. Within the institution it was noted that she was totally disoriented in time and place, delirious and hallucinatory at times.

Alzheimer found that her short-term memory was greatly affected. She was able to name objects but could not recall what they were after only a few seconds. She often would substitute the use of an object for its label—example, milk-pourer instead of cup (*Milchgießer statt Tasse*). In addition, she showed difficulty in recovering words from memory. Sometimes she was unsure of the use for certain objects. By contrast, her physical condition was normal.

Her illness progressed rapidly; she died four years later, completely incapacitated. Such rapid decline, seemingly early death, and the peculiar symptom pattern served as a suitable reason for autopsy. Her brain had atrophied generally, with evidence of arteriosclerosis. Neurofibrils in cells were found to be enlarged and clustered into bundles. In many cells there were stored metabolic products that were pathologic. Alzheimer was unable to identify the substance and called for further research into its nature and meaning. Overall, he concluded, there was evidence of some specific disease process that precluded identification with diagnoses already accepted. In other words, he felt that here was something new and challenging that needed identification in its own right.

His publication hardly excited great interest or enthusiasm, even in Germany. His work did catch the attention of Kraepelin, the leading authority of the time, and was rewarded with a citation in Kraepelin's work on psychiatry (1910), where the suggestion was made to accept the new condition and name it after the finder. Limited follow-up by others continued for several decades. As older persons began to complain of symptoms now associated with the disease, and as families found increasing problems in their aging parents, the culprit was felt to be the very condition described by Alzheimer. In the past 40 or 50 years, the diagnosis has become increasingly popular, leading to major research efforts to determine causation and to develop treatment for symptoms if not for the disease. Still, there is the point made in Burns, Howard, and Pettit (1995, p. ix) that "Alzheimer's disease probably became a disease in the 1960s and 1970s and as such is beginning its long journey into the collective conscious."

Potential Causes. The search for a cause has produced a number of possibilities, none of which has been shown to be the answer. The first likely culprit was aluminum since abnormal quantities were found in diseased cells upon autopsy. This presumes, of course, that brains of "normally aging" persons of the same age had been autopsied and found to have some amount of aluminum present significantly less than in those who had Alzheimer's. This is debatable since the number of such autopsies has been, and still is, limited. In any event there was excitement created that control of aluminum buildup would reduce the number of persons developing Alzheimer's. Consequently, suggestions of ways of avoiding aluminum were generated and broadcast. Antacids were among violators, even aluminum cookware. One prominent gerontologist always checked the kitchen of a new restaurant, and if she found that they used aluminum, she would refuse to eat there. Such efforts were ineffectual, of course. Alzheimer's continued to increase. That does not mean that aluminum may not be implicated in some way, and so research continues.

The major thrust has been in other directions, however. The possibility of an infectious agent remains viable; the role of genetics has some strong adherents as well. By far the most popular and promising returns to a principal finding of Alzheimer: a form of protein that formed fibrils and rendered the neuron useless over time. Whether the protein (called beta amyloid) is cause or effect is still not known, but it seems certain that the amyloid forms the abnormal strands that accumulate on brain cells. Part of its action is apparently to alter another normal protein, tau, which joins in the destructive process that leads to the plaques and tangles seen by Alzheimer and still considered the clearest evidence that the disease is present. Findings can only be conducted microscopically, and so the actual proof of diagnosis is lacking in almost all cases.

Such research is the hope for finding a basis for halting the progression of the disease as well as discovering a means for reversal of the process. Best of all will be the eventual prevention of the condition. That would seem to be in the distant future. At present there is no treatment for Alzheimer's disease as such. Yet drug corporations are funding research to find a drug that they call "treatment" in order to alleviate the symptoms that distress both patient and caregiver. Such an endeavor is commendable as long as there is no confusion that such drugs are limited to temporary relief and do not affect the insidious course of the disease. Most such drugs are aimed at improving the short-term memory of patients so that they may assume part of the independence that has been lost.

The intervention is aimed largely at the role of the neurotransmitter acetylcholine, a vital assist in short-term memory function, depleted in its quantity as cells are diseased. By inhibiting the enzyme cholinesterase, the quantity of acetylcholine can be more effectively used by the neuron. Thus, the treatment is primarily as an inhibitor so that secondarily the neurotransmitter may be somewhat more effective. Such an indirect approach would seem to assure that the drug will be helpful only part of the time for only some of the patients under limited conditions. That has, in fact, proven to be true. One might ask, then, why not just increase the level of acetylcholine available to neurons? The answer is that the brain will not take up the neurotransmitter directly.

So the options are limited. The picture is complicated by the fact that side effects, some dangerous and severe, have resulted from the use of the currently approved "treatments." There may be about as far to go in finding an effective and safe drug for symptoms as in finding the cause of the disease.

Course of the Disease. The case reported by Alzheimer was unique in certain respects. First, the patient was 51 years old, not a rare occurrence but certainly not typical of the age group most at risk. Burns et al. (1995) report that 3.2% of those in their seventies and 10.8% of those in their eighties show evidence of Alzheimer's disease, with similar ratings for dementia arising in connection with vascular disease. The prevalence for those under 70 is much smaller. In addition, those who display the symptoms leading to a diagnosis at a younger age tend to die earlier than those who are diagnosed at a later age. (There is, of course, a limit to this statement just as to other such generalizations.) The point is that Alzheimer's may run a course of several years (say, 5 as in Alzheimer's own case) or as many as 15 or 20 years for those who display behavioral effects in the years following diagnosis. Predicting a terminal point is practically impossible. The most reasonable position is to say that a patient may live for a number of years and become progressively less mentally competent. The relentless nature of the condition places increasing burden on the caregiver, so the patient, who becomes less and less aware of stressors, may outlive the caregiver. Because professionals prefer order, and families want answers, it is not surprising that there have been attempts to provide "stages" in the progression of the disease. Butler (1990, pp. 934–935) has supplied such a scheme but makes the point that *"there is great variability and the progression of stages often is not as orderly as the . . . description implies"* (italics in original). Edwards (1993, p. 146) has critiqued attempts at staging in two ways: confounding of disease with outcome and an implication of a linear relationship between the course of the disease and the associated dementia. It seems more appropriate to inform patient and family that the disease is irreversible at the present and shows overall decline into senility so that dependence will become greater as the disease progresses. Of course, *how* one informs the affected persons is an important component. Nor is it reasonable to leave the situation at this level. There are skills that caregivers can learn, practice, use more and more proficiently, and achieve adaptability. Providing training and direction in building trust, problem solving, and assertiveness provide more assurance of positive outcomes than a list of changes to anticipate.

Behavioral Effects. Since the cause of Alzheimer's is unknown, and biopsy of the brain is dangerous, it is not surprising that presumptive diagnosis must occur. That places the burden on a set of behaviors that are commonly observed and accepted. The most common complaint by patients and caregivers concerns the changes in memory function that increasingly interfere with normal daily routine. It is, in fact, with one form of memory that overwhelmingly is reported and checked in the diagnostic procedure: short-term memory malfunction. As a result, the use of such measures has assumed almost mythic qualities.

Long-term memory seems not to be a culprit in this regard. In fact, the lore has it that memories from the past, particularly the far past such as childhood, remain stable far into the process of the disease itself. Eventually, of course, even remote memories are lost. Meanwhile, many incidents from the past may be rehearsed over and over by the patient and are assumed often to be accurate and complete. There is little evidence that such acceptance is warranted.

The question arises, in any event: What is there about this disease that it follows such a clear course about memory? Primary is the fact that patients and caregivers themselves find such losses introduce increasingly severe problems in dealing with life. They cite the memory problems as the chief concern, even though they may also note other difficulties. A secondary factor that may not be well recognized is that memory loss is a common feature of a variety of conditions, some of which are treatable. Certainly the dementias share the feature commonly so that it is not so clearly differentiating as the prolific use of the diagnosis might imply.

Short-term memory requires the input of a stimulus that is retained long enough for action to follow. This means a few seconds at the least, so the portion of the limbic system—in this case, the hippocampus—can effectively integrate and pass on the stimulus to the appropriate area of the forebrain. For this reason, some scientists believe that the destructive power of Alzheimer's begins in the hippocampus, interferes with short-term memory, and then moves on to the forebrain. Just how this process may eventuate is unknown at present. Since the hippocampus has been found to be associated with an ability to identify position in space in some animals, and since Alzheimer's patients present problems with spatial orientation, the argument may assume some greater validity. In any event the phenomenon is apparent and commonly reported.

Such an evident loss in memory would not seem to be sufficient to explain that Alzheimer's may be present. It is commonly noted that older persons begin to experience "slippage" in their memories, causing at least embarrassing and momentary problems. In addition, the elderly have greater difficulty in learning new material than they did when younger or when compared with cross-age samples. The fact that the material must be new is meaningful. Encoding such elements requires holding the stimulus in short-term storage for incorporation at a higher level. An example is learning the vocabulary of a foreign language. In German the acquisition of many terms corresponds directly or closely with English and so causes no difficulty. Others are somewhat like an English expression but may have a slightly different meaning and so will require greater practice. Then there are those that deviate widely from English. Practice must be intense in order to acquire facility and even then may be quickly lost to the forgetting procedure.

Memory loss, pure and simple, of whichever type is not a convincing evidence of the presence of a dementia. Just so, patients and caregivers report other problems that are increasingly recognized. These items may vary from source to source and authority to authority, depending on preference. Confusion, for example, is common and should be verified. The problem is that it is easier to test memory for facts than it is to test level of confusion. One may ask, "What is the date?" with some assurance (whether or not deserved), but "Tell me the difference between right and wrong" is less realistic. After all, even the questioner may not know the difference yet be able to give the date quickly and accurately. Yet dementia patients are confused, even in familiar circumstances. Evaluators must use observational data (or reports from caregivers) as the appropriate evidence. "She can't seem to remember where the kitchen is but has no trouble about the location of the bathroom" is an example.

Some patients demonstrate changes in personality traits significant enough to be included in some lists. Usually these are negative changes ("He has become abusive in the past year," an observation needing confirmation) since positive ones are not so often volunteered ("He has become calmer and nicer than he used to be," also needing confirmation). By and large, however, personality change does not seem to be a major feature of Alzheimer's in most cases.

This brings us to the topic of orientation. Psychologically, the term is taken to mean the ability to locate oneself in the environment in terms of time, place, and people. In the absence of dementia, one is aware of the mechanical features (clock time and calendar date) in most cases, although the aging person may not always be sure of the day or date. Similarly, spatial characteristics are part of consciousness, although any of us may be a bit confused if placed in a strange location. And, of course, we recognize others in our lives, the family and relatives and friends and acquaintances who are important to us. But sometimes we may develop a little problem recalling a name of someone known to us. In other words, degree is an important issue in deciding if the individual is *dis*oriented.

Unfortunately, we are faced with the same issues implied above: What are the norms for the population? Among the elderly, how much departure from orientation must there be in order to conclude that dementia is a fact? The tradition has developed that brief, direct test measures such as the Mental Status Questionnaire (Kahn et al., 1960) yield a sufficient answer. Consisting of 10 questions, the questionnaire requires the patient to respond to such items as current time (the "present" in the schema of past, present, and future). An example is, "What is today?" There are also questions reflecting the past ("What year were you born?") and even a probing of commonly known facts ("Who is the president?"). The technique has proved to be reliable and reasonably valid, as judged by diagnosis of dementia, but it must be supplemented by other observations and data. The psychologist must determine any hearing loss, medications that interfere with mental performance, even primary language and educational level.

As Alzheimer's disease progresses, space and time disorientation also increases, but not in a regular pattern necessarily and not with the same degree from one patient to another. The outcome over time is an increasing dependence on the caregiver as the patient is less competent to utilize the functions of mind: rational thought, planning, relating cause and effect, perceiving and carrying out appropriate actions, and so on. Since there is less awareness of inability the patient usually becomes less concerned about the shift from personal responsibility to total responsibility by the caregiver. As the patient becomes more dependent the caregiver gives up more personal freedom and control. Eventually, one person loses identity, whereas the other loses self. The cost is too massive to calculate. There can be no more profound acknowledgment of the role of space and time orientation in life.

Outcomes. Alzheimer's disease is not a "killer" in the sense of cancer or heart disease or respiratory conditions. Years ago the statement was made that Alzheimer's systematically "robs the mind." The physical body may continue to function, sometimes at high levels, as long as the directive functions are facilitated by someone else. In fact, patients may seem to gain physical stamina and competence as the stresses and cares of daily life are no longer recognized or expected. As damage to brain cells continues, of course, the ability to interpret stimulation from both within and outside the body will decline. Some patients will be unable to report pain or the locus of discomfort, and a few may not even be aware that they suffer in some way. Combined with such factors as declining immune system function, the signals that would alert the person to the need for medical attention will not be apprehended. The most common cause of death is reported to be pneumonia, the "old person's friend" in a general way as well.

The unfortunate fact is that many Alzheimer's patients die no longer able to recognize spouse, family, or friends. It seems likely that they are unaware of the death process itself since there is no longer awareness of one's place in time and space. The total devastation of the meaning of life, of the knowledge that one has accomplished many significant achievements during a long lifetime, that there are those who care and love and grieve at the loss of a significant individual testify to the cruelty and destruction wreaked by a condition whose cause is still unknown.

Multi-Infarct Dementia

There is a general agreement that most cases of dementia of the type described in this book are accounted for by Alzheimer's and vascular disease. Yet the two are distinctly different in several respects. Multi-infarct dementia (MID) has more deleterious effects on basic functions, whereas Alzheimer's shows its effects more profoundly on the higher mental faculties (Caplan, 1990, pp. 918–973. The former shows damage in the principal arterial supply areas, whereas the latter occurs in cortical areas that lie between arterial supply zones. Essentially, MID is caused by a stroke, most often "silent" in the sense that it is unrecognized despite its effects and compounding over a period of time. With sufficient neuronal damage, the patient becomes less competent to function in daily life. As Caplan has written, "Vascular disease 'bites the soma and licks the mind' whereas degenerative and toxic-metabolic diseases waste the intellect while sparing somatic functions until late in their course" (p. 971). He does point out that severe brain damage in vascular disease produces dementia. The process, Caplan says, is much like taking pieces and bits from a pie; eventually the pie is decimated.

There are several factors that dispose to MID. Chief among these is the set of conditions most commonly identified with stroke: hypertension, cardiac disease, high "bad" cholesterol, diabetes, and diseases of the arteries that block blood transmission. But there are less easily identified (by medical tests) factors as well. These include a history of transient ischemic attacks (TIAs) or strokes and signs of neurologic malfunction such as sensory loss, exaggerated reflexes, even incontinence. Indeed, insufficiency of blood supply (ischemia) to the neurons of the brain may be implicated in as many as 80% of strokes (p. 949).

The result is a fairly rapid disintegration of bodily controls accompanied later by a gradual loss of mental competencies. However, the locus of the stroke damage is a critical variable in determining the extent, even presence, of dementia. All stroke victims do not deteriorate mentally as Alzheimer's patients do, although they certainly experience permanent and often devastating behavioral effects. *If* MID occurs in addition to other stroke-related changes, the consequences described for Alzheimer's will show some corollaries.

There is a body of research that supports the view that there is a stepwise progression of the dementia in MID, whereas that for Alzheimer's is more irregular. However, the size and depth of the steps are not easily predictable, seemingly dependent on the number and extent of silent strokes. Generally, MID is diagnosed somewhat earlier in life than Alzheimer's, often first noted in the decade of the fifties and apparently related to the period when hypertension and other such factors become a significant risk. Patients may deteriorate at a faster rate as well. Males have been diagnosed more often than females, and the highest rate is found among those of African descent, perhaps a tribute to the degree and types of stressors in the lives of black males.

The picture is clouded by the possibility that diagnostic prejudice may be significant. Thus, there are more cases of AD than MID in this country, whereas England shows the opposite trend. Such differences call for caution in accepting generalizations that are based upon limited experience and research.

Causes. As mentioned, vascular disease is a significant factor in stroke and thus in MID. Hypertension, most common in males and often diagnosed around the age of 50, is a particular concern because of its effects on arterial flow. Yet the picture is not entirely clear, and vascular disease may be only a contributing factor in the final analysis. Still, there is a mixed bag in the sense that research does not consistently report a relationship between the condition and vascular disease, particularly hypertension. Further, there is some difficulty in differentiation between MID and AD. From autopsies there is evidence of diagnostic accuracy above chance levels, but there remain disturbing error rates. Since diagnosis is in question, there is a greater dependence on behavioral symptoms as a tool in decision making. Loss of body functions is one such criterion, occurring earlier in MID than in AD. Deterioration in higher mental processes occurs earlier with AD. But these, and similar factors, are hardly conclusive in their impetus.

Course. MID usually follows a stepwise progression, over a fairly short number of years. However, there is less than clarity in the data available to the present. Even so, there seems a good case to be made for the efficacy of early identification and treatment. Within the current view, intervention to correct vascular disease may be potent and effective. Diet and exercise, weight loss (when needed), and stress control may be as effective as medications, at least for some patients. The goal is to arrest the damage process and thereby stabilize the individual's condition. The result may be some avoidance of dementing symptoms.

Behavioral Effects. Complaints from patients and caregivers are frequently so similar to those of AD that differentiation is difficult. In some cases symptoms are reported as identical (Sunderland, 1990, p. 945). Certainly evidence of hypertension and other factors associated with vascular disease can help in some cases, but diagnostic confusion is nevertheless more common than might be expected. Sunderland notes that "there is currently no fool-proof diagnostic method. Even at autopsy, definitive diagnosis is impossible in some cases because of the neuropathologic overlap between MID and Alzheimer's disease."

The expressions of loss of competence in higher mental processes are to be expected in MID, then, particularly as the TIAs accumulate and infarcts become more widespread. In the forebrain, this leads to inability to reason accurately and quickly, think rationally, plan for the future, recover experiences from the past, and the like. Short-term memory becomes adversely affected, resulting in learning difficulties, and spacetime orientation is disturbed and eventually lost. Personality may show moderate change, perhaps even becoming major in expressions that are distressing and disturbing for caregivers. Essentially the MID patient becomes similar (and sometimes indistinguishable) to the AD patient.

Outcomes. Although progression will most often proceed faster than for AD, the MID patient must experience the same awareness of gradual but increasing losses. Such frightening events may be denied or ignored, but eventually they become manifest to caregiver as well as patient, particularly as the stepwise process becomes more evident and extensive. Still, death is more commonly ascribed to such factors as pneumonia unless there is evidence of an acute cerebrovascular accident.

Creutzfeldt-Jakob Disease

Among the few known infectious causes of dementia, Creutzfeldt-Jakob disease (CJD) has been the most often recognized. Present in only 1 person per million in the population each year (and so found in less than 300 citizens in the United States), it has previously been described as due to a slow-acting virus, most often active in those in their fifties and sixties, which causes death rapidly, usually in less than a year (Sunderland, 1990, pp. 946–947). More recent developments, however, have caused some caution to be expressed about the accuracy of the traditional descriptions.

Potential Causes. Today CJD is believed to be the result of an infectious agent called a *prion.* Not a virus, nor a bacterium, the prion is a hypothetical particle made up totally of protein, without a genetic component (*Webster,* 1996). Misshapen and destructive, these particles affect healthy protein so that nerve cells (neurons) become increasingly filled with more prions in a chain reaction. Cells are destroyed by holes that are inflicted by the prions, leading to the rapid loss of physical controls and mental competencies. Death results in a short time. Not only are human cells thus affected, but degenerative brain diseases similar to CJD have been identified in sheep, elk, mink, and cows. This last group is the one involved in the "mad cow disease" scare in England during the 1980s and 1990s.

A chronology has been prepared by Ratzan (1998). The first case of bovine spongiform encephalopathy (BSE, mad cow disease) was reported in England in late 1986. By 1995, over 150,000 confirmations were reported in some 33,500 herds within the United Kingdom. By the end of the next year the conclusion had been reached that the cause was due to ruminant-derived meat and bone meal in cattle feed. Thus, the cows were infected by eating protein supplements that contained prions activated in the living animals, increasing rapidly in their effects and spreading throughout the cow population. Even other animals (such as cats) have been similarly infected, suggesting that the condition may be able to move between species.

The exact relation between CJD and BSE is not clear, though the occurrence of CJD in young persons (a most rare event) has led to speculation that there may have been exposure to BSE. Enough cases have now accumulated to suggest that there may be a variant of the traditional concept of CJD that threatens the well-being of youth.

Regardless of the specific condition, the prion is the source of increased research in order to establish controls. Unfortunately, there seems to be no way to destroy it; its resistance has been called by some as the most complete on earth. There have been attempts to increase temperatures as high as 600 degrees centigrade, yet some of it survives after years of such treatment. Formaldehyde has not altered it, disinfectants are useless, and ionizing radiation has no effect. Biological scientists are unable to explain how such an agent can even exist.

Course. As mentioned earlier, CJD (and its variants) is slow to incubate but quick to bring death once the spongiform encephalopathy occurs. At autopsy, the brain shows atrophy and a degree of sponginess (Edwards, 1993, p. 175). In the course of development there is ataxia, muscle spasms, seizures, incontinence, psychotic behavior, and visual disorders (Fisk, 1981, p. 49). There is no treatment at present.

Behavioral Effects. Behaviors normally associated with dementia are to be expected in the CJD patient. Psychologically, apathy, a lack of concern about appearance and neatness, and psychomotor retardation are traits listed by Sunderland (1990, p. 947). Major clinical signs of CJD (Gibbs and Gadjusek, 1978, pp. 119–120) include insidious onset, normally without systemic illness; behavioral disturbances, noted as confusion, emotional lability, depression, and withdrawal; and progressive dementia. Some cases classified as familial suggest that there may be a hereditary transmission in at least a few cases.

Outcomes. As the condition progresses, patients lose the ability to move and to speak. A coma usually results, with death resulting from heart attacks, infections, or pneumonia.

Pick's Disease

As with other conditions leading to dementia, the cause of Pick's is un-known. Damage occurs largely in the frontal and temporal lobes, leading to memory loss and apathy. Attention deficits may become marked, leading to poor hygiene and seemingly careless behavior. Similarities to effects from Alzheimer's are marked, and it is difficult to assure accurate diagnosis until autopsy. Such diagnosis as does occur is based upon distinctive findings from a CT (computed tomography) scan.

Prevalence has been estimated at some 3 to 6 persons per 10,000 in the general population. This would indicate less than 200,000 cases currently in the United States (Edwards, 1993, p. 168). Although significantly more instances than for CJD, the condition is still much less prevalent than Alzheimer's for which estimates are around 4 million. In comparison, Constantinidis (1985, p. 72) has commented: "In psychological terms, we can say that in Alzheimer disease the intellectual faculties are disturbed, while in Pick disease their utilization is faulty." Although this is a meaningful distinction, it may be difficult for caregivers and even professionals to make the distinction in individual cases.

Pick's usually is expressed in the age range from 40 to 60 years. There may be a stronger case for heredity than with other causes of dementia. This is demonstrated in several studies. Gustafson (1987) analyzed 20 cases of frontal lobe dementia, of which 4 were diagnosed as Pick's, and found that half could be related to positive heredity. By contrast, the Alzheimer's cases in the sample had a 30% heredity relationship. From data with families, Heston, White, and Mastri (1987) agreed that the heredity probability is greater for Pick's than for Alzheimer's but that the risk over one's lifetime is greater for relatives of AD patients. They conclude that their evidence supports a genetic influence as the cause of Pick's.

Cause and Prognosis. There is a general problem in judging causation and diagnosis of dementia cases: Knowledge of the specific contributions that various brain areas make to dementia is clouded or unknown. Frontal lobe damage, in particular, is a hallmark of behavioral changes in almost all instances. This has led Chui (1989) to state that there is some over-simplification in classifying causes of dementia that masks a need to clarify roles of such systems as the limbic and paralimbic, the multimodal association areas, prefrontal cortices, basal ganglia, and so forth. She thus demonstrates the fact that knowledge is sparse. The old saw that further research (indeed, much further research) is needed must be spouted again. The unfortunate fact is that little such research is being conducted. Much more emphasis is placed on patient and caregiver adjustment problems, development of drugs to treat symptoms, and the like, than on basic brain/behavior relationships. This is not to belittle the importance of all areas; it is probable, however, that little progress toward delimiting cause and establishing prevention will be made by current emphases.

Current efforts at diagnosis of Pick's combines clinical data with technology. Unfortunately, clarity has not been achieved, so the mechanical procedures (such as CT scans or EEG [electroencephalograph] patterns) combined with psychometric measures (such as the Mini-Mental State or memory span) are suggestive rather than definitive.

Outcomes. Given the rare occurrence of Pick's, it should not be surprising that there are few studies involving groups of patients. Instead the literature more commonly presents case studies, both interesting and informative but hardly normative (for example, see Holland, McBurney, Moosy, and Reinmuth, 1985; Scheltens, Hazenberg, Lindeboom, Volk, and Wolters, 1990).

There are, however, a few postmortem studies of the brain tissue of Pick's patients. Johanson and Hagberg (1989) compared 20 persons for whom psychometric measures had been collected prior to their deaths with analysis of frontal lobe tissue. They found cognitive loss was less severe in those whose dementia had been recognized prior to age 56. Most commonly, the complaint had been dysfunction of expressive speech. As a result of the autopsy, 16 of the cases were diagnosed as "frontal lobe degeneration of non-Alzheimer's type" (and, thus, an example of a special expression of Pick's?). The other 4 cases appeared to the authors as clear cases of Pick's disease.

Pick's disease remains largely a mystery due to an insufficiency of research. There is little emphasis on cause, in large part because of its rarity. There need to be more definitive descriptions of the course of Pick's, including details of outcomes for patients.

There are several other conditions that may include a component of dementia but with recognizable instances where the primary states of memory loss, confusion, and disorientation may not be found. Two examples are Huntington's and Parkinson's.

Huntington's Disease

Huntington's disease (HD) is a hereditary condition where the genetic expression occurs only in the nervous system. The genetic trait in this instance is dominant, with complete penetrance and few mutations (Shoulson, 1978, p. 251). Within this context, however, the disease is diagnosed at different ages and follows an uneven course, leading to many individual differences in behavioral effects noted in patients. Loss of memory and reasoning are common outcomes, but significantly, language is unaffected. Intellectual decline varies widely from significant to minimal, so loss of mental competencies need not be expected. Depression, as might be expected, is a frequent manifestation as the patient recognizes the deleterious changes that accompany the syndrome.

Where dementia does occur (in 50% or more of cases), behavioral effects have been studied and detailed. Shoulson (1990), for example, reports that the dementia is relatively circumscribed and particularly involves certain (but not all) memory processes. But there are other complicating outcomes that must be recognized and treated: personality change, affective disorders, and psychotic reactions. Antidepressant therapies are helpful with these effects, according to Shoulson.

With data available, there has been a model proposed of the loss in mental abilities of the typical HD patient (Huber and Paulson, 1985). Language and perception remain intact during the course of the disease, whereas memory may be seriously disrupted. This differentiation is labeled as *subcortical*, leaving room for a *cortical* dementia, as in AD, where there are more global effects on mental abilities. There is some division among experts on the adequacy of such a distinction.

Cause and Prognosis. Due to behavioral expressions there is a case to be made for defects in the basal ganglia (Cummings and Benson, 1988). This leads to slowed thought processes (bradyphrenia), some loss of mental control for executive functions, definite problems with recall, disturbances in spatial relations, and increased depression and apathy. So far as this is true, a clear distinction may often be made with AD where aphasia is common, both recall and recognition are reduced, and increasing indifference about loss of control is found as the disease becomes more widespread. There are, of course, antagonistic views and data on the issue (Weinberger, Berman, Iadarola, Driesen, and Zec, 1988).

Outcomes. So far as the dementia that occurs with many HD patients is concerned, the effects will not differ significantly from that which occurs with any source of dementia. Life for the patient becomes increasingly disrupted and difficult, often with recognition that something is wrong but without any clear understanding by the patient. Caregivers will become burdened as the demands to protect the patient increase. Of course, HD itself will lead to such outcomes, and so one might consider the addition of any dementing factors as extrapolations of an already debilitating condition. There is evidence of personality disorders, with depression occurring often but also with explosive episodes as a reaction to the changes (Webb and Trzepacz, 1987). Alcohol abuse has been reported also and must not be unexpected both with patient and with caregiver.

Parkinson's Disease

Degeneration of the nervous system is the principal outcome in Parkinson's disease (PD) but seemingly caused by a deficiency in dopamine activity in the basal ganglia rather than hereditary causes (Edwards, 1993, p. 177).

In addition, cases in younger persons have been related to toxic effects of drugs. Usually PD is diagnosed in middle to old age and shows a gradual progression in its effects. About 1% of the population over age 50 (some 2.5 million) are affected. Dementia is a consequence in at least 25%, but some estimates run as high as 80%. Any dementia that develops seems to be complicated by side effects from drugs used for treatment. As with HD, then, there should be no assumption that dementia is inevitable, and the discussion that follows is limited to cases where dementia is found.

PD is a medical condition reflected in disease in the basal ganglia, leading to specific motor disability. Frequently there are cognitive losses that are identified, most often in association with damage in the cortex. Such cognitive losses are not unique to PD so that comparisons with other conditions producing dementia are inevitable. Such psychological problems as a patient may present may result, in part, from interference with the neurotransmitter dopamine in neurons (Dieudonne, 1984). Dopamine deficiency is probably necessary to PD, but that does not explain the mental losses that may occur.

When dementia is present in cases of HD or PD, then, its identification is based on the same behavioral signs as would be true with AD, MID, and so on. Looking for some relationship directly with the primary diagnosis is not a fruitful occupation at present. Why some patients develop dementia and others do not seems more likely due to locus of cell damage—and why that damage has occurred is unknown. The effects of the dementia on patient and caregiver deserve recognition and intervention in their own right. These will include supports of all types: psychological, physical, social, and educational. While treatment for HD and PD are ongoing, it would be unjustified to ignore the symptoms of dementia, just as it would be for AD or MID.

This brings us to the issue of equivalences and differences. This brief survey indicates that the conditions that may be associated with dementing symptoms are widespread (perhaps even more so than we are aware). There are certain effects that seem to be normative, albeit with wide variations from patient to patient in time and degree of expression. There are other effects that are often found but that are not universal. And there must surely be some effects that are unpredictable in their expression.

Equivalences

Dementia is defined as "severe impairment or loss of intellectual capacity and personality integration, due to the loss or damage to neurons in the brain" (*Webster*, 1996). More specifically, Sutherland (1989) has described the condition as

an impairment or loss of mental ability, particularly of the capacity to remember, but also including impaired thought, speech, judgment, and personality. It occurs in *senile dementia*, and in conditions involving widespread damage to the brain (such as *Korsakoff's Psychosis*) or narrowing of the blood vessels. (p. 112)

The *Diagnostic and Statistical Manual* (*DSM*) of the American Psychiatric Association (1994) follows much the same line. Thus, "The essential feature of a dementia is the development of multiple cognitive deficits that include memory impairment and at least one of the following cognitive disturbances: aphasia, apraxia, agnosia, or a disturbance in executive functioning" (p. 134). These must be severe enough to interfere with functioning in both social and work settings. There must also be evidence of decline from the person's previous functional level.

Such definitions put the emphasis on *effects* rather than *causes*, so dementia is diagnosed by behavioral signs. Of course, a number of these signs may occur from conditions that are treatable and reversible, making impermanence as possible as irreversibility. But most discussions (including this one) are concerned with dementia that occurs as a result of untreatable and irreversible conditions such as Alzheimer's disease. We deal, then, with a special case rather than a general one.

For any dementia, however, the most often recognized and cited behavior is memory loss. In the *DSM* it is the singular symptom to be paired with some other loss in language-communication skills. But as mentioned earlier in this chapter, memory may be expressed in a variety of forms and even in degrees. Among older persons the inability to retrieve certain names or facts is common—yet the individual is not considered demented. Function becomes a prime element of consideration as a result; if one's work is sufficiently influenced or if one's social accommodations are sorely stressed, there will certainly be suspicion of dementia and probably further investigation.

The "one of the following" category in the *DSM* points to diverse, puzzling but crucial circumstances in decision making about dementia. A case encountered by this author is representative. The patient was a resident in a state facility for veterans who had been diagnosed as having Alzheimer's disease. He was a puzzle to staff members since he had retained the ability to read and proved it by reading the newspaper to other residents who were now incapable of the skill for various reasons. The peculiarity was that he was unable to comprehend what he had read. He informed his fellow residents, who returned the favor by telling him the "news" that he had just read to them.

One of our major problems in dealing with dementia is our insufficient understanding of how the brain works. Important also is the fact that we speak of "mind" and know not what we mean. Current explanations place emphasis on understanding behavior in terms of structural qualities of the brain, without recourse to some more advanced, and perhaps mystical, quality. Research must continue in the present directions to disclose how accurate the rationalization is. If, in future, the cellular level does not satisfy the demand for explanation of complex behaviors, a search for "mind" will follow. Many of us believe that this result is inevitable. One avenue that will be involved is a more in-depth study of nonnormal conditions such as dementia. The remainder of this book will undertake an analysis of research done on disorientation and its meaning for our understanding of the dementia patient.

The equivalences among the several conditions considered in this chapter focus on behavioral effects, particularly memory but also language and communication. There is concern also about personality changes, when and if these occur.

Differences

As might be expected, differences among the dementias are largely of degree and direction, to a lesser degree in type. Memory, such a pervasive phenomenon in human behavior, is the apt example. With Alzheimer's the memory most affected is of short term, probably due to encoding difficulties in the hippocampus. Certainly long-term memories will have adverse features as well, but they are not so noticeable early in the process and preserve certain ones even late into the development of the disease. By contrast, the Pick's patient may show lesser effects on short-term memory (although the evidence in limited due to few studies and fewer cases for study). There is a genuine need for more normative studies of memory function in dementia to help clarify what problems develop, when, and their course.

There is even less clarity about associated variables, including personality change and language/communication, although observation indicates the presence of frequent and sometimes severe effects. There is only a limited corpus of data in these areas about conditions other than Alzheimer's due to restricted funding and consequent interest. Documented changes are spotty and lead to danger in attempts to generalize.

THE TREATMENT OF DEMENTIA

Without knowledge of cause, details of treatment will be suspect. What happens with dementia as with other medical conditions is that "treatment" is directed to relieving symptoms without effect on the course of the disease. There are now drugs available and prescribed that are designed to alleviate some of the effects of memory loss, but unfortunately only with indifferent success even in that limited context. Such drugs focus on the fact that the neurotransmitter acetylcholine is deficient in brain cells of Alzheimer's patients. Retrieval becomes increasingly more difficult and spotty. The rationale of the treatment with such drugs was described earlier.

For some individuals, particularly early in the disease process, this procedure can be effective—at least until the progression increases significantly. For other individuals the treatment is ineffective. There is the added limitation that the drug itself may have side effects that sometimes are too detrimental to permit its use. Gradually such limitations are being reduced, but we are still a long way from effective intervention in this direction.

What is needed, obviously, is to find the cause of a dementia and develop a preventive. There are foundations and governmental support for basic research into causation (again, particularly with Alzheimer's disease) but with limited success so far. One reason is that there is no clear model of where to look. Is the condition genetic, viral, systemic, or something else? The amount of funding is too small for such widespread efforts, leading to extended searches. Much has been learned about dementia, but the most important and engrossing questions have yet to be formulated and investigated.

THE BEHAVIORAL IMPORTANCE OF DEMENTIA

Incidence of untreatable dementias in this country is unknown. Estimates, however, indicate that there may be as many as 5 million persons who are deteriorating mentally (some in a matter of months, others in years) at a tremendous cost to society, family, caregiver, and patient. And the numbers will increase as people continue to live longer lives and there are more and more surviving to adulthood and old age. It is not inconceivable that costs in lost revenue and care are in the billions of dollars each year.

What may be even more distressing is the personal element of patient, caregiver, and family. Dollars mean little here; the psychological costs are insurmountable. Although any disease can exert pressures on spouse, children, and relatives, those leading to dementia are especially destructive. The most notable and noted is Alzheimer's, primarily because the process lasts on average about 8 years and may run on for as many as 20. The patient becomes less and less emotionally involved as awareness is lessened, while physical status remains stable and may even improve. The caregiver slowly but surely gives up a personal life and, first, labors for two, then more and more for patient alone.

Even with diseases that destroy and kill more rapidly, the devastation leads to consequences that are irrecoverable. Such matters are complicated by worry about the possibility of heredity and genetics, by loss of social contacts and pleasures, by strains on intrafamily relationships and responsibilities. To project the cost of such events in monetary sums would merely mock the severity of the problem. Yet society, and its leaders, ignores the realities and pretends not to see the verities. The future must bring one of two alternatives: either prevention as a result of adequately funded research or amelioration of effects (social, psychological, and physical) on patients and caregivers by trained and efficient personnel who can reduce stress and help bridge problems. The former seems highly unlikely unless citizens become involved on behalf of others and demand governmental responsibility. The latter requires education in the broadest and highest sense.

CHAPTER 8

Disorientation in Perspective

At the conclusion of Part II the case was made that psychologists have been concerned about time orientation across the life span. Emphasis, however, has centered on measurement and evaluation, with the assumption that time and space are absolute and need neither justification nor proof. The results have been helpful but leave much room for definitional postures. Lack of knowledge about storage mechanisms for experience and intellectual competencies related to the past-present-future concept of time hampered the generalizability of findings from the many hundreds of studies conducted and published. What resulted many times were inferences and predictions that were insular and, worse, exposed no real relationship to time as such.

Danziger (1990) described the history of psychological inquiry as one that has led to what he calls "methodolatry." Quantification has been the principal goal in research so that sophisticated statistics have been developed where significance is equated with probability levels. This is reflected in the many studies of time awareness surveyed in Part II (and others that could have been included) where time is the dependent variable and the variety in independent ones has been myriad. Although one may defend the procedure and gain considerable knowledge by its adaptation, such studies have contributed little to our information store about the role of time in human behavior.

What is lacking in such research is commitment to what Danziger calls "elaborate deductive procedures," which are a significant feature in the natural sciences. Psychology has opted to utilize procedures where "theoretical constructions have seldom been marvels of logical sophistication, and pessimism about the likelihood of reaching rational consensus on the basis of theory has long been widespread" (Danziger, 1990, p. 5). Universally valid generalizations are not a major part of psychological research outcomes so that idiographic explication is much more common than nomothetic.

What is lacking are models that present an opportunity to promulgate theories and design research pointed toward universal generalizations. Three general models are proposed in Part II, including the conventional one. If we are to comprehend time orientation (and especially time disorientation) in human behavior, the time has come to venture into dangerous and murky waters. The quote from Novalis at the beginning of this Part III was chosen deliberately to reflect the mood and ambience that should be found in league with continuing traditional efforts.

There is a need to make clear the position taken in this book relative to time, its measurement, and meanings in human life. Some reference was made in Part I, but here there will be a more consistent effort to define behaviors found in persons with dementia. Given the practical circumstances of our society, greatest emphasis will be given to Alzheimer's disease, but comments should be relevant to other causes of dementia as well. In all cases, what is intended is the application to irreversible and untreatable conditions and not to such conditions as depression, which may lead to symptoms that can be corrected with proper identification and treatment.

The course of the differing dementias leads to differing patterns of deterioration, and this is complicated by the individual patterns that develop among individuals sharing the same diagnosis. Thus, typically we see a gradual and irregular slope of decline in the Alzheimer's patient, on average over about 8 years but with recorded instances of 15 or more years. Such declines may be marked in certain behaviors (for example, arithmetical competence) but to a lesser degree in others (for example, recalling the names of objects). Short-term memory function is the most frequently cited problem, whereas certain long-term memories may persist over several years. Eventually, of course, all such abilities will be severely reduced to the point that the patient is dependent on a caregiver to direct, supervise, and protect behavior. Death is usually reported as caused by pneumonia or a similar condition.

By contrast, multi-infarct dementia usually proceeds more rapidly (on average, about five years) and with a stepwise progression of decline. Regularity is the more common pattern, although the depth and extent of a given step will vary. Short-term retention will be less affected than long-term but with the caveat that all memory function may be lost before death occurs. In all cases the cause of death is usually a major stroke or system failure leading to pneumonia. In other words, conditions leading to dementia are not often cited as a cause of death except incidentally.

Details for other dementing diseases are less well detailed, largely because numbers are small and research on them has been limited. It seems reasonable that the overall picture is not different for any of them, however.

THE PROCESS OF DEMENTIA

This brings us to the conceptualizations that will permit the development of a model that permits scientific inquiry and prediction. The general case of dementia will prevail, although specific instances from given conditions may be cited as illustrative.

It would seem reasonable that a person developing dementia would have identifiable symptoms. However, these are not likely to be physical in nature, and with our ingrained views of illness and medicine, they may be ignored even when worrisome. The symptoms, then, are mental: There will most likely be brief episodes where some essential and critical feature for behavior and action is impossible to recover. The patient may be distressed and inconvenienced, but the brevity of the episode and the seeming complete recovery to normal memory function will lead to a successful attempt to explain away the incident. A spouse or child or employer (someone at least who is close to the patient) may notice some of the lapses but ignore them in the belief that they do not have great significance.

With time, the irruptions become more frequent and last for longer periods of time. At some point, probably after a period of years (perhaps two or so), there will have accumulated enough disruptive behavior to force recognition of a need for professional analysis, diagnosis, and treatment. Examples are myriad, from becoming lost and requiring help to get back home to errors on the job that become costly to a company to leaving a stove on and causing a fire. Now a doctor will be consulted, a complete physical conducted, and screening (perhaps by another professional) when no physical disorder or cause can be located. By this time, almost inevitably, a diagnosis will be proposed. And, under normal circumstances, counsel that implies a now-hopeless prognosis will be given.

What is described above is based upon observation and reports from patients and caregivers and centers on the central problem experienced: memory loss. Yet the screening done by a physician or psychologist will disclose other behavioral difficulties. Increasing confusion and disorientation in time and space are apt to be present to some degree and will certainly increase in the future. The memory loss becomes a focal point, necessary but not sufficient to indicate the extent of major behavioral effects. We need to consider what disorientation in time means to daily life and action.

There are various considerations that must be included in a conceptual model of time and human behavior. Several of these will be surveyed, but, first, a rationale used by this author seems appropriate. As the process of dementia begins, the signs of its presence are muted. Brief, inconvenient gaps may occur where thoughts are lost or a sequence of events is incomplete. But this is so ordinary in human behavior (and not only older persons) that the instances may be ignored or explained away. The behaviors are easily and often linked to an inconvenient memory loss so that we have no information on time orientation as a part or adjunct to the incidents. With progression, however, the incidents become more critical and eventually lead to a referral to a physician for evaluation and diagnosis.

Behavior has been so adversely affected by this point that the dangers and effects are self-evident in most cases. Unless some treatable cause can be discovered the most likely diagnosis will be dementia and, because of awareness and interest, as Alzheimer's disease. Examination will include some assessment of mental competencies including at least some crude estimate of orientation in time and space. It is usual to find that there are difficulties in awareness of orientation when a diagnosis is being contemplated or has been made. This suggests that memory loss has been accompanied by loss in orientation as well, although no evidence may have been noted or reported by patient or caregiver. There seems a presumptive case that disorientation has been a developing and continuous facet of behavior over some period of time. It would seem worthwhile to assess time and space orientation periodically in examination of older persons. We do have evidence that in those older persons who have not shown signs of dementia orientation is as good as that of younger adults (Edwards, 1998).

Effects of Existence in Time and Space

In the circumstances, then, there is the suggestion that a person developing Alzheimer's disease lives increasingly in a *timeless* world. One of the most direct connections of consciousness with reality is to realize where and how one exists in space and time. Loss of orientation is represented in decreasing connection with reality. As a result, space is apt to be misunderstood and misinterpreted. There are many instances cited by caregivers of patients who are unable to function in their own homes. The patient may be unable to locate the bathroom in the house where he has lived for years. Placed in unfamiliar settings, the patient may not be able to maneuver at all without close supervision and help. The result of a loss of spatial orientation is confusion, demonstrated by an inability to maintain independence. This leads to increasing dependence on a caregiver. Since space and time are intrinsically linked, the patient can no longer retrieve the basic elements of time orientation when questioned about the day, the date, the year. Even highly familiar and personal elements such as age and date of birth are apt to be affected and lost.

The importance implicit in such behavioral deficiencies has tended to be lost in the pursuit of memory defects. Essentially, they have become enfolded into examples of memory loss so that their intrinsic meanings are mere corollaries of memory or are ignored altogether. This seems a misguided effort. We should be as concerned for evidences of disorientation in behavior as we are of memory loss. We may become more directed to the presence and growth of dementia from a close study of orientation/disorientation than is possible from attention only to retention facets. This will depend, however, on more extensive and precise measures of time and space orientation so that codification is achieved. This should lead to efforts to objectify the patient's time orientation and the development of treatments to return the individual to contact with reality. Current developments in drug therapy to treat symptoms of memory loss should not cease, but they should be only one direction of effort.

THE NATURE OF TIME ORIENTATION

Our first steps should be to determine what time orientation *is* and the role it plays in daily adaptation, how it is *developed* (part of the purpose of Part II in this book), how it may be *measured* (only partially met with present tests), and how it may be *changed* (trained) to meet functional demands, psychological and social in nature.

Definition

In common parlance, *dis*orientation seems to represent an absence of orientation. Such a position is seductive because it seems so straightforward and congruent with absolute notions. But it leaves untouched such matters as why some persons with dementia are more globally disoriented than others and why individual differences in direction and amount of disorientation are so demonstrable. Relationships among variables in dementia are often confusing and subject to misinterpretation.

In this vein, a study by Pruchno and Resch (1989) is relevant. They examined the relationship of burden for the caregiver to the behaviors displayed by patients. When the caregivers perceived burden, caregivers expressed greater concern about personal mental health. Pruchno and Resch concluded that there may be some type of "wear and tear" explanation. Frequency of disruptive behaviors increased caregiver stress. As that most common complaint of dementia—memory loss—was cited, burden increased but in a nonlinear fashion. But the greater the forgetting, the less burden felt. In fact, Pruchno and Resch say that stress among caregivers who reported little or no memory loss was similar to that where a patient had severe memory loss.

The problem is complicated even in memory loss. The various causes of dementia share the symptom, but there is research that indicates that for the more specific types of memory such as semantic and episodic there are differences among the several causes. Confusion and disorientation are often cited as symptoms of dementia, but it is not clear how these states may manifest themselves, how they progress, or whether interventions may reduce their symptomatic pressures. The overall picture is clouded, making it difficult to explain to patients and caregivers. A central fault is the fact that few models or theories that have been tested are available. Disciplines, and subdisciplines, differ in research foci, making it difficult to make comparisons and draw valid generalizations. It is no wonder that professionals dealing directly with patients and caregivers complain about the lack of practical research.

What, then, is time orientation, and what is the nature of its antagonist, disorientation? The answer for this author lies in the concept of spacetime. Space and time are not independent and absolute dimensions. Traditionally, we have accepted space as the three-dimensional model of length, height, and depth—interrelated and providing structure to a universe of complex parts. Time, traditionally, has been described as an arrow moving straight through space and consisting of present, past, and future. Its role is independent of space and equally absolute.

These time-honored notions must now be questioned. We may preserve the dimensionality concept, but it must be expressed by spacetime. Four dimensions are the result: length, height, depth, and flow (without regard to direction). Centuries ago humankind began to develop the physical attributes assigned to space and to apply and extend their meanings through mathematics. Although arbitrary in expression, the means to perceive space were taught and practiced from childhood in order to assure competence throughout life. The arbitrary nature of time has not been so clearly articulated and developed in terms of physical characteristics. Certainly we have instruments to measure time—but they have been and continue to be largely inconsistent and in conflict. In space, an inch is an inch; in time, a second is more or less a second, depending on the quality of the timepiece used. It is no wonder that we have trouble perceiving a nanosecond if we aren't even sure of the meaning of a second. Precision has been largely assured with the current cesium clock that is the scientific standard, although Duncan (1998, p. 234) points out that recalibration is needed because the earth has random fluctuations. Its practical applications appear to be far in the future.

Orientation in spacetime requires that we view the characteristics of space within the medium of time. Space cannot exist in the absence of time; time may exist in the absence of space, however. If one accepts this principle, it is manifest that time is the essential element in being oriented or disoriented. One is oriented to the degree that awareness and relation to time are present. Given this, spatial awareness is present and permits one to perceive the universe in which each of us lives. Because there is overlap in the universes created by individuals, it is possible for us to perceive the same phenomena largely as others do. We can communicate to an extensive degree even though that communication will have some variations and inconsistencies about the same phenomena.

Spacetime may be defined as the medium within which each of us develops awareness of place and meaning of self within the universe of experience called life. *That awareness may be labeled orientation.*

By the same reasoning, *disorientation* is the label that may be assigned to the circumstance where awareness of place and meaning of self are so different from that of other persons that communication is fractured or even absent. What must be remembered is that the orientation of an individual in such a case is not absent; there is no timelessness. Instead we must attempt to perceive the state(s) of awareness in such a person in order to understand the consequences, perceive reality as recognized, and perhaps bridge the gap.

Development

Part II of this book was an extensive review and assessment of many of the studies done on the teaching and learning of time concepts and measures. The variety of approaches and assumptions makes it difficult to describe a consistent and regular pattern of how time awareness evolves and develops. However, there needs to be some statement of trends that are consistent with the positions taken in this book.

There is, first, the question of the presence of time awareness in the human infant. Much has been written of the biological clocks displayed among animals (Block, 1989, pp. 67–68), a number of which are found in humans as well (Melges, 1989, p. 106). A case may be made, then, that there is some predisposition toward adaptation to features of light and dark, changes in temperature, dangers from the environment, and the like, even at birth. The various experiments on conditioning might be explained as a variant on time awareness. Beyond such basic but important adaptations, there is little to suggest that very small children live in any time mode but the present—and that only to a limited degree that would not allow survival.

The educational efforts to bring children to cognizance of time measures and their meanings are intentional and have been shown to be successful in varied approaches. With Piaget, the emphasis was on the relationship to the mental periods of development that he displayed in former work. Other investigators, using different models, have found concordance with a developmental process that may be related to intellectual gains. Such work has concentrated on the ability of the child to understand and use the common measures of time rather than on assessment of spacetime awareness.

Generally, such experimental efforts have ended during the adolescent years, and the research on adults has focused on time frames according with the linear "arrow of time" evolving from Newton. There is solid agreement that our time sense may be focused on the present, past, and/or future and that discrimination among these is necessary at the same time that balance is the desired outcome. What may be concluded from research results (at the same time where disagreements in findings are reported) is that different adult life periods may show different points of emphasis. Young adults are said to be more future oriented than older ones, middle-aged persons are focused on the present, and the elderly look increasingly to the past. There are sufficient inconsistencies in results to indicate that such generalizations must be taken with a considerable grain of salt.

A solution to the dilemma must rest in a consistent defining of the meaning of such labels as present, past, and future. Again, for the purposes of this volume, a recapitulation of what has already been stated in several ways is worthwhile.

The "present" may be defined as that transitory moment between past and future. Thus, its existence is so instantaneous as to be practically non-existent. It is impermanent and explicitly finite. The present lacks reality except as compared to past (what was) and future (what will be). It is the basis for identifying space in time, in part as a function of the role of measures (clocks) in perceiving space and in part as a source of experience for action as well as possible storage for future actions. Jason Brown (1990, p. 145) refers to this idea when he speaks of "the Now" as "a brief segment with an indefinite duration and unclear boundaries." In the most practical sense, the "present" is what we call Living. As soon as it occurs, life has moved on to a new "Now" with possible storage of experiences in the past.

Our "pasts" are our permanent records of experience. Their quality and effect are finite, depending on experiences, what is actually stored, and how they are stored. The past is the record against which all experience can be verified. Obviously, then, the more experience, the better equipped the individual to be able to act appropriately. There is a rough equivalence with age, but not a very significant one. The past is reality in the only sense known to human cognition. It is the basis for anticipating a future and affects the experiences desired and accepted. The past grows by encompassing the manifold presents that follow it.

"Future" is a concept that involves predictions based upon both fact and fiction. It is an "anticipated present," derived from the prejudiced expectations established by the mind's cataloging of the past. It is infinite within those boundaries but limits the perceived nature of the presents allowed mentally. The prediction of a future can, however, be altered by an unexpected element in experience that then becomes a different present than was originally expected. The result is a new present that becomes integrated as a part of the past so that mental equilibrium will be maintained.

As mentioned, time awareness is limited, perhaps absent, at birth. We must *learn* what time is and how it impinges on us. Experience influences development in this dimension as in any other. But we may modify our concept of time as we have greater experiences during life. Most persons consider time only in terms of the experiences of childhood and youth. A few, however, encounter experiences that modify prior learning. The nature of these experiences influences (prejudices) the view held of time. Whether that view is more or less accurate, more or less true, more or less consistent depends more on the nature of the experiences than it does on the nature of time.

Nowotny (1994) has related such a view to the concept of the future. She notes that there is longer life expectancy today than at any time in history, yet the future has no projection space as it formerly did (p. 50). The discrepancy is meaningful as we consider that length of life averaged 45 years in 1850, a period when the future seemed remote to citizens. In 2000, the length of life was about 75 years, so there is a much longer future to anticipate and plan. Yet today people find the future too imminent and pressing. There is not enough time to accomplish what seems necessary in a succession of presents.

The issue is not time so much as it is the retooling of generations to accept lack of future for immediate gratification. The alternative is to restructure the future so that individuals can tolerate delay of gratification that may never come. The *key* is the monolith of business—not the nature of time. This circumstance has its roots in the changes brought about by the Industrial Revolution. The meaning of time changed as a result. Workers became bonded to the clock and lost the identity of proper time in order to conform to industrial pressures. Revolt—of several types—resulted.

What became necessary next was for industry to develop generations of workers who had been educated to conform to "company" goals and needs. That millennium arrived by the late twentieth century in the industrialized societies all over the world. Workers, from the assembly line to the executive washroom, have abandoned revolt for conformity. Labor unions, of whatever type or degree, have become more impotent than powerful. Proper time today has come to mean company time. Psychologically, workers have lost the sense of self-importance implied in the term *proper time*. It is not unusual today to find young persons who are willing to behave in any fashion ordered by the company in order to achieve wealth— seen by them as the essence of power. As Flaherty (1991, p. 83) has stated: "Surprisingly little cognitive engrossment is necessary if one assumes an instrumental attitude and aspires to nothing beyond simple practicality." What this portends for the future may be the principal social problem of the twenty-first century.

In the general meaning, *time orientation* is the consciousness of one's place in space relative to other possible relationships (other places in space), both past and future *and* real and imagined. One develops time orientation by defining arbitrary demarcations of spacetime relationships within the limitless boundaries of time. These arbitrary demarcations are idiosyncratic and may or may not accord with the demarcations defined by others. Once defined, the demarcations represent the nature of consciousness for the individual. Reality for that person is represented by the several demarcations defined. The structure of this consciousness varies for the person according to the integrity of the brain.

In the "normally" integrated brain, there will be many demarcations shared with other persons, leading to shared consciousness and compatibility in the nature of reality. In the "diseased" brain, there will be fewer shared demarcations and less compatibility of reality. The more extensively damaged the brain, the greater the differences. Yet the process is the same in all cases: Reality exists in the consciousness of each individual.

MEASUREMENT OF TIME ORIENTATION

Psychological measurement of dementia patients has centered on the ability to function in the everyday world. This includes a considerable emphasis on space and time awareness and relationships, as has been shown by the most popular of the instruments used in the evaluation process. Yet there have been questions about the role and evidence of utility of such instruments since their first usage over a quarter century ago.

Typical of such judgments is a literature review undertaken by Cooper and Bickel (1984) on early detection of dementing disorders. Their principal interest was in screening of the general population in order to detect dementia as early as possible. Within this view, however, they considered "what may be broadly termed 'psychological' screening instruments, where evaluation in terms of applicability and accuracy in case-finding is now assuming an increasing importance in preventive geriatrics" (p. 88). As they note, such tests were devised and applied for differential diagnosis, measurement of any changes (positive or negative) in terms of treatments, or defining more precisely a particular form of psychopathology. Today, those uses are still the most frequent, particularly the first two. Cooper and Bickel included a table that listed and described the dementia scales available at the time. These include: the Mental Status Questionnaire, the Abbreviated Mental Test Score, the Short Portable Mental Status Questionnaire, the Mini-Mental State Examination, the Cognitive Assessment Scale, and the Cognitive Capacity Screening Examination. It is worth noting that several of these scales are still the major vehicles used in the professional setting, for both diagnostic information and notations of change in performance.

As Cooper and Bickel noted, there was little to choose between the scales at the time since differences in mental functions assessed were largely minor. In all there were efforts to measure orientation of time and place as a part of the procedure. Their question became, How effective are these scales for their purposes? This suggests data are needed about reliability and validity in particular. And these authors found that, with the limited data available, these scales were acceptable. They were less sanguine about case yield, however, since results indicated dementia and depression could be confused, especially in early stages of the disease process. They advocate, as a result, screening for each separately, a step still recognized as important since depression is treatable in a way that dementia is not.

The matter of validity has most often been considered in studies that have compared dementia scale scores with external measures. An example is found in a work by Creasey, Schwartz, Frederickson, Haxby, and Rapaport (1986) where correlations were computed between dementia scale scores and CT scans indicating atrophy and ventricular dilatation. The authors concluded that severity of dementia (as reflected in the scores from dementia scales) was related to the physical changes. Even among dementia patients, greater cognitive loss was associated with greater atrophy. By contrast, Nagaratnam and McNeil (1999) compared patients (n = 4) with global aphasia without hemiparesis for their performance on dementia scales. The results indicated to the authors that such scales were not very useful, and they called for guidelines that would yield more reliable criteria for diagnosis. Although such studies as these two contribute to knowledge, it seems clear that generalizations are suspect unless one accepts the scale scores as an accurate reflection of degree of dementia present. That step, at present, is ill-advised.

There remains an issue concerning comparability among scales and sources that might bias generalization from scale scores. Gurland, Wilder, Cross, Teresi, and Barrett (1992) examined five widely used scales, compiled a compendium, and evaluated both absolute and culturally relative rates of cognitive impairment from their data. The sample of 550 subjects included approximately equal numbers of African Americans, Hispanics, and whites. But the tests used produced several critical differences in their predictive efficiency (judged by clinical diagnostic criteria). A central difference among the scales was the variation in sensitivity to dementia criteria for the sociocultural groups. With adjustments to equate the scales in their cutting points, Gurland et al. succeeded in eliminating a large portion of the errors built into the instruments.

The scales used by Gurland et al. were those still common in their use today. They included the Mental Status Questionnaire, the Short Portable Mental Status Questionnaire, the Blessed Memory-Information-Concentration Test, the Mini-Mental State Examination, and the Comprehensive Assessment and Referral Interview. Since these tests are still being used in their same form, it seems clear that users and test designers were not influenced by the deficiencies found by Gurland et al.

It is of more than passing interest that the tests produced greatest disagreements in classification with Hispanics and least with whites. And the greatest point of conflict applied to early expressions of dementia, the point in time when there is the greatest hope for intervention that may delay the development of the dementia. Beyond this point, all the scales had lower internal consistency, lower interscale correlations, and more false positives for African Americans and Hispanics than for whites.

Since the criterion was clinical judgment, the issue of bias on this front must also be considered. "Where expert neurological diagnosis was taken as the criterion ('true and unbiased') rate of dementia, it reinforced the evidence that sociocultural bias in conventional scales is a remaining limit on cross-cultural method" (p. 112). A case in point is the often cited difference in incidence of multi-infarct dementia and Alzheimer's disease by race, a difference that has not been tested adequately.

Current Popular Measurements

There are two tests that have had a long and useful history.

1. *The Mental Status Questionnaire (MSQ).* The MSQ published by Kahn et al. in 1960 is widely used, in part because of its brevity and its apparent correlation with competence in mental functioning. The simplicity of the procedure has led to its employment, often with modifications, by professionals in many fields outside psychology.

The useful element in the MSQ is the almost exclusive focus on orientation in time and space. Ten questions pursue awareness of the place where the person is at present, the current time (such as day of the week), one's historical place in time (say, date of birth), and a few common facts related to understanding spacetime relationships (such as the current president of the United States). Zarit (1980) has clarified the relevance of responses made as they may reflect language changes in patients.

A patient who is asked these mental status questions can give three possible responses. He can answer correctly, suggesting intact brain functioning. He may respond that he does not know or give a wrong answer, which is often indicative of dementia. Or the person may respond to conative, rather than denotative, aspects of the question. (p. 142)

Obviously, the person with an intact brain and normal experiences in our society will have little or no difficulty with the 10 questions asked. It is important to consider factors that might reflect lack of opportunity or interfering qualities when there is a poor performance, especially in elderly persons. Hearing loss is one example, medications still another, and basic language or educational deficiencies still another. In the absence of any such interfering matters, more than 3 errors of the 10 may well lead one to suspect loss of mental competence. It is important to remember as well that language ability and expression may remain present in the individual who suffers a dementia. Errors may need to be followed by some exploration of the depth and quality of response. These should not be part of the scoring of the test performance, however.

2. *The Mini-Mental State Examination (MMSE).* The MMSE was published by Folstein, Folstein, and McHugh in 1975. It has wider scope than the MSQ, consisting of 30 items yielding information about orientation in time and space as well as short-term memory, calculation skills, and language function.

The MMSE serves its best function as a screening device that offers clues about the patient's strengths and limitations mentally. This offers an opportunity for more extended investigation as well as decisions on interventions that may be useful and successful with the patient. There are no norms as such, nor do they seem to be needed. Many psychologists consider the MMSE to be valid for their purposes even though reliability data are sparse.

This brings us to the issue of what is to be gained by using one or more so-called dementia scales. For some professionals, these tests are accepted as legitimate reflections of abilities present or lost; they thus give an indication of the degree to which dementia, if present, has progressed. To others, the scales contain items concerning traits adversely and uniquely affected by whatever causes the dementia; this would include disorientation in time, place, and person. Still others believe the scores serve as a confirmation of a physician's diagnosis of dementia of whatever type; they confirm the conclusion drawn by the doctor from other (physical) data. Still others will attest that the mental competence of a patient is the basic factor in dementia; to ignore such information will be unfair, even injurious to the patient's well-being. Surely, also, some will say that any or all of the above are covered by the content of dementia scales. Folstein and Folstein (1990, p. 929) proposed that the purpose of a mental status examination "is to determine the patient's mental capacity *at the time of the evaluation*" (italics added). To them the medical history will focus only on the past and thus miss a current view. Folstein and Folstein also state that this mental exam must be conducted and evaluated separately from the traditional examination. Further, "The MSE and its quantified derivatives . . . can be used for case finding, diagnosis, and assessment of treatment. The MSE alone does not provide a diagnosis; that requires a history, physical examination, and laboratory tests as well" (p. 929).

Obviously, there is a strong perceived need for measures of mental competence to be applied to patients diagnosed with some condition that predisposes to dementia. Additionally, several test authors have applied their skills to developing tests to serve the purpose, no matter how poorly defined that purpose may be. Certain of these scales have been and are widely administered and interpreted for the various needs expressed. The question becomes, how valid are the scales for the conclusions that are drawn from them?

Analysis of Content. As interesting as this question may be and as important as it is to find an answer, this is not the source for it. The emphasis here is the role of orientation/disorientation in spacetime. Without assuming that the analysis to follow answers any general questions about dementia scales, the matter is cogent for discussion.

Let's begin with a review of what currently used scales include as items that may reflect spacetime measures. First, we must be aware that space and time in these tests are assumed to be independent and absolute in their expressions. It is the space and time of the public that has held prominence since the nineteenth century. Space is three-dimensional; time is an arrow. Measurement is based upon the devices that reflect these principles. Second, the items are limited in number, scope, and depth. The space questions include such sampling as, "What is this place?" and the time ones deal with, "What is today? How old are you?" and the like. Beyond this, the content moves into cognitive abilities and awareness. Thus, there can be questions such as, "Who is the President of the United States?" or items dealing with computation, registration and recall, and language. Orientation, thus, is a minor part of the examination in part and in whole.

This is not to say that the information gleaned is unimportant or trivial. Indeed, experience has shown that it can be helpful in diagnosis and denoting severity *if the dementia process is sufficiently well progressed.* It is insufficient to disclose loss in competence until it is clear that the patient has a distinct and personal loss in ability to cope in the environment in which that person lives and/or works. Screening, particularly early screening, is not helped very much with these dementia scales. Add to that the fact that few such tests concern themselves with exploration of function in the present, past, and future. Nor do they tell us much about space beyond the immediate and obvious to the nondemented individual.

If orientation in spacetime is an important component, perhaps even the important element, to communication with others and dealing effectively with daily tasks, the question becomes one of what measure should be available to serve the purpose of disclosing early signs of dementia and to demark its progression. Norms must be established and reliability and validity demonstrated. To date, such a measure has not been proposed. It is possible, however, to describe how such an instrument might be devised and evaluated for the purposes needed.

Given current attitudes and values, measures of time awareness and spatial orientation should be provided on separate bases. Each should consist only of items related to the trait being measured and not include items that require other intellectual skills and knowledge. It is important to determine how the individual interprets stimuli and experience directly related to time and space. In addition, items of time orientation must include three components: present, past, and future. The items used must be demonstrated to be so common and meaningful that persons without dementia will be able to answer all, or virtually all, without error. Edwards (1998) has taken preliminary steps in this direction with a scale meeting these standards. Items include such questions as: Is it night or day? Is it summer or winter *or* Is it fall or spring? Is it A.M. or P.M.? Each of these reflects present awareness and accommodation to time variables.

Examples of past time relationships include: Which came first: World War I or World War II? Which comes first: Twice or once? Which comes first: Never or soon? For the future, there are items such as: Today is (use correct day). What will tomorrow be? If this year were 1990, what would next year be? This is (give current month). What will be the month one year from today? In each instance, the item is structured so that a choice is given, one of which is the correct one, the other being wrong. Through such series the examiner can gain basic information about time awareness and the flow of time. With such items, a preliminary sample (n = 54) of older adults (ages 60 to 91), answered with at least 92% accuracy. The task remains to use these same items with persons diagnosed with dementia. If they discriminate, the next task is to administer them to a large sample and follow them over several years to see how scores correlate with later diagnoses for any individuals developing dementia.

Spatial orientation follows somewhat the same format, but adjusted so that three-dimensional characteristics are sampled. For example, Which is higher: a foot stool or a chair? Which is taller: a man of 6 feet or one of 75 inches? If a train goes 100 miles per hour for 4 hours, how far has it traveled? To date such a measure has not been subjected to empirical test, and so such items may not work to the purpose intended.

Eventually, as our cultures become more cognizant and adept with the practical import of physical progress, items that sample spacetime might replace both the examples above. Spacetime is defined as: "The four-dimensional space whose points are events" (Hawking, 1996, p. 243). This concept has been delimited further:

Minkowski . . . had now discovered that the Universe is made of a four-dimensional "spacetime" fabric that is absolute, not relative. This four-dimensional fabric is the same as seen from all reference frames (if only one can learn how to "see" it); it exists independently of reference frames. (Thorne, 1994, pp. 87–88)

We, and particularly those of us in the discipline of psychology, have not yet learned how to "see." As a result, we must move in the direction of rather than directly to.

CHANGING THE ORIENTATION

Much effort has been expended on attempts to find ways of helping dementia patients deal more effectively with the "real" world, that is, the world as most of us view it. Patients show increasing disorientation in time and space, and professionals often want to return mental functioning to the present. Such techniques as reality orientation (Taulbee and Folsom, 1966) are frontal assaults on the problem, whereas others such as reminiscence therapy (Butler, 1963) use life review to resolve conflicts that interfere with adequate adjustment. Still others emphasize accepting the person in whatever mode, with an attempt to aid the individual to be as happy and adjusted as possible. Nonjudgmental, such approaches tend toward benign neglect. Unfortunately, none of these has been as successful as the therapists have wished and are largely futile with dementia patients beyond a very limited floor.

The hope for a return to the norm through the use of psychological techniques seems to be unlikely. This, in large part, is due to the fact that changes in neuronal cells are irreversible. We do not know what is "cause" in the change of physical events resulting in dementia, but we can recognize some of the circumstances present in the process. In the case of Alzheimer's disease, there is evidence of the collection of beta amyloid in cell bodies, leading to an accumulation of neurofibrillary tangles (NFTs). Is this the cause of Alzheimer's or merely the ultimate outcome from a true cause? The result is predictable, whatever may be the answer. By contrast, there is considerable recognition of the role of strokes, small and "silent" in their aggregation but fairly rapidly inducing the behavioral changes leading to dementia. This latter is potentially treatable and preventable; the former is too much a mystery for such a statement to be made. Other explanations for the occurrence of dementing behavior have been offered for other labeled conditions: One current one is the incidence of prions in Creutzfeldt-Jakob and similar brain diseases.

The list could continue but without any particular resolution to the problem. We must speculate and extrapolate from that to a premise that offers the possibility of generating hypotheses that are testable. Let's go back to Alzheimer's disease. We can accept the role of NFTs as a reality. Thus, every case must show evidence of NFTs in diseased neurons. Yet there is evidence, as well, that NFTs occur in brain cells of persons who do not show dementing symptoms. Certainly fewer in number, there is still the engrossing possibility that should the individual live long enough, every person on earth would eventually develop dementia of the Alzheimer's type. But this must mean that there are differential rates of development and differential effects from NFTs. Does this mean that there are disease processes (perhaps many in number) that produce effects that can be lumped under the label "Alzheimer's disease"? If not, what is the possible explanation?

At this point, a net in the search for hypotheses must be cast. Take the proposition that we have oversimplified the problem. We have considered only the three-dimensional world that assumes absoluteness and unidirectionality. If we enlarge our perspective we open the opportunity to incorporate the universe of others in our considerations of problem cause and effect. What we see as absolute and one-directional does not include the view of the person observed. It should be possible to include that perspective along with our own so that we are able to communicate (but not imitate) with the dementia patient. Behavior may become rational in a way that was not possible before. Instead of viewing the patient as disordered, we view the patient as rational within a spacetime context that differs from the traditional one.

The Role of Neurofibrillary Tangles

Regardless of one's acceptance of the possibility and importance of such an approach, we are faced with a need to describe the presence of NFTs and the effects that they sponsor. The data are clear that NFTs interfere with "normal" cell function. The transmission of a stimulus is altered or blocked as a result. Action in response to the stimulus cannot occur in consequence. There have been attempts to increase stimulus transmission through artificial means, but these have been largely or totally ineffective. Based upon the use of dopamine uptake by the brain in Parkinson's disease, for example, there were attempts to supply the neurotransmitter acetylcholine directly to cells in Alzheimer's patients. The efforts failed. That suggested that some less direct effort might succeed in improving the mental competencies of patients.

Overall, as NFTs increase in a cell and the disease invades increasing numbers of cells, interventions of any kind become less and less effective. This not only proves the obvious conclusion but also points to the need to find alternative solutions if "treatment" is to be effective. There are efforts in laboratories and research centers throughout the world that may culminate in success. We should applaud and support such efforts at the same time that other doors should be opened to include alternatives outside the research efforts.

With time, of course, and depending on condition and patient characteristics, the NFTs become sufficiently dense that the cell collapses and forms a plaque. When the cell body is so invaded, regeneration is impossible. Again, this is a demonstrable fact that is not obviated by the fact that dendrites may be regenerated and proliferated. When the cell body dies, behavior patterns in which that cell was involved are disrupted or lost. The cell may contain the essence of energy that can no longer be used by the brain, since the force is trapped. It would appear that, effectively, the brain has had created within it a "black hole" that sucks up the energy that impinges on its surface. This leads to the interesting question: Is there some way to tap the energy (if there is any) within the plaque?

Increasing numbers of plaques continue the degenerative process and lead to more extensive behavioral changes. The result is greater incompetence in daily life on the part of a person who at one time dealt effectively with life. Dependency on a caregiver increases to the point that the patient can no longer function effectively in the real world. And we are not capable at the present time of communicating about the reality of the world in which the patient currently lives.

This suggests that "Alzheimer's disease" is a concept of convenience, not a true disease process. Care must be exercised to ensure that decisions are not made solely upon traditional and convenient prejudices.

OTHER PERSPECTIVES ON ORIENTATION

There has been some interest, both with empiricism and theory, in the concept of orientation and its applications for many years. However, the published papers and books have not had the influence on psychological efforts about time that one might expect. Nevertheless, a review of some of this work is apt if for no other reason than to permit some assessment of the positions in the preceding section. Additionally, alternatives to what has been presented will become apparent at well.

Cerebral Disease

One of the earlier empirical efforts dealt with time awareness in cases who had been diagnosed with cerebral disease (Benton, van Allen, and Fogel, 1964). The authors reported that their intent was concerned primarily with the temporal orientation of such patients instead of the ability to "guess" temporal duration (as was popular in such studies of the day). How frequently did disorientation occur in such cases, and to what degree? was the stated objective. This was augmented by the position of some authorities that memory loss derived from an inability to encode information due to lesions in the hippocampus, whereas others believed that retention was impaired even when information had been adequately registered and stored.

The experimental group was nonpsychotic (n = 60) persons who had a diagnosis of cerebral disease. The controls (n = 110) were patients with various somatic disorders but without cerebral disease. The groups were equivalent in mean age and educational level. Time orientation was measured by questions about the day, date, month, year, and the current time. The controls performed with little error; in fact, some 61% made perfect scores. Among the experimental participants, only 45% had perfect scores; there was also a much wider variance in scores. Interestingly, both groups showed the same rank order of type of mistake: day of the month most frequent, current time next, and day of the week.

Benton and associates conclude that "a direct relationship between defective temporal disorientation and significant general mental impairment seems evident. Nevertheless, that such impairment was not a sufficient precondition for the appearance of defective orientation is indicated by the finding that a number of grossly impaired patients showed quite adequate temporal orientation" (p. 115). The authors had put their finger on a relationship for which we have no adequate explanation. They do report that patients with bilateral disease were less able to maintain time orientation than either those with lesions only in one hemisphere or the controls. This was modified by the fact that the bilateral group had more significant general mental impairment as well.

In their discussion, Benton, van Allen, and Fogel advocated that clinical neurologists needed to use a standardized test of time orientation with objective scoring. At the same time, consideration should be given to factors such as geographical location and cultural influences that might affect performance. Their data persuaded them that defects in time orientation represent the integrity of recent memory and largely, though not totally, due to lesions in the hippocampus.

This study identified major problems in defining and measuring negative changes in time orientation when brain cells are diseased. It might have served as an impetus to theory and empiricism that would lead to resolution of such difficulties. Unfortunately, it seems to have been largely ignored.

Korsakoff's Syndrome

A more general analysis of information about Korsakoff's syndrome gives us the theoretical perspective (Rosenfield, 1992). He notes that the discipline of neurology has traditionally ignored the subjective nature of the conscious self (p. 67), leading to a model of the brain that disregarded time as a fundamental variable. In more recent years, clinical evidence permitted the view that the temporal nature of memories relied on storage in different parts of the brain. To Rosenfield this suggests the question: How does the brain create the notion of time in the first place? A critical question, still far too unique to have deserved investigation for an answer. To him, subjectivity is the basis for our concept of time. Indeed, it is some part of the idea of consciousness (p. 67).

In a chapter entitled "In a World without Time" (pp. 68–87), Rosenfield discusses the demonstration of memory loss in Korsakoff's and its relationship to short-term and long-term memories. Rather than being types of memory, to him they are merely ways in which the brain structures experience. They differ from each other both in quality and in structure. He contrasts our experiences of the past and their relation to the present and points out that the memories are not the same as the experiences appeared to be at the time of action. This leads Rosenfield to conclude that we judge time in terms of qualitative differences that we infer between new and old memories (p. 69).

Much of what was assumed to be true in the past will not fit well with this view. There are no different kinds of memories, no different parts of the brain involved in storage of experiences. Instead, there are different kinds of subjectivity, which leads to different kinds of knowledge, the two being interrelated (p. 69). The matter of subjectivity (seemingly analogous to relativity) has not been employed by psychologists as it should be. For example, in measurement the assumption is held that the answer to a question about the name of an object reflects the belief that both examiner and patient share a harmony of meaning. However, Rosenfield believes that the subjective worlds of the two persons are different—and largely because the patient has now lost the sense of time (at least as viewed by the examiner).

The observation has frequently been made that Alzheimer's patients keep and use long-term memory, while short-term is problematic. Rosenfield makes the apt point that recalling the past is not a re-creation of the past experiences involved since the past has meaning only in terms of the present (p. 73). If one is unaware of the present, what does past mean?

When we recall the past we think in a more general or abstract mode than when we recall recent events. Distant experiences become specific—refer to a specific event in our past—*when we can relate them to our present world.* (p. 75, italics added)

This expression of time as past and present accords with the position presented in the preceding section of this chapter. Rosenfield reinforces this idea when he notes that the past has specificity only in relation to the current "now," the present (p. 77). He goes further to state that time in any immediate sense is determined by our physical relation to the environment and its myriad experiences. Memory, as he stated earlier, is not the crucial element; time is.

Rosenfield expands these ideas in the remainder of his book. He offers definitions of widely used terms and illustrates his own interpretations. Having pointed out that neurophysiological evidence has demonstrated that the brain interprets stimuli in terms of coherent patterns of responses, he stresses that these coherent responses are not conscious. There can be no consciousness without the dynamic interrelations of past and present, interacting with the personal body image. This means that consciousness as a state reflects a general dynamic state. This state is the process of change. As we become aware of change, we are conscious regardless of the stimuli perceived.

As brain damage, from whatever cause, occurs, there may be destruction of certain elements of self-reference. This destruction not only alters the structure of consciousness; it also modifies knowledge. Language is a tool that benefits the higher forms of consciousness, yet language cannot prevent the loss of conscious awareness that comes from neurological disease (p. 87). Alzheimer's disease patients are apt and poignant examples of this fact. Clinicians encounter cases where the language function is still seemingly available, yet conscious awareness is altered. The case of a man who was asked the questions on the MSQ is illustrative. He admitted to being unable to respond accurately but also stated that he "knew" the answers. Unfortunately he was unable to retrieve any of them. This is more than memory loss; it is a loss of temporal awareness that alters the self.

Rosenfield has provided a cogent analysis of the role of the brain in consciousness. Even more important, he has redefined concepts of past and present to fit a mental structure of self that reflects the conscious state.

A Contrasting Model

More direct to the psychology of time awareness, and evolutionary in its focus, is the work of Jason Brown (1990). Spacetime is not pertinent to this model since it is physical in its expression, whereas Brown is concerned with the psychological. Psychological time involves, in part, the recognition of succession that may suggest that there is some sort of physical time order just as perception carries an implication of some object in physical space. This presumption aside, there are similarities to the positions above. One major difference between Brown and Rosenfield, however, concerns the role of memory and its relation to time awareness.

Brown speaks of the present, which he labels the Now, as some fluid transition in a world of constancy. The person thus observes time as it progresses through this world. There are two aspects to the Now: the phenomenal present, which lasts only a second or so, reflecting the experiences of the moment, and an absolute Now, which is very brief, wherein signals cross levels that represent the structure of the mind. From these are built what we see as a past, stored so that they may be recovered as needed. We feel time as an awareness of the growth and decay of life that is refined in the growth and decay of mental life. The essential element, the "glue" that gives meaning, is memory, itself dependent upon the experiences that make memory possible. Without memory, there can be no awareness of time. On this basis, then, Brown differs from others of the writers surveyed. This idea also suggests that there is no time awareness until there is accumulated, stored experience—and the greater the experience (life) the more awareness of time the Self potentially may achieve. To Brown the events that lead to memory function determine our time awareness (p. 145).

Brown allies himself with Bergson (1965) in his differentiation of time and space. This is reflected in an analysis of duration of time. The phenomenal Now endures in the interpretation of the mental state given to the absolute Now—that is, to the interval between present and the Nows of the more or less immediate moments. Such duration is not longitudinal, however; it is not a time line since that would represent space rather than time. He illustrates this idea figurally (p. 147). He defines duration as an intuition that occurs when we compare the present with the remaining stage of a past mental state. The greater the perceived distance between the two, the longer the duration (p. 148).

There are two different mental times proposed by Brown (p. 150). One consists of the events, duration, and succession during a dream state, the other in a waking state. Brown speculates whether they share mental time or occur in different mental times. He concludes that time in a dream state is associated with and perhaps dependent on a different space than while awake, and employing a quality of timelessness, thereby affecting perception of duration and relationship. This leads to the conclusion that the problem revolves around different times in different worlds, not different times in the same world (p. 150). He points out that this has nothing to do with a question of whether there are various streams of time in the same environment. Yet the question arises, and the possibility of parallel, coexistent time streams is a fascinating one in its own right.

Within the framework established by his basic contentions, Brown explains the past, the substance of events, succession of events in time, rate at which time passes, the accuracy of duration judgment, and expectation for past and present since psychological time moves in only one direction: past to present. There is a movement toward the future, based on expectations and other forces. But its role in time awareness is not comparable to that of past and present.

So how does time awareness originate? There are natural rhythms involved, such as biological clocks, circadian rhythms, and the like. A prime basis is succession, often involving cyclical behaviors that lend stability to duration. But mere recurrence is not enough. What must be present is an evolution of memory. Our pasts must exist as content, not altered thresholds.

"Time and space are separately woven into the mental state, time through iteration and the traversal of events in decay, space through the process of object formation. Time is in relation to memory, space to perception" (p. 161). This sums up Brown's position, with the elements more fully fleshed out in the body of his article. He believes that psychology is concerned only with the limits of the absolute Now.

The distinction of time and space revolves around the content of each. Brown believes both are incorporated into the mental state of the individual, time through repetition and space through object formation (p. 161). As stated earlier, time equates with memory, whereas space equates with perception. Time awareness can only develop through perception of space, and both time and space depend on objectification of the world. He raises the interesting questions: Are the components relevant to the universe an analog of the mind observing the universe, or are they implicit to the universe alone? Is it possible that the physical laws that govern the universe (still poorly understood) are applicable in some way to the laws that govern the human mind (almost totally a mystery)? Further, Brown notes that the universe has a structure with no absolute center. Is the mind of a similar organization? To him, the center of the mind can only be understood in a world where the mind is active, where one mental object relates to other mental objects in the same mind.

Social Models

Brown has challenged some of the traditional limits that have become sacrosanct in psychology. Perhaps it is time for more of us to move on from the repetitive nature of psychological research and become more innovative and challenging in seeking answers. Still it seems reasonable that such an approach can employ specific types of behavior; it must not be global only.

One example of such an approach is a study by Flaherty (1991), who has given his attention to the subjective nature of time, especially in social situations. The conventional model in sociology, he says, has been to focus on the social organization of time, thereby emphasizing time as reflected in clocks, calendars, and schedules. However, knowledge of how time is organized for the individual does not provide any knowledge about time as a part of living experience. The emphasis on hours, days, months, and so on, Flaherty says, gives us an expectation of the length of a 10-minute segment, say; the expectation gives a feeling that 10 minutes of duration is 10 minutes lived. This is called *synchronicity*. But certain periods are not so stable, and so their duration seems longer or shorter than the actual elapsed clock time. This he labels *protracted duration*. These two elements are studied in social situations in the paper reviewed here.

Using undergraduates as his subjects (the second favorite experimental group for psychologists), Flaherty found that the perception of the objective nature of an event played an important part in the subjects' estimate of time. This principle eventuated from the fact that the greater degree of time embeddedness, the greater the amount of stimulus complexity. Either relatively eventful or uneventful situations were the bases for a perception of protracted duration. Events that are more routine do not bring this reaction, indicating that it is the unusual circumstance in life that appears to take a longer-than-actual time, and it does not matter whether there are stimulating or nonstimulating natures to the event.

There is an interesting parallel in Nowotny (1994, p. 32). She describes the need "to belong," to "join in" as a social obligation. Today this force has become economically mediated, and this has been equated with temporal inequalities. She sees society as moving on two tracks: A "fast" group is accepted and rewarded, whereas the "slow" group is ignored or rejected, certainly not rewarded. Achieving complementarity between these groups seems impossible in such a world. Socially, this outcome would seem comparative to Flaherty's remarks about personal time evaluation and to the traditional "folk theory," as he labels it, which states that busy time passes quickly, whereas empty time is slow moving. His data actually refute such a difference.

There can also be some analogy in the meaning of time to the dementia patient. In what ways may time seem to pass quickly? Is the principle that Flaherty advocates applicable directly? If not, how does it differ? Indeed, is the "passing of time" merely a misstatement for an Alzheimer's patient? A case may be made that there is a psychological equivalent for the physical statement that relativity demonstrates that observers, no matter how they move, see their world in the same way in their own frame of reference (Fagg, 1995, p. 32). Einstein referred of course to the speed of light; the shift from the absolute frame of reference to the speed of light as the absolute may surely have its psychological counterpoint in meaning if not in fact. We must keep in mind that "our familiar ideas of simultaneity are seriously challenged. That is, two events that are seen as simultaneous by an observer in one frame of reference can in general be observed as one occurring after the other by an observer in another frame moving at an appropriate relative velocity" (p. 33). There is no intent here to do a misservice either to physics or to psychology. Instead, what is sought is a new way of viewing behavior, a push for models that enlarge what has already served the psychologist who sometimes finds discord between the traditional and the current (see Jackson, 1989, p. 44, for a similar view).

Flaherty (1991, pp. 81–83) concludes and elaborates five sequential elements that lead to his findings: extreme circumstances, emotional concern, cognitive engrossment, stimulus complexity, and density of experience. Only one of these is external to the individual completely, although two (stimulus complexity and density of experience) are external variables moderated by internal perceptions. The other two are personal variables and may vary in intensity from one occasion to another, even within a single experience. Much work remains to be done.

Perhaps one of the minor tragedies of life is the fact that only a small part of the time do we experience protracted duration (p. 83). Synchronicity is the more common parlance of life, again recalling remarks of Nowotny (1994) in her analyses. Flaherty believes that the seminal element is that subjectivity has been socialized, with society providing redundance as the chief form of engrossment. The rewards await those, as Nowotny says, who learn the socialized relation of experience to temporal units of societal importance.

Other examples of studies focusing on more restricted aspects of time awareness, pertinent to the position that the scope of investigation must be broadened in the social sciences, are available. And they vary widely in the focus used (for example, Boscolo and Bertrando, 1993; Bouffard, Bastin, and Lapierre, 1996; Golander, 1995). Such researches will be surveyed in Chapter 9. The unfortunate part of this comment is that each such effort is largely isolated: Most frequently there is no model and thus little generalizability.

There are examples of models that focus on subdisciplines in the social sciences as well, thus delimiting but developing generally within that sphere. Such an example is Nowotny (1994), a blend of social psychology (with emphasis on the social) and industrial-organizational psychology. She has not only traced the concept of time as it has developed historically in the economic and social sphere, but she has also explicated the meanings and effects on the individual within given societies and in a world that is becoming more global for the person. She relates her ideas to current developments in technology that continue to give us more time to accomplish less. It is of more than passing interest, for example, that the purchase of a new computer, which performs more rapidly and with greater applications than its predecessors, is obsolete for the same things by the time it is unpacked and activated. We may be gaining many small victories while we are losing the war in the personal sense. Aging has long been measured in chronological time but, as Nowotny notes, there is now a cultural definition of aging that corresponds to obsolescence (p. 66).

Time as a theoretical or a real entity has not changed. What has changed is our increasing dependence on our awareness of time as a construct of the Self. If we do not find answers to personal questions and continue our dependence on the mechanistic world to provide us answers, it will take no future wars or alien invasions to destroy what cultural attainments have accomplished over thousands of years.

CHAPTER 9

Physical Properties of Time Relations

The contention of this book is that time and space exist in dementia in the same way that they do in our so-called real world, even though psychologists have largely opted to look at differences rather than similarities. The similarities may be used to infer that the meaning of time and space is equivalent regardless of mental competence as well. Psychology needs to change the focus from abnormality to normality in order to appreciate the implications of orientation in all aspects of life.

THE MEANING OF TIME AND SPACE

Jaspers (1959) synthesized the meaning when he wrote:

Space and time are always present in sensory processes. They are not primary objects themselves but they invest all objectivity. . . . They are universal. . . . Everything in the world that is presented to us comes in space and time and we experience it only in these terms. (in Sims, 1998, p. 52)

The experiential form of Jaspers's conception and its meaning has been illustrated by case studies reported by Shomaker (1989). She notes our tendency to label as "abnormal" the person who alters (in some sense, self-determined) the reality perceived by others so that communication becomes difficult or impossible. Particularly for the Alzheimer's patient, where time disorientation becomes increasingly the norm, Shomaker asks, "if such misrepresentations reveal a logic and insight into the patients' perceptions of reality" (p. 91). She concludes not, instead opting for a complex arrangement that contains a strong structure of logic and organization. That structure needs to be determined, not ignored.

Shomaker's case studies are illuminating and persuasive. In one she describes a 61-year-old man who thought himself to be 45, regressing so that he recognized few of the persons, including his son and wife, previously well known to him. In fact, he regressed to such a level that he believed himself a young adult, a period when he was happiest. Other cases could be cited from Shomaker, but they would differ only in content, not context. Her point of a complex structure is well taken from such reports, and they are not limited in the experiences of professionals working with Alzheimer's patients.

However, seldom is there any attempt to analyze or understand the meaning of the behavior to the patient. A student doing a practicum in a nursing home reported to me an incident illustrative of this fact. She was walking with a resident along the hall where there were pictures of various bucolic, relaxing, unobtrusive scenes. One was a painting of a blacksmith shoeing a horse while a small boy looked on. The patient stopped at this picture and told the student: "This is a picture of me and Dad." Later the student asked an employee if, in fact, the picture was as told to her. It turned out that the patient's father had indeed been a blacksmith and that the son often stayed with him in the shop, but this was merely coincidental. Why the patient made the "mistake" in identification was explained as the way elderly people lived only in the past, were confused about reality, and had to be oriented to the present.

Such incidents raise questions that should be researched for answers. For example, how are diseased cells involved in the representations of past-present relationships among patients? Indeed, are cells programmed for events at various times of life? If so, does this mean that cells holding old memories are less affected by the disease process? (Admittedly, an unlikely prospect, but our knowledge is so limited that no question is really absurd at this stage.) Shomaker speculates that as the patient loses short-term memory potential, there is a loss of present age and situation awareness. This is supplanted by fragments of long-term memory. How would such a process work? And why in the general sense? Is it possible to have the mind move into a future perspective? (There have been no such reports, but that doesn't deny the possibility.) One could even speculate whether there is further movement into the past as the disease progresses. This would then lead to the possibility of the time period being utilized as a marker for degree of dementia.

As bewildering as such cases may appear and regardless of speculation about them, Shomaker maintains a belief that there are logical explanations. As she says, "Time regressed and moved within the limits of the disorientation creating what seemed to others to be an irrational association between ideas and a random array of elements. . . . But the fragmented and chaotic time perspective masked continuity and predictability" (p. 96).

The more typical current view of alterations in time awareness is portrayed by Sims (1988). He refers to the mechanical nature of time, clock time that is objective and independent of the emotional self. Yet he also notes the presence of personal time, which is subjective and perceived in terms of the way time seems to be passing (p. 52). For these types of time, there may be disorders of time sense.

An ability to separate events into past, present and future, even if limited; capacity to estimate duration; and the ability to put events in sequence, is necessary for intellectual processes to be carried out. Disorder of time sense is closely associated with disturbance of consciousness, attention and memory. (p. 53)

Whether one adopts the viewpoint of Shomaker or of Sims can have a major effect on interpretation of behavior and implementation of treatment. It is not a matter of which approach is the right one to take: both are important and deserve continued investigation, including models as well as empiricism.

Autobiographical Memory in Dementia

One, perhaps special, instance of the process of disorientation in dementia can be found in autobiographical materials. An example of the approach has been reported by Fromholt and Larsen (1991). They compared aging adults without signs of dementia with a group that had been diagnosed with senile dementia of the Alzheimer's type (SDAT). They point out that dementia patients are commonly described as having problems with memory but that the effects on remote memories have been variously interpreted. Some experts believe recent memory is impaired, but remote memory is unaffected, whereas others take the position that long-term memory can be as adversely affected as short-term. Fromholt and Larsen, in this study, focused on the availability of memories across the lifetime of both groups in their sample. There were 30 persons in each group, matched on age, education, health, and similar variables.

Interest here is in the group with SDAT. Three subgroups were formed to reflect degree of dementia: those with minor memory problems and loss of competencies (n = 7); others with moderate degrees of memory loss and lapses in orientation (n = 13); and a subgroup with severe limitations in memory and social skills (n = 10). All were interviewed privately and asked to tell about the important events of their lives. Significant differences between the normally aging group and the dementia group were found on number of words used and memories reported. Those with dementia also repeated themselves significantly more often.

Within the dementia sample, the most severe cases used significantly fewer words than the other two, which did not differ from each other. A more serious effect was found for memorable events in lives. Here, even the least severe cases performed less well than the normally aging. Number of repetitions did not differ among the dementia cases, but the group as a whole differed from the nondemented group. Details reported about the memories deviated significantly between total groups and within the dementia sample. For the latter, the mild group was significantly different than the other two subgroups but performed at the same level as the normally aging. This led the authors to conclude that richness of reported detail within their samples was not discriminated until later in progression of the disease. Two other findings are of more than passing interest: demented subjects related more transitional (that is, life-changing) events such as marriage than did normals and more negative experiences from their lives.

So far as greater reliance on the distant past for memories, Fromhart and Larsen found evidence that belied that position. Those with dementia recalled less well the memories from the first fifth of their lives. This deficiency increased in the second fifth. By contrast, memories of more recent vintage were not so adversely affected. In addition, interjections that had no bearing on the task of reporting life events occurred more often among the dementia sample. Thus, such statements as "Society takes good care of old people, nowadays," "I think of the flower over there," and "I cannot remember any longer" were significantly more common. Such statements may be as much a control mechanism in the face of a demanding task than a change in direction of deliberate thought.

One comment from the discussion by Fromhart and Larsen is particularly pertinent to the topic at hand.

We found a progressing inability to recollect an integrated personal history. . . . This suggests two relatively independent structural levels, single events and relations between events, in the process of autobiographical deterioration in primary degenerative dementia. The eventual outcome . . . can be an ahistorical existence fixated in the present context. (p. 91)

This is a fearful reminder that dementia eventually leads to a return to the most basic, animal "eternal present." Dependency is paramount in behavior at this stage, and there is a lack of recognizable orientation in either time or space.

There are other studies of autobiographical memory that do not report consistent findings with those of Fromhart and Larsen. The point here is that a process of deterioration is continuous if sporadic, that we need to define more critically what that process is and to determine such elements as time and space in its expression and as its cause. Only then will we be able to develop remediating, even preventive, interventions.

PHYSICAL CHANGES IN THE BRAIN

Dementia is progressive and, in its final form if the individual lives long enough, encompasses various areas of the brain. Developmentally, however, there is a progression that has been observed and mapped that is more restricted and directly related to the behaviors that have become the hallmark of dementia. Such a statement oversimplifies the complex relationships that make up the process, its markers, and its effects. Part of this oversimplification can be explicated and defined, but our understanding of the brain and its functions is still too rudimentary not to require speculation, albeit educated by other facts, and supposition.

Most writers in this arena have, therefore, elected to restrict themselves to more specific (although complex) components in presentations. There is a large corpus of literature extant that serves this purpose, and to some degree, a comprehensive reading will help to elucidate the scope of the process and its outcomes. Perusal of Damasio, Van Hoesen, and Hyman (1990) will yield information on the memory retrieval process in humans and its disruptions when Alzheimer's disease occurs. These authors explain such outcomes in terms of the corticocortical connections involved. If one reads DeKosky (1996), by contrast, there is great emphasis on structural changes that "cause" the resultant effects of neurofibrillary tangles, senile plaques, (SPs) and loss of synapses. He also delves into neurotransmission changes, amyloid metabolism and its alterations in dementia, and even the genetics that might explain the protein properties.

As important as such a complete survey may be, it is beyond the scope of this book. A more selective approach will be followed, focusing on the early developmental changes and the brain areas affected and allying those with behavioral expressions commonly recognized by patients, caregivers, and professionals.

Brain Structures Involved in Dementia

The most common complaint (and often the first) of developing dementia involves memory. In a few instances these may be major, even critical events related to job or social functioning, but that is not the usual case in the beginning. Instead, these will be more personal instances where requests or instructions are seemingly ignored, causing irritation or minor discomforts. The reaction may be varied but almost always involves emotions, a feeling that the person is deliberately behaving in this perverse fashion, causing hurt feelings and perhaps emotional outbursts. Given such a sequence it seems reasonable to look for "early signs" to involve the limbic system in some manner.

And that is precisely where we should begin. The evidence has now accumulated to the point that the hippocampus and amygdala are areas where there is some disturbance leading to the behaviors. Since new instances of input are involved, even if commonly rehearsed sequences make up the pattern, the hippocampal formation almost certainly must be central. With stimulation, there must be input that is stored on a momentary basis, one function of the hippocampus. If this part of the sequence does not occur, there can be no memory and consequently no forgetting. Damage to cells used for momentary storage may well be the first step that will lead to eventual demented behaviors.

The rest of the sequence will not follow, but if the system is intact to this point, there is some mechanism by which "processing" occurs that takes the input beyond the moment. This process is unknown but is the subject of some investigation. Once processed, the brain (or mind) makes the decision as to whether the event is to be stored on a permanent basis. This procedure is also part of the great unknown. Overall, what has occurred is a move from short-term to long-term memory in some way. As dementia develops, there must be a spread in damage to cells in areas where events are stored. And thus the individual not only has problems in encoding "new" events but in retrieving "old" ones as well.

As detrimental as an inability to encode new information may be (and with increasing losses in retrieval as well), one still could function in some respects in the daily world. Assistance from others would become more and more necessary, but there need not be the losses to society that currently occur with advancing dementia. As the disease spreads to cells in the prefrontal cortex, however, the effects become more massive and destructive. Neurons are lost that are part of the ability to plan, to analyze, to organize, to solve problems—all the things that make the human capable of functioning in a complex world. The horror of dementia is not just a loss in memory but that plus the loss to behave in a truly human way.

The process that causes cells in certain areas to be destroyed is not yet known, but the change itself is clear. Within cells, there is an increasing development of amyloid protein that is expressed as neurofibrillary tangles. These strands have been and are being investigated extensively, along with other effects associated with dementia such as senile plaques and loss of synapses (Kazee, Eskin, Lapham, Gabriel, McDaniel, and Hamill, 1993). Such physical expressions are being evaluated as well with genetic risk factors and genes that may be predisposed to the development of lesions (Hyman, 1994). To date, the answers are less obvious than the questions, and the questions are multiplying with the increase in the search for answers.

Papolla and Robakis (1995) have surveyed a number of these factors. They begin with an incontrovertible though disturbing fact: the characteristic lesions of dementia are found in all persons who live into old age. There may be a difference in amount or extent of such factors, but the characteristics are shared. Thus, autopsies have disclosed NFTs (and other features such as amyloid beta protein) in the brains of persons who aged normally as well as in those who have been diagnosed with Alzheimer's or other dementing conditions. There are authorities who believe that whatever the process may finally be proven to be, it is age-related. If we live long enough, we will become demented. Despite the lack of proof of such a statement, and despite its depressing nature, it must be recognized as a possibility. There is an associated question that arises from the acknowledgment of NFTs in all aging persons. In what ways, if any, do these "normally aging" individuals show problems with spacetime awareness? Is there merely a matter of degree rather than kind?

There are two types of senile plaque: the "classic," where the central core is amyloid surrounded by glial cells and neuritic processes, and the "diffuse," where the characteristics are not so distinctive or clear (Papolla and Robakis, 1995, p. 5). Diffuse plaques precede the development of NFTs and are "the earliest detectable alteration in the pathogenic sequence of the AD neuropathology" (p. 6). There is evidence that diffuse plaques arise in neurons, and Poppolla and Robakis speculate that during the process by which debris and waste from the brain are being removed through blood vessels, any amyloid present may collect on vessel walls. Over time, this amyloid material, being highly insoluble, will accumulate, although its relationship to the development of diffuse plaques is not clear.

The assumption has been that the production of amyloid beta protein (AβP), results from the processing of amyloid precursor protein (APP). The latter seems to play important roles in cell physiology, such as modulating growth and receptor functions, and so is essentially normal in its expressions (p. 9). Regardless of the eventual resolution of this issue, AβP is involved with the death of neurons once its presence is manifest in the cell. Perhaps this amyloid itself is the reason for cell death, but this position is supported only by certain studies and in conflict with others. Indeed, NFTs have been found in areas where no amyloid is present. This leads Poppolla and Robakis to the position that AβP may be only an early marker or the actual cause of dementia (p. 10).

There are a small percentage of cases of AD with a clear relationship to genetic mutation (on chromosome 21, for example). These instances are called "familial Alzheimer's disease" (FAD) because they seem to occur within families and across generations, again without complete predictability. In such cases investigated to date, a small percentage of persons have mutations in the APP gene itself. This might suggest that the AD found in FAD is caused by some alteration in the way APP functions in FAD. But as with so many other results from research on dementia, there is no clear and certainly no conclusive basis for claims and generalizations. Papolla and Robakis include reference to studies that point to the role of environmental factors in the development of AD, indicating the broad scope still needed.

The possibility that AD may progress along pathways within the brain has been proposed by Unger, Lapham, McNeill, Eskin, and Hamill (1991).

They believe that the amygdala may be a central unit within this process (p. 389). Further, they propose that there may be a bidirectional set of interneuronal influences that is pathogenic and leads to the disease and its expression. To them, "This hypothesis would extend the notion of trans-neuronal transport participating in the pathogenesis of neurogenerative dis-eases characterized by system degeneration" (p. 397). Certainly several authors have stressed the importance of this process in transport in the dementing process.

For all of us, the amygdala plays a part in long-term memory, especially where the emotions are involved (McGaugh, Introini-Collison, Cahill, Munsoo, and Liang, 1992). "Viewed from this perspective, the amygdala may be part of a brain system that serves to insure that memories of sig-nificant experiences are well retained" (p. 431). Alzheimer's patients are frequently characterized as becoming increasingly dependent on the past, with remote memory well preserved into the dementing process. At the same time, notable lacks and modifications in long-term memories have been noted in patients. Perhaps the gaps and the retentions may be traced to the role of the amygdala in the selection and storage of experiences.

Mann (1992) gives us an extended picture of this role in the normally aging as contrasted with those suffering dementia. Patients with Alzhei-mer's disease usually show a large loss in size of the amygdala, and partic-ularly for those who die before age 75. This amounts to 40% on average and as much as 60% in some cases (p. 576). To lose so much mass must play some effects on the control of emotions and the retrieval of remote experiences, even though at present the relationship has not been defined empirically. This is accompanied by neuronal losses amounting to as much as 70% in cortical and medial nuclei. Mann points out that these match the level of losses reported for the hippocampus, temporal cortex, and nu-cleus basalis of Meynert (p. 578). He concludes that such losses emphasize the critical involvement of the amygdala in the pathology that occurs as Alzheimer's disease progresses.

As is to be expected, the occurrence of NFTs and SPs in the amygdala are significant as well, even exceeding their total in other cortical regions such as the hippocampus (p. 580). Mann concludes that neurons die in a nonselective nature as lesions develop and grow within a pattern of con-nections to other centers of the brain. For AD patients, the accumulation of APP is significant, but it is also found in aging individuals without de-mentia. Mann hypothesizes that the deposit of amyloid is more likely linked to aging and genetic factors than to the disease process itself (p. 585). AD must be defined in terms of the degeneration of neurons along with amyloid deposition, he believes, ultimately leading to the outcomes noted in AD. The role of the amygdala is significant to Mann since there is an implication that the disease is most destructive because it originates and spreads from the amygdala.

How do the lesions prominent in AD begin? Mann makes a case for the entry of some causative agent through the olfactory epithelium, which is then transferred into the amygdala (p. 587). From there is dissemination to other regions, and the lesions grow and spread. There is no evidence as to the nature of the "causative agent" at present, but Mann speculates that neurotoxic agents such as aluminum or viruses may be the culprit. There has been a strong predilection on the part of some authorities for the role of aluminum in AD for many years now, a position that is still being investigated. Perhaps, Mann thinks, whatever the agent may be, it interacts with tendencies toward degeneration that are present already in the individual to cause the neuronal degeneration that then occurs and produces the effects called Alzheimer's disease.

The role of the amygdala is not confined to AD, however. Mann discusses other dementing conditions, such as Pick's, Huntington's, and even supranuclear palsy (p. 587), and concludes, "Disconnection of these areas [the amygdala and hippocampus] via neurofibrillary degeneration of neurons (in AD) or through Pick-type lesions (in Pick's disease) may contribute to the totality of the memory deficit characteristic of AD and the mnestic deterioration common in Pick's disease" (p. 588).

Progress in understanding the relation of brain areas to the dementias has been significant and is still growing. It is apparent as well, even with such a brief review of research as in this section, that the task is far from completed. Physical data will help clarify and specify psychological data, leading to more complete and general models of dementia.

DEMENTIA AND BRAIN STRUCTURE

There is a topic more specific to the functioning of parts of the brain that deserves consideration and that has been researched extensively. Mention has been made already that neurofibrillary tangles are common to several dementias, whereas senile plaques represent a conclusion to the death of neurons. Autopsies have been conducted increasingly on brain tissue of elderly persons for the presence of tangles and plaques as well as amyloid protein (see Bouras, Hof, Giannakopoulos, Michel, and Morrison, 1994, for example). Generally, these have shown agreement in the presence of tangles and plaques (even among normal controls) as a common feature of dementia, with differences from controls mainly in amount. The hippocampus has been most often cited as the site of such matter, and some researchers have proposed that NFTs (and accompanying amyloid) in the hippocampus are necessary components for dementia.

Specifically, Bennett, Cochran, Saper, Leverenz, Gilley, and Wilson (1993) followed four cases of Alzheimer's patients from biopsy through autopsy. For the years following biopsies, mental competence showed marked decline on clinical measures, but there were no consistent changes in density of plaques or tangles. This result surprised the authors, leading them to speculate that unless their results are artifactual, there are several possibilities to explain the outcome.

First, the density of plaques and tangles in those who are mildly demented may be as intense as those with much greater incompetence. This possibility has received support from other studies as well. Second, progression may be more a matter of increased effects in several cortical regions rather than an increase in density within a given area, such as the hippocampus. Third, plaques and tangles may not be the important component frequently assumed. In fact, Bennett and associates note that studies have shown a decrease in plaque density with progression of the dementia. There must be considered, also, the phenomenon of what are called "ghost" tangles, found outside the cell body of the neuron. Perhaps these are residuals of tangles that are being catabolized. Fourth, neurites in plaques and tangles may reflect some more generalized cytoskeletal disorder as a part of Alzheimer's disease. Fifth, there has been speculation that the severity of dementia may be correlated with density of tangles in the nucleus basalis, or loss or shrinkage of large cortical neurons, or loss of synapses. Obviously, the physical presence of tangles with amyloid and plaques leaves us with a fact that explains little about the disease process itself.

A study by McKee, Kosik, and Kowall (1991) approaches the topic from a slightly different viewpoint. They point out that Alzheimer's is the leading cause of dementia in North America, with an annual incidence of 123 new cases per 100,000 population each year (p. 156). Neuropathologically, the primary signs are SPs and NFTs. However, the relationship between these and clinical dementia is debatable, as evidenced in several studies. They compared a control group (n = 22) of normally aging adults with a group (n = 34) of elderly demented patients with SPs and NFTs, using antibodies raised against amyloid SP cores and tau protein as well as thioflavine S. All of this group demonstrated abundant β/A4 protein but divided into two subgroups on the basis of density of neocortical NFTs. One subgroup had a predominance of plaques but relatively few NFTs, whereas the other had widespread SPs and NFTs.

As compared with controls, the Alzheimer patients showed a significant increase in dystrophic neurites. The number of these neurites and NFTs correlated with the clinical severity of dementia in a positive direction. Evaluations showed a clear distinction between functionally demented and nondemented brains based on the presence of dystrophic neurites (DNs). They speculate in their conclusions, "The formation of DNs may accompany disruption of fine neuronal processes, including axons, dendrites, and synapses, leading to NFT formation and eventual cell death. DNs may, therefore, be an earlier and more sensitive correlate of clinical dementia than NFTs" (p. 164). And so another dimension has been added to make a complex arrangement even more complex.

Judging clinical dementia requires functional assessment, usually based on accepted measures with known statistical properties. An instance of a study that compared the severity of dementia with the rating on such a scale is found in Bierer, Hof, Purohit, Carlin, Schmeidler, Davis, and Perl (1995). They investigated the relationships between the severity of dementia and the presence of lesions in several areas of the brain. The scale used to assess severity was the Clinical Dementia Rating Scale (CDR) of Hughes, Berg, Danziger, Cohen, and Martin (1982). Bierer et al. include a description of the characteristics of the scale and the adaptations they employed to fit the characteristics of their sample and the purpose of the study.

With 70 cases of confirmed Alzheimer's, Bierer et al. found that only NFTs had a significant correlation with the CDR scores, and then only in the neocortex. They found no significant relationships for the amygdala, hippocampus, or entorhinal cortex. Thus, SPs were not correlated significantly with CDR scores in any brain region. They comment, "These results suggest that the involvement by NFTs specifically of the neocortex is a key factor in the appearance and progression of dementing symptoms in AD. Moreover, they indicate that this association exists independent of the effects of age" (p. 84). This conclusion must be evaluated in terms of the statistical procedures (partial correlations controlled for age) as well as the measure of severity of dementia.

The data gathered by Bierer et al. indicated to them that the medial temporal lobe is the primary site of NFT formation, which then spreads to the temporal, frontal, and parietal cortices (p. 87). To them, this indicates a strong possibility that Alzheimer's develops in specific cortical areas, whereas others are only slowly involved as disease progresses to its ultimate destruction of tissue and behavioral competence.

The comparison of dementia severity measured by psychological scales with specific areas of the brain was investigated also by Samuel, Terry, DeTeresa, Butters, and Masliah (1994). Their measures included the Information-Memory-Concentration (IMC) scale of Blessed, Tomlinson, and Roth (1968), the MMSE, and the Dementia Rating Scale (DRS) of Mattis (1976). Their sample was small (n = 13), all having been diagnosed as "probable" AD, which was confirmed at autopsy. The scales were administered to eight subjects between three weeks and 40 months before death (median = 11 months) or over 16 months before dying for the remaining five individuals. No differences in scores were found between the two subgroups. At autopsy, Samuel et al. assessed NFTs, SPs, and neuronal and synaptic density (SD) in the midfrontal cortex and nucleus basalis of Meynert.

Their results differed somewhat from those reported by Bierer et al. in the preceding study. Samuel et al. report that SD was the largest correlate of dementia severity as measured by the scales in the midfrontal cortex, followed by NFTs. In the nucleus basalis, NFTs had the strongest correlation, followed by SD. In neither brain region were senile plaques a significant predictor of scores overall. They conclude that the decline of synaptic density in the midfrontal cortex and NFT accumulation in the nucleus basalis are major contributors to dementia of the Alzheimer's type. Thus, "our results imply a remarkable specificity of association between the type and locus of pathology on the one hand and particular neuropsychological tests on the other" (1994, p. 776). They further note that, in agreement with other studies, SPs have a lesser relationship and importance to the severity of dementia as judged from performance on commonly used and accepted scales.

With a sample of 16 "probable" Alzheimer's premortem cases who were administered the same scales as in the preceding study, autopsy information from the hippocampus and entorhinal cortex was examined by Samuel, Masliah, Hill, Butters, and Terry (1994). They found that NFTs correlated most strongly with dementia severity scores in the CA1, subiculum, and CA4 regions, whereas synaptic loss was the greater contributor to dementia in the dentate fasciculus and stratum lacunosum, CA2/3, and CA4. From their results, they conclude that correlations between lesions in the hippocampus and the severity of dementia depended upon the type of pathology and the region where it was observed. In addition, a total pathology "score" correlated significantly with mental status scores throughout the hippocampus except for the entorhinal cortex. The most independent predictor of dementia with their neuropsychological tests was pathology in the CA4 region.

Samuel et al. use these results to advocate a two-component model of the role of the hippocampus in Alzheimer's. First involves the input processing of stimuli by the hippocampus, a recognized component in intrinsic memory and to action. Here, the hippocampus is conceived to summate excitations of neurons, and this influences cognition, degree and level of which depend on the density of synapses available for the process. The second component of their model involves the output mode where the processed signals are received in the CA1 and subiculum, passing the result on to other subcortical and cortical regions. Now, cognition is affected by the numbers of NFTs in neurons used for the purpose. Thus, progression of the disease will affect both components with consequent memory loss and increasingly impoverished cognitive competence until the patient eventually becomes too demented to function in the everyday world.

There are two considerations to understanding the changes occurring in the brain of the person suffering Alzheimer's disease. Since various, though restricted, areas of the brain are involved (principally the hippocampus, frontal cortex, and temporal lobe), results are dependent on analyses for physical changes in all of these. The changes to be evaluated are well agreed upon: NFTs, SPs, SDs, and their interrelations. There is some agreement that "amount" is a principal component in the process.

At the same time, there must be attention to the conclusion of the severity of dementia that is present. Rather than use only "counts" of the changes, an independent measure of "amount" of mental loss is desired. For this purpose, tests have been developed and are widely used because they are accepted as adequate measures of the criterion. Most have a long history, at least as is usually found for tests, without modifications. This raises a question about the quality of these measures and their demonstrated evidence as reliable and valid reflections of the criterion: severity of dementia.

THE STUDY AND EVALUATION OF DISORIENTATION

Disorientation in time and space has occupied the attention of professionals dealing with dementia for many years. Some persons consider the outcome as a special case of memory loss (Hussian, 1987, pp. 185–186) and have designed training techniques to help overcome memory deficiencies, assuming that the disorientation will be corrected as a part of the recovery of memory. The problem with this approach is that disorientation is a more generalized state, leading to a dependency that eventually restricts the ability of the person to exercise executive functions such as planning and problem solving. Short-term memory loss is circumscribed in its effects and may be improved by training. There is no known way to change the adverse effects of disorientation.

The study of disoriented behavior in dementia has most often focused on clock time and immediate spatial surroundings (see Pattschul-Furlan and Retschitzki, 1990, for example). This view is supported in a proposed procedure to assess functional status reported by Loewenstein (1990). Among the functional domains advocated by him for judging competence is time orientation. He advocates this be measured by "testing time at increasingly difficult clock settings and answering questions pertaining to year, month and day" (p. 62).

Certainly the current environment is the medium where problem behavior will be noted most quickly by patients and caregivers. Rarely have there been efforts to extend the research into cognitive competencies involving prefrontal lobe integrity, however. There are exceptions, as found in a case study published by Petty, Bonner, Mouratoglou, and Silverman (1996). Generalization must be limited since there is a single case, but details are intriguing and may lead to research involving larger samples.

Their case involved a 67-year-old man with a history of diabetes and peripheral vasculopathy who was found wandering along the London Underground. He appeared confused to police and was found to be "grossly disoriented in time, place and person" (p. 237) upon examination. A CT showed evidence of infarctions in the caudate nucleus and thalamus. He was treated with drugs and later given a complete psychological assessment. He was judged to be suffering an acute dementia of the frontal lobe type, an atypical diagnosis considering the lack of neurological signs. The psychological tests indicated a subcortical type of dementia that is consistent with cases of Huntington's disease. The onset of his condition was unexpected and sudden, probably reflecting some catastrophic event in his life that was not known.

Petty et al. present a lucid picture of the relation of the caudate nucleus (CN) to behavior. Projections to the CN come from the higher association cortex, the hippocampus and the amygdala. Consequent effects on behavior when there are lesions in the CN are thus likely and may prove detrimental to the memory and language as well as problem-solving abilities. As Petty et al. point out, there are five frontal-subcortical circuits that connect specific regions in the frontal lobe to the thalamus by means of circuits in the CN (p. 239). Lesions there operate to disconnect the frontal cortex from subcortical and, perhaps, the limbic system. If lesions occur in the third of these circuits, executive functions and motor competence are affected. If the fourth circuit is affected, there are personality changes, including inappropriate behavior, irritability, and other signs of overdependence on environmental cues. Both circuits were affected in this man, and the CT scan disclosed a lesion. Petty et al. conclude that the lesions discovered through the scan explain the adverse behaviors shown by this man and reflected in the psychological testing. Although the subject's condition improved with treatment over a period of some two months, he remained severely cognitively impaired.

Hussian (1987) approaches the matter of disorientation from a more general perspective. Further, he proposes that the cause of temporal and spatial deficiencies may be due to insufficient stimulus discrimination, a case where training may be beneficial. He sees temporal disorientation and wandering (an instance of spatial disorientation) as "the classic and most heavily researched areas that exemplify the overall problem of poor stimulus control" (p. 177).

Disorientation is defined by Hussian as a general term that includes the usual inability to identify correctly such items as the day, year, current location, and the like, or to locate specific areas in the environment and to use these in terms of their intention. An example of this would be either to be unable to locate the toilet in a familiar setting such as the home or, once there, to be confused as to the proper receptacle to use. This latter situation (locating specific areas) is less often tested than the former (testing day, year, etc.), perhaps because of its ease more than its relevance. Hussian proposes, then, that the functional approach may be more pertinent and useful to gather information about patients who are impaired (p. 178).

With this orientation, Hussian advocates that problem behaviors of the type cited should be viewed in terms of management, especially when there are significant problems of control for the patient and caregiver (p. 178). There are very practical outcomes from lack of time orientation, such as missing necessary medication, irregularity in taking medicines, and missing meals and activities. Most of all there is the implication for loss or prevention of independent functioning in the home and community, perhaps leading to institutionalization, unemployment, and restricted efforts at treatment (p. 178).

Deficient stimulus control is one possible result of progressive changes in the brain (p. 182), including dementia resulting from Alzheimer's, Pick's, Creutzfeldt-Jakob, and similar diseases. As he states, the more global the effects on brain tissue, the more often does stimulus-free responding occur. With restricted, focal damage there is a lesser chance for such responses to occur or at least to be more restricted in their consequences. The stimulus-free response is defined as one that is inappropriate and apparently free from stimulus control by the patient. To the time of the publication of his chapter, Hussian reports that differential diagnosis within dementia types has been equivocal (p. 182). This is partly due to the fact that reliable and valid measures of behavioral indices have not been used in studies and in fact have not been demonstrated in those that are currently popular.

The difficulties inherent in making differential diagnoses may be of small consequence, Hussian believes, if functional analysis indicates that disorientation is due to poor stimulus control by the patient. One may move directly to techniques that will assist the patient in developing and using improved stimulus recognition and control. It is important that appropriate cues in the environment be present before beginning attempts at treatment; supplying missing cues may solve a nonproblem before efforts start. There must be a realistic assessment and analysis before beginning training as well. Hussian mentions such instances as extreme disorientation in a person that would be impossible to overcome and that may increase problems associated with the condition, such as agitation (p. 183). This would mean that severe dementia cases may not be suitable for intervention.

Among the techniques that Hussian lists and discusses are reality orientation, remotivation, resocialization, attitude therapy, reinforcement therapy, sensory stimulation, sensory retraining, memory retraining, and milieu therapy (pp. 185–186). Each is suitable for limited purposes and conditions, and each has its limitations even there. This fact leads him to alternative methods and modes. One of these is to consider disorientation as a memory problem. Where short-term retention is the only difficulty, training techniques are particularly useful. With dementia, however, the intervention is time limited in a realistic sense and perhaps should be avoided because of the associated problems (such as anger) that may be generated in a confused patient.

Beyond viewing disorientation in a memory framework, one may also consider the problem from a learning standpoint (p. 185). Operant conditioning may be suitable and successful for some cases when used judiciously and appropriately. All memory retraining focuses on strategies that may be used by the patient, not materials as such. There is a shift from the more popular techniques such as reality orientation as a result. What is proper and fitting should be the first consideration, not loyalty to a given technique or method as the more appropriate one in all cases.

Hussian concludes, "Disorientation and wandering, then, can be viewed as special cases of responses to inappropriate stimulus control. Although the literature is small, the use of stimulus enhancement and stimulus control techniques appears promising" (p. 187). Once again we are left with the promising caveat that "more research is needed." Unfortunately, many psychologists have opted for more of the same rather than an innovative perspective.

Relationships with Daily Life

There have been several studies published that illustrate the relationship of disorientation as one variable with various activities of daily living (ADLs). An example of such efforts is found in Venable and Mitchell (1991). They used patients with AD who had difficulty with keeping track of time so that they were unable to organize their daily lives, thus yielding dysfunction in performance of daily living activities (p. 32).

The authors measured temporal adaptation with two measures of time orientation and compared the results with a measure of instrumental ADLs, including the physical self and maintenance. Further, Venable and Mitchell assessed the severity of AD using a clinical scale designed to reflect stages of dementia. Their sample consisted of 19 persons who had been diagnosed with AD, 15 of whom were living at home. A Spearman rank-order correlation coefficient between measures was computed and accompanied by descriptive statistics.

Their results were mixed and their explanation somewhat obfuscated. In any event, positive relationships were found for one measure of temporal orientation and both activities of daily living and stage of dementia. Negative relationships were obtained for all other comparisons. Such outcomes are difficult to interpret, although judgment must include the inadequacy of the measures used for the purpose for which they were created. In any event, Venable and Mitchell conclude that significant relationships were found for temporal adaptation and performance on ADLs, and between severity of AD and performance on ADLs (p. 49). It would seem, then, that persons with AD will have increasing problems acting in a purposeful way on life's demands as the disease progresses. Such a finding would seem to prove the obvious but does stand as a verification of observations.

A similar emphasis on important and necessary daily tasks such as sanitation, laundering, transport, dress, and values was used for communication purposes by Holland (1987). Ten women in a nursing home with a diagnosis of dementia were used to test a short-term therapy program for language loss, which was complicating the lives of these patients. Their language problem was attributed to dementia and not reflective of sensory loss, stroke, health problems, lack of education, or bilingualism. The therapy lasted for six weeks, with measures taken before and after treatment.

Three treatment techniques were developed and applied to "connect past and present reality, and to elicit problem-solving and functional communication" (p. 62). Orientation for place was reflected in encouraging labeling of personal items, making notes and lists, maps, and floor plans of residences, and scheduling trips to unfamiliar places within the nursing home. Temporal orientation used clocks and calendars to supplement birthday books, checklists, menus, and church bulletins. Goal setting was a final activity in each session (p. 64).

Holland reports that the results were encouraging and followed up for several weeks after conclusion of the six weeks of therapy (p. 64). "Both longitudinal data and testing of related means on two standardized tests demonstrated treatment efficacy for both individual subjects and for the group as a whole" (p. 64). In addition, observations by staff and family supported a position that language behavior was improved and accessory behaviors (such as emotional reactions) were reduced.

There has long been a concern about identification of dementia earlier in the process than commonly done. As it is, most diagnoses are made only after some critical incident and a fairly long history of increasing complaints about behaviors. Morris, McKeel, Storandt, Rubin, Price, Grant, Ball, and Berg (1991) attempted to distinguish mild AD from normal aging, using psychometric testing, clinical observations, and pathological findings. "Very mild AD" was based on information supplied by informants, buttressed by judgments of experienced clinicians. Ten subjects met the criteria and were compared with 4 persons who tested for cognitive normality.

Morris et al. note that such features of AD as NFTs and SPs are found at autopsy in the brain cells of persons who have not been diagnosed as demented, who in fact seem to have lived cognitively normal lives (p. 469). To these authors, one problem with such a position is defining and determining "cognitively normal." After all, norms for those who live into old age are notably in short supply, with no real agreement on how to proceed with the task of gathering them. By contrast, of course, norms on infants and children are common and even used to direct the efforts of parents and family in rearing a child. In any event, Morris et al. propose that, among persons judged to have aged normally but having plaques and tangles, many represent cases of unrecognized, although obviously very mild, dementia.

Among their sample with AD they found some evidence of losses in memory, language, and psychomotor performance. They also found NFTs and both classic and diffuse SPs in this sample, but such exemplars were lacking in the normal controls. From their results they conclude tentatively

that performance on psychological tests by those with "very mild dementia" will overlap scores of older persons who are aging normally. Determining mild dementia cases depends on decline observed by caregiver and
professionals, and they are verifiable neuropathologically. In fact, even
while it is mild, there is already histopathological evidence of AD. They
also report that tangles correlate more highly with dementia severity than
does plaque density. Interestingly, they conclude as well that plaques and
tangles were not always found in their control subjects. Morris et al. later
make the comment that " 'benign senescence' may not be benign" (p. 476),
a thought to be considered carefully and fully.

One of their suggestions is a call for developing psychometric tests that
are more sensitive to the earliest signs of dementia. This accords with the
view in this book that the tests currently popular are restricted in their
coverage and not sufficiently robust for the job undertaken.

Relationships with Nerve Cell Degeneration

There are several studies in the literature that relate the presence of physical changes (NFTs, for example) with disorientation. In some instances
they are specific to a restricted area. An example is found in Foglia, Perini,
and Vanzulli (1991) where a woman showed, among other symptoms, a
confabulation with disorientation of time. A CT scan revealed a change in
the right thalamus, reflected in a loss of density that had occurred after the
healing of an ischemic lesion. Her condition, fortunately, improved over
time.

All such cases do not have such a happy ending, however. A case reported by Green, Goldstein, Mirra, Alazraki, Baxt, and Bakay (1995) presents a more disturbed picture. The 66-year-old man involved here was
diagnosed with Alzheimer's disease and demonstrated a slowly developing
apraxia. At the time of his diagnosis, he had already lost finger-hand coordination and coordinated movements of the left hand. Writing ability
was found to be severely impaired, and he was unable to determine the
shapes of objects by feeling. With time he showed increasing deficits in
memory and language. A biopsy of his right temporal lobe disclosed large
numbers of NFTs and plaques. Neurological exam suggested that the right
parietal lobe had damage interfering with contralateral communication and
cooperation.

Such individual case studies offer only suggestive clues about the relationships between brain regions and effects of deleterious changes. Yet with
the continued occurrence of such cases we are gathering an impressive notion that, with all its diversity, there is a consistent though ill-defined pattern of losses that exert themselves in the behavioral symptoms that we call
dementia. Finding the links between the diversities and defining the consis-

tencies among seemingly unrelated outcomes should assume a major role in research programs in the future.

The findings with a sample of 32 cases by Beer and Ulrich (1993) focus on a more discrete element of the process by examining the number of neuritic plaques with proportions of tissue affected. Their purpose was to determine the length of duration of dementia based upon the presence and proportion of plaques, without regard for such features as NFTs. "Length of duration" of AD was judged on two bases: time since the first low score (23/30 or less) on the Mini-Mental State Exam and time since the family first detected detrimental behavioral changes in the patient. The two did not accord and offer interesting bases for speculation.

Beer and Ulrich acknowledge that duration of dementia may seem less important than the severity of the condition for the patient, yet information gained about the evolution of the condition in duration is the central issue. "A comparison of the duration of the illness on the one side and the numerical density of the various plaque-types [early, classical, burned out] on the other side might eventually give more information about the evolution of AD" (p. 2).

There were equal numbers of men and women in the sample, with an average age of 82 at death (range = 62 to 102 years). The average length of duration of dementia was 33 months as determined by the Mini-Mental State. The range of severe symptoms was 1 to 148 months. Plaques were counted without regard to type (classic, for example). Brain weight correlated most strongly with the months of severe dementia, an expected result. However, neither the number of plaques nor the area of stained tissue showed significant correlations with total duration as described by those who had closest contact with the patient during the development of the disease.

Significant results for duration were found with brain weight, number of plaques per area unit, and the ratio of plaques to the total area of cortical tissue—but only if the onset of the disease was defined in terms of first finding of low Mini-Mental State score. And not one of the variables correlated significantly with the onset defined as the behavioral moment when the observer noted sufficient abnormality to consider a severe problem present. To Beer and Ulrich this difference can be explained by a cultural factor: Some families are more open to changes than others, so progression is greater in some instances and earlier in others when a problem is recognized.

Insofar as this explanation is true, it reflects a lack of education and understanding about AD and its expressions. Clearly, earlier education about "warning signs" and mental changes in higher faculties (such as recognizing and solving problems) could be valuable in this regard and might bring the results from tests like the Mini-Mental State more in line with observation. Yet there is a worrisome affair to the difference found: What is it that the Mini-Mental State does or contains or ignores that leads to significant differences in prediction? Or perhaps a better question would be: What is there in the mental makeup of professionals making diagnoses that predisposes to the acceptance of a test without independently demonstrated validity? What constitute the "seven mystical signs" that are answers to questions on the Mini-Mental State? Where is the evidence of brain functions, or mental capacities, that indicates that an individual is now mentally incompetent as compared with some prior time and/or some specified group?

In any event, Beer and Ulrich conclude that dementia leads to more and more plaques as long as the patient continues to live. Apparently, then, once plaques form, they are persistent or, even if they have a terminal life period, more plaques form faster than will disappear over a time unit.

There has been an increasing interest in the role of a protein called tau that acts to stabilize certain structures of a cell in normal conditions. In the case of dementia, the structures concerned are found in the axons of a neuron. When phosphorylated abnormally, however, tau becomes toxic to the cell in the sense that the axon does not transport normally, and the cell dies (Holzer, Holzapfel, Zedlick, Brückner, and Arendt, 1994). It is possible that such phosphorylated tau in different parts of the brain is a signal event in the development of neurofibrillary tangles. Holzer et al. have reported data from a comparison of abnormally phosphorylated tau proteins compared to normal tau and to the reaction of structures in areas of the brain where both are found. They further compared results to judgments of the severity of AD as measured by the Global Deterioration Scale of Primary Degenerative Dementia (p. 500).

Their sample consisted of 12 persons with AD and nine age-matched controls without evidence of mental impairment. These authors found that, in members of their control sample, normal tau deposition varied by brain region and by age, with a decrease in amount with increasing years. The same was true in the AD sample, with significant decreases in normal tau deposits in different brain regions. The higher the tau content, the more seriously affected were the cells, and there was a significant correlation with the accumulation of abnormally phosphorylated tau. They point out that the total amount of tau, both normal and abnormal, was greater for AD cases than for controls. This gave evidence that supported the view that such abnormal tau is a constant and early marker for detection of AD, particularly in the hippocampus and nucleus basalis of Meynert.

Holzer et al. offer support for the position that AD is a progressive disorder that spreads over an increasing number of cortical areas from its limbic and paralimbic base. It may be that different areas of the brain have different susceptibilities to the disease, although they urge caution in accepting such a premise. More important, the authors suggest that what is regarded as different "stages" of AD may more accurately reflect different forms of the disease instead. There is certainly evidence to support such a contention when individual cases are considered for particular defects and disturbances. Correlating such differences with the location of lesions in the brain would support a case for subtypes of AD and bring a closer relationship of behavior to physical signs. (See Jones and Richardson, 1990, for an extended argument for the premise that AD is actually a blanket term for several different diseases.)

Based upon their results, Holzer et al. note that there was a higher correlation of abnormal tau in the basal nucleus with severity of the disease than was true for any other brain region. Further, the abnormal tau correlated more strongly with neuropil threads than with NFTs and may be a central feature of the loss of synapses and subsequent neuronal disconnection.

As already noted, there are differences in normal tau levels in different regions of the brain, a finding that is related as well to the amount of abnormal tau in different regions of the brain in AD patients. One suggestion of this fact is that different brain regions are structurally organized for functions of that particular cortical area.

Within the framework of this hypothesis, it can be predicted that primary sensory areas should evince a higher degree of structural stability than limbic and paralimbic areas, which are related to processes as memory formation and which might, therefore, involve a higher degree of "event-related" synaptic plasticity throughout life. (Holzer et al., 1994, p. 512)

This attitude presents a possibility for relating behavior to brain function in a fashion not often considered before.

The role of amyloid protein in AD and its relationship to dementia have been examined more closely in recent studies. McKee, Kosik, and Kowall (1991) compared a sample of 34 dementia patients with 22 normal controls for NFTs and SPs along with beta amyloid. They point out the traditional relationship shown between NFTs and SPs in AD but note as well that there has been considerable argument over their relationship with clinical dementia. New techniques have indicated more refined, specific, and detailed components in NFTs and SPs than had been realized. One such component is dystrophic neurites, which are defined as "altered neuronal processes, i.e., axons, dendrites, and/or synaptic terminals" (p. 156). These occur in normally aging as well as demented patients, although there has not been a thorough examination of degree and influence. McKee et al. extended their research to include tau extent and distribution within their sample as well.

Within the group (n = 27) that they labeled as "classic AD," they found that β/A4 protein immunoreactivity and neuritic pathology were more frequently occurring and more severe than in a group of AD patients with a predominance of plaques. But they found no evidence that neurites or neurofibrillary tangles in the hippocampus was a reliable predictor of behavioral changes, even though those with functional problems could be clearly differentiated from normal controls so far as neocortical dystrophic neurites were concerned.

Controls showed a considerable number of cases (54%) with amyloid or SPs even though clinical dementia was not present. All AD patients showed the presence of the amyloid and plaques. Neuropil abnormalities were a strong feature of brain tissue in AD patients. Overall, they conclude that dystrophic neurites may occur earlier in the process of AD and be more related to clinical dementia than are NFTs.

Perhaps the most cogent, and certainly the safest, remark that may be made is that the physiological elements in AD and dementia are too complicated for conclusions at this point. One outcome is a move toward a more global view of the relationships between disease and effects, an enlightened and encouraging trend.

Other Conditions and Disorientation

Although the literature is limited, there have been some studies published that describe disorientation in other conditions than AD. Frequently these can only be cited as interesting rather than definitive since the depth of study necessary has not been completed. For example, McGilchrist, Wolkind, and Lishman (1994) reported a case study of a young woman with Tourette syndrome who had shown maternal neglect for her child. One of the associated features of her behavior was an inability to sense the passage of time, accompanied by a loss of skill to read or draw a clock face.

Similarly, Cutting and Silzer (1990) did an extended review of time sense in the literature on schizophrenics, concluding that two themes can be seen. First, schizophrenics share with brain-damaged patients the same kinds of time errors. These are expressed in a disordered sense of time passage, as in the Tourette patient above. Second, schizophrenics display a unique understanding of the meaning of time, expressed in a discontinuity of events related to time. Cutting and Silzer collected data on 350 schizophrenics, reporting substantial evidence of a disordered sense of time in their lives. The meaning of such findings for comparative purposes with AD patients who become increasingly disoriented is subject to question.

Closer to the topic here, Kawata, Suga, Oda, Hayashi, and Tanabe (1992) have presented a case study of a 60-year-old female with Creutzfeldt-Jakob disease. They report that "our results indicate that CT scans or the more sensitive MRI might reveal the white-matter changes characteristic for some types of CJD and may be helpful in detecting the disease process before death" (p. 851). This woman had displayed disorientation to time as well as impaired memory in her behavior. Their suggestion of the role of the brain white matter in CJD is applicable to AD as well, but the use of scans has not proved to be the tool that provides answers.

Directly to the point with Parkinson's patients is a study by Vriezen and Moscovitch (1990). They used a sample of 20 persons, 14 of whom were males and all with a diagnosis of Parkinson's but without the symptoms of dementia. A control group of elderly volunteers were matched with the patients on a vocabulary test as well as age and education. They found that the Parkinson's patients differed from the controls on a measure of temporal time order and an associative learning task. This difference they attribute to fronto-striatal disruption from lesions in the basal ganglia. Recognition was not affected, implying some regional differences in types of memory tested.

In a few cases there have been reports of cases where time disorientation without place disturbance (or vice versa) occurs. Heilman and Fisher (1974) described a 56-year-old woman with hyperlipidemia who suffered time disorientation but who had no problems with person or place. Kirchmeier, Lee, and Schwartz (1988) found a 68-year-old woman who preserved her orientation in time but was disoriented to space. They propose that this outcome may be due to a diffuse encephalopathy. What is needed, they say, is evaluation of nondominant cerebral hemispheric function. Few such studies have been reported to this date.

The period when time and space disorientation begins, and its progression from that point, is an issue yet to be resolved. Grewal (1995) grappled with this matter by testing time awareness at two degrees of severity of the AD. He used 35 patients, subdivided into two groups based on severity of their dementia. The Mini-Mental State was used to distinguish 16 patients who were mildly demented from 19 who were moderately demented. His time test consisted of two questions: How old are you? and Do you think that it is possible for you to live another 200 years? The groups differed not only on Mini-Mental State score but on his time test as well. The mild group made no errors on the two time questions, whereas the moderate group had a mean score of 0.9 (out of two). The two sets of scores on each person correlated .85, a significant outcome. Grewal proposes that his results suggest that mildly demented patients retain time awareness, which they begin to lose during the progression of the disease to a moderate level. Suggestive as these results are, they encourage a more refined design and testing to help pinpoint when and how time orientation declines.

TREATMENT OF DEMENTING CONDITIONS

Treatment is a concept of varied meanings. One approach is to intervene in some fashion in order to correct an ailment: surgery or medication or change in environment or diet or any of many other possibilities. In this case it is necessary to know the cause of the ailment before beginning the process. A second meaning involves intervention in order to stabilize a condition. This does not require knowing cause, even though that would certainly be an advantage. The ailment is still present in this case; the intervention prevents further progress and consequent worse effects. We see the presence of this approach in controlling a condition while requiring other action to bring amelioration, if any. A third possible meaning involves reversal for the sake of achieving cure. Here, there is a stabilization of the condition followed by intervention that brings change leading to improvement and eventual restoration to the original state.

The conditions that cause dementia, with its detrimental effects such as disorientation, are little understood. In most cases, the cause is unknown with the consequence that the options discussed above are only partially or tangentially achieved. Finding a cause is often a difficult, long-range, and expensive endeavor, dependent on political forces more than scientific acumen. Such "basic" research efforts may be uncoordinated and directed by personal preferences as much as by critical analysis of alternative options and probabilities. This is exemplified by the attempts to find the cause of Alzheimer's disease: some researchers are disposed to focus on a genetic cause, others on the nature and role of prions, still others on viruses or other biological hazards. To deny any of these would be foolish in our present state of ignorance, but the issue becomes then: how should resources be allocated and applied?

There is even more effort at finding some intervention that will accomplish one of the other approaches: stabilization or reversal. Such research also requires heavy investments of time, energy, genius, and money—particularly money. For this reason, the majority of research efforts in dealing with dementia and its effects comes from the pharmaceutical industry. The major emphasis is to develop medications that will control some effects so that a degree of relief for patient and caregiver is achieved. In this sense the treatments are intended to be symptomatic. They will not affect the progress of the disease, so their effects are transient. They may well be unsuitable for a sizable number of victims of the condition.

Such a view of treating dementia may be unacceptable to many. Certainly it would be a disservice to those patients who can benefit from an intervention, time and impetus limited though it may be, to deny the development and application of such treatment. Objectively, it seems reasonable, however, to question the service to the many others who cannot benefit from a particular treatment for a limited purpose. When comes their day in benefits?

There have been a number of reports of "treatment" or strategies for treatment in the literature, most often focusing on effectiveness of particular interventions. This reflects two elements at least: First, there is greater interest in finding more basic information that may yield wider benefits for more people; second, the so-called treatments currently available and used are not valid enough to warrant extensive study and reporting.

An example of this state of affairs is found in a discussion by Leonard (1990) on medical research strategies for Alzheimer's disease. He concentrates his effort on the neurochemical factors that are involved in the typical signs of Alzheimer's, the NFTs and plaques. Underlying these changes are the cholinergic changes that have now been studied for some years but with increasing efficiency and reliability. Leonard notes that the nucleus basalis of Meynert (NbM) and related areas show losses in cholinergic cell bodies for AD patients. But current evidence indicates that such losses are not the most probable cause, perhaps not even a leading cause, of the dementia that reflects behavioral changes. Indeed, he proposes that there is insufficient evidence that a specific neurotransmitter system is the responsible agent for the symptoms and outcomes of AD.

The most successful efforts at treatment that alters neurochemical balance are the several drugs developed using tacrine (tetrahydroamino acridine). Leonard notes that some amelioration of some symptoms has been found for some patients when such drugs are prescribed and supervised by physicians. The latter point is important since sometimes severe side effects, especially in liver function, have been found in patients who appeared suitable for the treatment. It seems to Leonard that neurotransmitter system changes are perhaps secondary to other more fundamental changes that are not yet clearly defined.

Nevertheless, Leonard assesses the efforts made with treatments using neurotransmitter alterations to achieve behavioral improvements in function as a means of suggesting treatment strategies. He considers, first, the cholinergic system. Here, four major attempts at treatment are reviewed. Acetylcholine precursor dosage has proven to be unsuccessful, but there has been modest success with efforts to release acetylcholine. It would seem profitable to use a direct-acting cholinomimetic drug, but Leonard reports that, by the time of his article, the results have been disappointing. Finally, medications that inhibit acetylcholinesterase (such as physostigmine) would seem profitable in the sense of permitting present acetylcholine efforts to act more beneficially. Still an active approach in the current drugs being prescribed, the results have been modest and limited to a selected portion of the Alzheimer's population. Until something better appears, it would seem that this approach will continue since pharmaceutical firms have invested heavily in the procedure and will continue its practice.

A second area of research surveyed by Leonard looks at biogenic amines, compounds that can enhance noradrenergic or serotonergic transmission. Unfortunately, the results have been disappointing. Some improvement in emotional quality of AD patients has been found with antidepressants, but these have no effect on the course or severity of the dementia resulting from the disease process.

Leonard also surveys what he labels "novel approaches." Somewhat successful with animals, neuropeptides (such as are found in ACTH [adrenocorticotropic hormone], vasopressin, beta endorphin, and the like) do not produce benefits to humans with AD. Still, efforts continue to develop drugs that will enhance the cognition still available to patients. The mechanism believed to operate in this procedure is some release of acetylcholine, the neurotransmitter most often cited as deficient in AD.

Some scientists believe that degeneration of the cholinergic neurons in the forebrain results from the insufficiency of nerve growth factors (NGFs). Evidence indicates no particular losses in the concentrations of NGF during the progression of Alzheimer's, but there is a case to be made that NGFs may prevent premature degeneration of neurons. The difficulty is finding a means whereby synthesis of NGFs can be directed to brain regions (such as the hippocampus) in the early stages of AD—assuming that one can identify an early stage in the first place.

Some drugs have been touted as working to improve the integration necessary to mental performance. Called "nootropic," such a drug would enhance memory and learning, allow better communication between the hemispheres, and aid resistance of the brain to destructive forces yet produce no adverse effects on the peripheral system nor introduce sedation, neuroleptic or analgesic activity. Again, the process involved is an increase in release of acetylcholine, particularly in the hippocampus. An example of such a drug is Hydergine, which Leonard cites favorably for its effects on social functioning but faults for its inability to improve memory and cognition. The further point is made by him that there is little or no consideration of the alterations in drug effects among aging persons in the research conducted with such drugs. This brings us back to an earlier issue: What is the norm for an aging brain (or any of the rest of the body for that matter)?

Leonard concludes that "the discovery of the defect in the forebrain cholinergic system has led to a treatment strategy which, though limited so far in its clinical value, raises the prospect of rational drug development" (p. 665). Although progress has been made in some respects since the publication of his article, matters remain essentially as they were. The major difference is that we have more drugs approved by the Food and Drug Administration. These follow the same basic modality developed with the first such agent: inhibit the role of acetylcholinesterase in order to maximize utilization of acetylcholine present in the brain of the patient. This should assist in relieving short-term memory problems, the most frequently cited complaint by patients and caregivers. Such relief is to be commended, but its success has been limited to intervention early in the disease process and thus is time limited. Side effects have restricted its benefit to some patients, and those with more advanced degrees of dementia do not benefit much if at all with the use of the drugs.

Perhaps a final quote that demonstrates the status of a realistic position about the relationship between brain status and dementia will serve as a cautionary note.

Our data suggests that markers indicative of cytoskeletal changes, e.g., NFT and PHF protein accumulation, correlate well with dementia even in a mixed sample of causes of dementia and that with univariate analysis these structural changes are a better correlate of dementia than are declines in synaptic protein immunoreactivity. (Dickson, Crystal, Bevona, Honer, Vincent, and Davies, 1995, p. 296)

This statement is not quoted so much to be discouraging (although it is typical enough to suggest such an attitude) as it is to encourage an open attitude to more innovative and global approaches to research and model-building about dementia.

CHAPTER 10

Restructuring Past, Present, and Future

Dementia is a terrifying, destructive process: It leaves the physical body basically untouched (although obviously other debilitating, even lethal, conditions may occur) while the brain is systematically, even if slowly, destroyed. What one observes as a result is the mental dissolution of a once-capable individual. The fact that it devastates the mental qualities while the physical self is preserved is difficult for many people to understand and accept. After all, it flies in the face of "illness" as it has been and is still conceived, diagnosed, and treated.

Dementia may even go unnoticed by those who have only a transient contact with a patient. The superficiality of many of our social contacts makes it easier for a casual observer to question any inference that something is wrong. After all, the so-called patient can be polite, answers questions such as "How are you?" with a sensible response, be well-dressed (by the caregiver perhaps), unobtrusive, even obsequious. "What is wrong with such a mannerly presentation?" the uninformed may think.

Only as one begins to observe more closely and in greater depth does an appreciation for the behavioral destructiveness associated with dementia occur. One may begin to notice the inseparability of patient and caregiver, the subtle but consistent appeal to the caregiver for answers to some questions asked of the patient, the inability to comprehend and answer many questions that probe a fund of information normally available, the inconsistencies in comments, the acquiescence with almost any statement made by the observer. Then there comes some inkling of the extent and depth of dementia's presence and ravages. Then, also, may begin an understanding of the need for some means to understand the condition and find means for intervention.

The first step in such a process requires explication of the general components needing identification and study. There may be at the same time a strategy developed that will explore and exemplify the specific elements that constitute the general components. This stance was considered at the end of Chapter 6 with a brief argument for three related but distinct approaches to study of dementia.

THE STUDY OF DEMENTIA

There is a need to explore and find nomothetic generalizations in order to explain dementia as a process. Models must be constructed and hypotheses generated to ensure as scientific an explanation as possible. That task lies far ahead, perhaps, but there are beginnings already and avenues where data exist congruent with the purpose.

The first possibility, and one already rich with potential as demonstrated in Part II of this book, is the experimental approach begun by Wundt and Ebbinghaus and having a consistent and expanding history ever since. Essentially, in research on dementia as well as other psychological phenomena, this approach represents a means-to-end method. The procedure involves a paradigm, designed to allow an answer to an (often) limited question. There is no reference to nomothetic outcomes, usually not intended as a purpose of the study. The technique involves basically a correlational approach, although more sophisticated statistics may be used.

Examples of such studies, relating to dementia and orientation/disorientation, can be found in various fields: economics and work situations (see Amyx and Mowen, 1995; Verma, 1992); gender studies (Bouffard, Bastin, and Lapierre, 1996); psychological effects (Bascue and Lawrence, 1977; Beiser and Hyman, 1997); planning and actions (Buehler, Griffin, and Ross, 1994; Zimbardo, Keough, and Boyd, 1997); estimations (Carrillo de la Peña and Luengo, 1994; Sawyer, Myers, and Huser, 1994; Shaw and Aggleton, 1994); social situations (Flaherty, 1991; Shmotkin, 1991; Venable and Mitchell, 1991); and the listings and citations could be continued at considerable length. Similar analysis could be applied to the many studies of brain components and areas described in the literature as well.

Such studies are invaluable assets to the particular and specific aspects of the investigation and may hold value for a more general meaning if differences in sampling, measures used, and the like, can be ameliorated or controlled. As is, of course, this outcome is not likely or recommended. There needs to be a classification system devised that does provide some measure of stability for the differences in procedures so that outcomes may be compared for appropriate generalizations. This implies a series of master's theses and doctoral dissertations, conducted under conditions that will avoid the pitfalls already present in the type of studies to be consolidated. The principal difficulty in utilizing such reports at present is that they reflect a "symptomatic" approach since only an effect is studied and the cause left undisclosed. This makes it impossible to draw comparisons and conclusions for the general case.

A second model moves into a conceptualization of basic elements of psychological phenomena. It is a refinement of Model I in that studies are done within a context of overlapping and extended relationships toward an outcome of demonstrating the relevance of concepts. Examples of such an approach include the work of Block (1974, 1989, 1996) and that of Zakay (1993a, 1993b) and his associates (Zakay and Block, 1997; Zakay et al., 1994), among others.

Such studies represent an improvement over the one-shot, focused, and individual reports. But they suffer a lack of relation to a more general picture. Thus, they provide pieces to a mosaic that amplifies their roles. Unfortunately, however, we do not know just where they should fit in the complete picture. And without the nomothetic quality, they remain restricted in their contribution.

The third model is a deductive proposal of essential and testable elements of psychological phenomena. It follows the concepts explicated by Danziger (1990) and should be based upon a theory derived from research and observation, allowing a testing of hypotheses to yield validity for its components. This means that there must be a blending of research, test, and observational data gathered on individuals and most often published as case studies.

An apt example is found in Weiner (1996, pp. 34–35). He describes a 51-year-old woman who had shown less initiative and greater memory loss over the past 5 years. She also showed inappropriate behavior, had difficulty understanding verbal communication, and used the same label for different objects. Examination yielded no evidence of emotional disturbance or head injuries and no history of significant illness. Her symptoms had been noted in other family members.

Her mental status was mixed. While she was alert and cooperative, knew the year and month, she could not name the day, date, or season. She also knew where she lived, including city and state, but could not repeat names of objects or subtract serially. Neither could she name a watch or a pencil or follow a three-part command.

A neurological exam was normal. Intellectually, she scored a Wechsler Adult Intelligence Scale verbal IQ of 53, performance IQ of 58, and full-scale IQ of 52. She had great difficulty understanding directions and often said she did not know the answer to items on the test. Overall, neuropsychological examination indicated diffuse brain dysfunction, perhaps particularly severe in the left and anterior lobes. Both computerized tomography and magnetic resonance imaging gave evidence of atrophy. Blood tests were normal, but there was reduced blood flow in the frontal lobes despite adequate vascular blood reserves. Her death in three years was followed with an autopsy. The diagnosis from this procedure was multiple systems atrophy due to deterioration of the brain stem and severe loss of neurons in the cortex.

Such a study offers the possibility to catalog both physical and behavioral stigmata, including specific brain damage identified at autopsy. With a large number of such complete reports, systematic detailing of elements will disclose similarities and differences among individuals and, at the same time, allow a more complete picture of the details of dementia as a general state.

In such cases there is the reporting of medical and psychological data that give a holistic picture of a patient and permit the drawing of specific characteristics that may be essential parts of a complete model. Obviously, many such reports are necessary and, fortunately, are receiving more attention in the literature. Examples include Weiner (1996, pp. 35–36, 36–37), Paulman, Koss, and MacInnes (1996, p. 226), and Shomaker (1989). A similar approach is found in Edwards (1994, pp. 9–17), including an analysis of behaviors observed and reported.

The impetus for detailed case studies had its start with Alois Alzheimer (1907) with his behavioral, physical, and histological description of a 51-year-old woman. With the autopsy he performed, which displayed neurofibrillary tangles and senile plaques, noted by him for the first time, the door opened to a "new" condition.

Using the translation provided by Jarvik and Greenson (1987), several excerpts provide the detail that later case studies would emulate. For our purposes, we can examine first the history of problems reported by her husband.

Initially, there was a developing "suspiciousness of her husband," closely followed by "rapidly increasing memory impairment" and spatial disorientation, even within her own home. She also personalized feelings, dragging "objects here and there and hid them" and "believing that people were out to murder her, started to scream loudly." By the time she came to the attention of Alzheimer she had become "completely disoriented to time and place." Several examples of such behavior are cited by Alzheimer, followed by personality changes. At times she displayed delirium and auditory hallucinations.

Examination of this patient was trying at best and required great patience and persistence by Alzheimer and the staff at the institution in Frankfurt. However, over time a clinical evaluation was possible, leading to both psychological and physical findings. It was determined that her powers of memory were severely limited. (The term used by Alzheimer was *Merkfähigkeit*, translated as "the ability to encode information" by Jarvik and Greenson.) What would be helpful would be information on her conduct before the disease began its process. For example, how did she read and speak before she became ill?

Physically Alzheimer reports that her reactions were normal. And this level was relatively maintained for the remaining 4.5 years of her life. At the time of death, when she was 55, she was "totally dulled, lying in bed with legs drawn up, incontinent, and, despite all care, developed decubiti."

An autopsy was performed and produced the findings that later led to the condition being labeled Alzheimer's disease. There was consistent atrophy throughout the brain, with arteriosclerosis in the larger cerebral passages. What was even more striking were "peculiar changes of the neurofibrils." Alzheimer noted their appearance as unusually thick and with an unusual ability to accept staining. In further views, even more fibrils were found, with similar appearances. Eventually, the fibrils were so numerous that they collected into bundles. At last, the nucleus and cell itself had fallen apart so that the only evidence of what had once been a ganglion cell was a tangled bundle of fibrils. This represents the classic portrayal of neurofibrillary tangles, along with plaques, the principal features for a diagnosis of Alzheimer's disease.

The changes in the fibrils, Alzheimer reports, would seem to be accounted for by the "storage of a pathologic metabolic product in the ganglion cell." The need for research into this issue is called for by him. In this particular brain, Alzheimer found that one-fourth to one-third of all ganglion cells in the cortex were adversely affected, accompanied by numerous losses of cells in the upper cell layers. He also reported finding a peculiar substance in cells of the cortex.

Alzheimer makes his case for his findings to suggest a new disease process. He supports this by pointing out that a number of new disease processes had been identified in the period before this article (that is, before 1907). He urges that efforts not be made to force unusual processes into the accepted lexicon. Histologically examinations can disclose the characteristics of unusual conditions and thereby establish refined and more complete disease categories. Alzheimer was justified in just a few years when Kraepelin described the condition in the leading textbook of psychiatry of the time and labeled it Alzheimer's disease.

Using such complete case studies plus the observations of caregivers and patients themselves (as in Weiner, 1996, p. xix), a more complete picture of the diverse ways of debilitation in dementia may be cataloged, compared and contrasted. The complexity may then be reduced by locating similarities and disparities that must be accounted for. The result, eventually, would be a model to which research findings may be applied for refinement and elaboration. A final, but essential, goal will be the development of interventions.

TIME AND DEMENTIA

The tradition has been established in psychology to artificially segment time into three periods: present, past, and future. This has nothing to do with the nature of time itself, only with the focus of study: the brain and understanding of its function. Emphasis has been placed on basic processes and their relation to brain areas as a means to understand behavior. Nowhere is this more evident than in the explanations of selection for responding to some stimulation in the present while ignoring others.

At any moment in time the human is bombarded with untold numbers of stimuli—and the opportunity to respond with whatever possible responses are available in the individual armamentarium. Some of these are innate and unlearned, others are learned from experience, and still others are motivational. Whatever their source, they are means to adjust to the environmental demands imposed in the process of remaining alive.

The question arises: How does the brain decide which stimuli must be responded to, which should be but are not essential, and which may be ignored safely? The answer to this question is unknown at present. But the brain areas involved have been identified and incorporated into a model of consciousness that is the domain of cognitive psychology. So between the *structure* of afferent admission and selection to the *perception* of environmental accommodation lies an answer to our question.

The brain stem, part of the old brain, is the beginning point. There, in the central portion of the brain stem from the midbrain to the medulla, is found the reticular formation. Virtually every sensory system feeds input, both internal and external, which can then be redirected to other areas of the nervous system, depending on complexity or need for security. Within the reticular formation there have been several different functions identified: control of heart rate and respiration, motor functions (including muscle tone), consciousness (by access to the thalamus and cerebral cortex), and even cerebellar function. There may yet be other functions involving this old but significant formation.

More important to this book is the fact that stimulation may be random but is interpreted systematically even at an elementary level. Channeled from that base to the limbic system and beyond to the cerebral cortex, we begin to see how the brain operates to ensure that our security is maintained by alerting us to dangers as well as perpetuating pleasure and well-being and even lending the necessary stimuli to augment and support planning, problem solving, use of past responses, and anticipation of a future.

All this occurs in the ubiquitous Present. There can be no meaning to a past nor reference to a future unless the Present furnishes the constituent elements. Reality consists of our total of experiences and their interpretation on a moment-to-moment basis. In a perfect world, of course, there should be a balance between the Present and both the Past and Future that is equally inclusive of all elements. But that arrangement seems unlikely to ever occur given the individual differences that are found in brain function.

For that reason, most psychologists acknowledge an imbalance in the components making up our individual time relations. The reasons for such imbalances are unknown, although age differences are most often cited. In any event, the literature describes preferential expressions of time relations, depending on characteristics unrelated to time. Thus, some persons will be *primarily* present-centered in their adjustment to the environment and perception of reality. Still others will be past-oriented in their adaptations. And at least a few will prefer to accommodate to the future in most of their adaptations.

In fact, it is probable that most of us are not so dependent in our behavior as such characteristics would indicate, instead opting for the relationship that best serves our drives, needs, and preferences of the moment. One may momentarily concentrate on the present but continue to extract from the past what is relevant and perhaps accede to the future in final actions. Or one may dwell in the past at times, yet still accommodate to the demands of the present and even extrapolate to future behaviors. At another time, the future may present the challenge that stimulates contemplation and action, whereas the past becomes a reservoir of potential responses influenced by the stimuli of present events. Such possibilities deserve research to judge their meaning, weight, and worth in understanding what time awareness means to human behavior.

The measurement of time has become a refined technique. The meaning of time is still an issue for debate. In Chapter 1, the point was made that "present time" must be distinguished from "past time" and "future time"; otherwise, the present lacks any meaning beyond the reaction to immediate stimuli (a level common to the animal world). Basically, "present" is transitory, so instantaneous as to be almost nonexistent. This assures importance and finiteness. The meaning of Present (the use of the upper-case letter identifies the concept as used in this theoretical proposal) rests in its comparison to the Past (what stimuli were responded to and recorded from previous "presents") and to the Future (what may be). The Past becomes our permanent record of experience, finite in quality and effect, serving as a record for all succeeding events. The Past is our only and personal reality, often congruent with that of others but sometimes not. As our reality, the Past also serves as the basis for anticipated Futures, expectations prejudiced by the mind's cataloging of the Past. Infinite in nature, the Future still serves as a limiting factor to perceptions of the nature of Presents allowed mentally.

One may agree or disagree with the definitions offered above. Where agreement is plausible, a further problem arises. How may one depict a Present, Past and Future to give them dimensionality verifying their validity and communicating their nature? The difficulty in doing so involves our ability to visualize beyond three-dimensional space, sometimes even restricted to two dimensions (Tufte, 1990). When we add a fourth dimension, called "time," the task is above present mental capabilities. That, however, will not prevent an attempt in this book.

Figure 10.1
Theoretical Conception of the Present

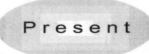

The search for a solution is certainly not unique to this volume. Gould and Shearer (1999–2000, pp. 43–44) both defined the problem and suggested a solution. They describe what they call a "pseudo-postcard" by Marcel Duchamp, an attempt to visualize in four dimensions when limited to the three spatial ones. They quote him as questioning, "What is the meaning of this word 4th dimension since it does not have either tactile or sensorial correspondence as do the 1st, 2nd, and 3rd dimensions?" The solution to this conundrum, Gould and Shearer propose, is to represent the time dimension *spatially* as a fourth axis at right angles to those of length, height, and depth. Admittedly, this axis cannot be drawn in three-dimensional space, but the concept merits consideration. *Mentally*, we may succeed in "seeing" the possibility and promise for such a conception. Eventually, that mental presentation will become actual (Greene, 1999, pp. 49–50).

In an experimental, still theoretical vein, Jason Brown (1990, p. 147) portrayed his concept of the "absolute Now" in terms of a triangle viewed from above. Since he believes that duration is not longitudinal but one of height, the succeeding Nows are associated with a change in height of the preceding ones, leading to differences that are phenomenal in nature. Brown, indeed, states, "The idea that duration extends over a limited time, like the sum of a succession of moments, is a confusion of the spatial with the temporal" (p. 146).

Such disparate attempts at explanation and explication encourage only another attempt, the one of this book. Here, an ellipse (Figure 10.1) is used to signify a moment in time during which multiple stimuli impinge on the organism. The shape used is merely a convenience and does not imply any particular relationship to a moment in time. Unfortunately, also, such a graphic is two-dimensional, displaying only length and height. Shading has been introduced to create the illusion of depth, thereby making it possible to visualize the three dimensions. Since a Present is succeeded instantly by another Present, there must be a conceptualization of a continuous process. That may take the Newtonian form of the "arrow of time" and thus be presented as a linear succession. However, time is not influenced by directionality: It may, theoretically, move in *any* direction: forward, backward, even sideways. You may recall that Hawking (1996, pp. 184–195) considered this matter and posited three options, logically reducing them to a

Figure 10.2
Theoretical Conception of a Succession of "Presents"

Figure 10.3
Theoretical Conception of the Relationship of Present and Past

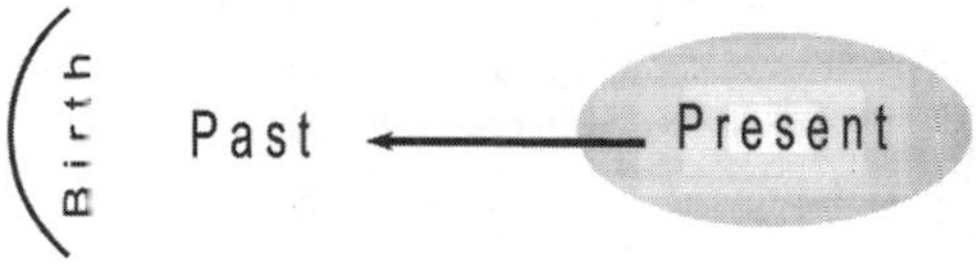

single direction. If he is right, that does not mean that the Newtonian version is the only possible one. It is possible that time continues to move forward even as overlap occurs in some Presents.

This possibility is the focus in Figure 10.2. Several ellipses are displayed, with an overlap in two cases. The overlap signifies some conditions compatible in restricted features: environmental, where experience reoccurred in a previous site; psychological, where experience reoccurred in a mental state; social, where experience reoccurred in a social relationship. The overlap, however, does not mean that time has changed direction since all such examples will be *spatial*. Each is new and independent and so without any real contact. Only as they are assigned to the past and recorded in the mind is there a basis to interpret the experiences as related. (See Greene, 1999, pp. 204–205, for a similar discussion.)

This brings us to the Past (Figure 10.3), our basis for establishing personal reality. Potentially, the past is an accumulation of experiences beginning at least at birth and continuing into each succeeding Present. The process permits the establishment of a fund of experiences, by some process stored in the brain and available for recall in some form or as needed to interpret a given Present and/or predict a potential Future. There is a joker in the process, however, since only an unknown portion of stimulation in a given Present will be accommodated, and only an unknown portion of those will be stored in the brain. Those experiences stored are not necessarily faithful to their original form, and there may be alterations even then over time. This may be due to the influence of succeeding Presents that influence the nature of the stored experience, some personal factor such as emotional context that assumes importance to the person, or to some adaptation by the brain itself. With time, also, alterations in cell integrity

Figure 10.4
Theoretical Conception of the Relationship of Present, Past, and Future

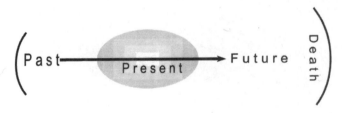

(and consequent brain plasticity) may exert an influence. Certainly nerve cell destruction must be accorded a major role in our ability to utilize in some form the experiences stored in our past. Within such caveats, the construction of a personal reality is available to permit the individual to adapt, in the fullest meaning of that concept, to the forces, stresses, opportunities, and pleasures of life.

The Future (Figure 10.4) is anticipatory, accommodating to the potential in our Past and the succession of Presents that contain information useful to the Past in making predictions. Thus, the Future must include the Past and be extrapolated to the remainder of life. Many predictions are relatively safe, easy, and accurate. For example, if I must be at work at 9:00 A.M., and I have been employed in the setting for several years, it is no dangerous act to assume that I must wake up at a certain time in order to complete chores (such as breakfast, bathing, driving) to arrive on time. On some days I may get a shock because something goes wrong, but generally I will be successful without incident.

The most accurate predictions about the Future probably occur for more immediate circumstances in the Present, that is, short-term prediction. The further in the Future the predicted outcome, the more likely one is to be inaccurate. Caution must be exercised. (Some research supports this view, but it is not unanimous.) Long-range prediction is, nevertheless, a common feature of human behavior. It is in this context that the so-called executive functions of the mind operate. We show evidence of an ability to plan, to create, to solve problems, to seek out or avoid situations, and many other future-oriented behaviors. Accuracy may differ from one person to another and even for the same person from one Present to another.

Within the context of Present, Past and Future, we behave in respect to our orientation in time and space. Table 10.1 depicts the relationships between these orientations and the physical and mental activities demonstrated experimentally and/or as conceptualized.

The Present, in its evanescent and transitory phase, focuses on discrimination among the multitude of stimuli impinging on the organism at any moment. There must result some decision about a response/no response, followed by a choice of response if the decision is positive. In this schema,

Table 10.1
Time Orientation and Behavior

Time Orientation	Physical/Mental Abilities Involved
Present	1. Discrimination of stimuli and decision making about responding
	2. Transmittal to storage of experiences
	3. Analysis of utility of responses
Past	1. Storage and retrieval
	2. Analysis of stored experiences for current behavior
	3. Application of stored responses to decision making
	4. Use of executive functions based on experiences
	5. Making available experiences for use in future time orientation
Future	1. Tapping of executive functions
	a. Seeing cause and effect
	b. Planning
	c. Problem solving
	d. Realizing means to ends
	e. Analyzing experiences
	f. Rationality and reasoning (e.g., among alternatives)
	g. Decision making
	h. Evaluation (e.g., of concepts and ideas)

for the human, experiences stored in the Past may be evaluated for a choice. If the Present experience has no history (that is, is novel), the organism must react in some protective manner until more evidence is available. In large measure, then, this behavioral level is used as a means to ensure security in the interest of continued well-being. At this level, the human equates with the animal's "living in an eternal Present."

Following a reaction, the behavior is transmitted for storage of an experience, either at a short-term or long-term memory level. The effort transcends, but still includes, the Present. This permits a form of analysis of utility of a given response that may result in a directing to either short-term (and therefore expendable) memory or a long-term (and therefore suitable for future experiences) memory storage.

There are considerable data already available in the literature and some norms that describe temporal orientation in Present-encountered situations. Age norms, particularly, have been published for various experimental tasks, reflecting this level of orientation. An example would be the many

Figure 10.5
Influence of Limbic System Losses in Normal Aging

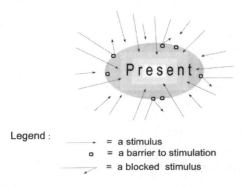

Legend :

→ = a stimulus

◻ = a barrier to stimulation

↗ = a blocked stimulus

studies designed to test reaction time. Instructions for responding are given in a simple ("Press the key when the red light goes on") paradigm and leads to several trials that permit the storage of experiences and greater accuracy as a result with practice. The task may be extended to increase complexity both in stimulus and response variables.

More complex behaviors may be sampled in the Present orientation mode as well. An example could be accepting or declining an invitation to have dinner at the home of an acquaintance. Of course, if one is an inveterate eater, the decision may reduce to what is today called a "no-brainer." But for a more sophisticated being, there must be some analysis and evaluation. This would mean a rapid scanning of experiences stored in the Past (perhaps at the level of nanoseconds?) before deciding and replying. "Is that evening free or is another engagement already planned?" "Are these people pleasant to be with for an entire evening?" Maybe even, "Do they serve good drinks, hors d'oeuvres, and entrees?" Whatever can assist the Present in answering yes or no may come into play. If the time is too short, some important factor may not be screened. That will require re-evaluation and perhaps embarrassment.

Figures 10.3 and 10.5 present graphics that illustrate parts of this concept model. A Past orientation requires the implementation and extension of the Presents that contribute to a fund for behavior. Basic is the storage needed to provide a source or sources for retrieval. Both storage and retrieval require an order that allows analysis; storage and retrieval are not arbitrary, or they will be less than trustworthy (although this may be an analog for many of the "unreasonable" actions found in dementia patients). In the "normal" brain, sufficient order is found to preclude errors in all but a few cases. It is possible, for example, that experience is stored in one's brain in an orderly fashion but that a Present occurs where that order seems inappropriate. It may even be that the stored order bears so little relation to

Figure 10.6
Influence of "Early" Dementia on Present and Past

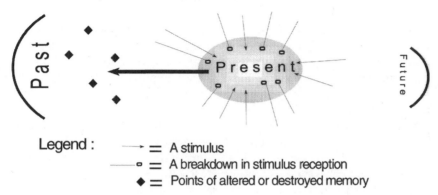

Legend :   ——→ = A stimulus
            —— ◦ = A breakdown in stimulus reception
              ◆ = Points of altered or destroyed memory

that demanded that the person will not realize the connection. Under ideal conditions, the individual will become aware of the apparent discrepancy that was not seen as usable. Then reordering becomes a possibility and will help responding in future similar settings. Perhaps this is saying nothing more than that the Past may be a strong component in generalization.

The Past includes, then, a potential for analyzing stored responses for current behavior, for those Presents where the storage is pertinent. This suggests that applications of stored responses to decision making are a role of a Past orientation. This can be conceived as occurring at any level of Presents but extended to any level of storage and retrieval in the Past. If this is true, then those higher-order mental activities called "executive functions" must begin in the person's Past, evolve at least partially, and be passed on at an appropriate time to Future time orientation. There, they will be developed to a more complete and precise degree, applied as the individual finds a need for them. The applications may vary in pertinence and precision, depending on both the fund of experience and the intellectual competencies of the person.

There are few data on these roles for the Past, and what is accepted currently is observational, and often idiosyncratic, at best. No norms have been developed as a result. Figures 10.3 and 10.4 depict basic relationships, whereas Figure 10.6 portrays some elements where dementia is present.

A Future time orientation makes special demands on the brain since it involves executive functions in coordination with intellect. As depicted in Table 10.1, the results, when successful, involve a number of higher-order behaviors. Planning is a requisite and employs data from the storage in the Past in order to realize cause-and-effect relationships. These must lead to conclusions that are either accurate and useful or inaccurate and deleterious to behavioral competence.

As the process, regardless of outcome, continues, there must come a selection of means to accomplish ends that are desired. This is a part of a problem-solving technique that may be learned but that is not eventuated by such. Problem solving in its highest form requires both an acquisitive and inquisitive mind, intellectually capable of analyzing experience, deducing ideals from facts, and applying the result to experiences both real and imagined. Rationality and reasoning are employed so that alternatives are considered as possible problem solutions. There evolves an interaction that will lead to a decision. The more complex (novel and original) and the more esoteric (abstract and imaginative), the greater the need for intellectual competence combined with manifold experiences relevant to the task. What brings about such a level of mental behavior has not yet been disclosed. On a physical level, however, it may consist of number of dendrites in order to encompass more experience, accompanied by integrity in neuronal status and function. On the intellectual level, the components may consist of such elements as curiosity, speculative willingness, and both deductive and inductive competence. The end result leads to an evaluation to test concepts, ideas, and actions that result, carried out in either a mental or expressive manner. Typically, both should appear over time. An example of such a combination of qualities (both physical and intellectual) was found in Albert Einstein (Clark, 1984), whose mental competencies outpaced his social qualities. In other words, the product and the mind that produces it may not fit the social model that is sought in current societies.

The role of emotion is important to Present, Past, and Future time orientation. There can be positive effects when emotional states assist awareness and persistence. If too strong or too weak, the search for appropriate behavior in each orientation is apt to be inconsistent or inappropriate. All efforts are a part of consciousness even when there is no awareness of the fact. What Ferris (1992) calls "unconscious" (pp. 73–74) in his discussion of mind and what Greenfield (1995) describes as "parallel processing" (pp. 32–34) by the brain may be examples of rumination. By this, I mean mental behavior that has not yet reached the level necessary for the outcome to be palpably conscious. Of course, some psychologists might respond, "Oh, you mean an 'aha' experience." Whatever the answer may finally be, Future time orientation requires some employment of executive functions.

Figure 10.4 reflects the direction of relationships among time orientation dimensions, whereas Figures 10.6 and 10.7 reflect diminution of Future time orientation when dementia is present. There are few data, observational and inferential when reported, and no norms for this dimension.

In summary, each form of time orientation must be conceived as attempts by a conscious brain to put experience to work in order to deal effectively with the environment.

Figure 10.7
Influence of "Late" Dementia on Present and Past

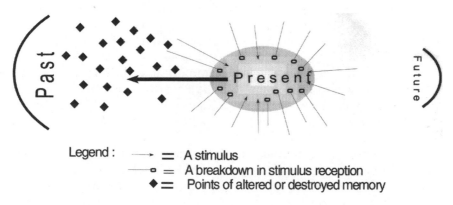

Legend :   ⟶ = A stimulus
           ⟶◦ = A breakdown in stimulus reception
           ◆ = Points of altered or destroyed memory

DISORIENTATION IN TIME

Departures from the "ideal" or complete patterns of time relation are found throughout life but increasingly with age. Particularly is this true with the Present, where changes in cell integrity in the hippocampus lead to problems with short-term memory even in the healthy aging. The problems must be confounded in dementia where slowly accumulating debilitation eventually leads to the recognition that the person is having difficulty in adapting to daily demands. It would seem probable (a hypothesis that needs investigation) that stimulation correlated with danger to security must exercise an increasing threat even before executive functions are affected. Since we have no measures that will identify and quantify such changes, this issue must remain at the theoretical level for the present.

Yet there are the many evidences that short-term memory begins to suffer with age and leads to more severe effects than minor forgetfulness in the demented. In some ways the balance of time relations must reflect such effects beginning in early dementia. Figure 10.5 projects a theoretical indication of such a set of changes. Notable is the need for some breakdowns to be occurring in the Present in such cases, breakdowns that cannot be reversed and will accumulate as the disease progresses. Even the Past must begin to show functional decline, despite the stereotype that the past remains intact and increasingly utilized in Alzheimer's and other causes of dementia. More profoundly (and perhaps a proper point of first attack) should be the adverse effects on future orientation. If this proposal is proper, the dementia patient should show identifiable impact on both amount and quality of Future thought projections.

The ways to measure such changes are more numerous than could be covered in this book, but there are some suggestions of what might be useful. For example, an examiner could supply the individual (or potential patient) with the current correct day of the week. This could then be followed by asking what tomorrow will be. An extrapolation would suggest that today is some other than the correct one, then ask what the following day should be. More complex questions, involving executive functions, might be included in such an examination as well. For example, an examiner may ask: What route do you follow to get to the grocery store? Which medications do you take in the morning and which in the evening? (As dementia progresses, questions should be more focused and less complex.) Data would not only test the adequacy of the time balance theory proposed here but, if the model holds, lead to earlier identification of possible dementia in the future.

Where dementia has been identified, the effects on the time balance for the person become more apparent and more easily objectified. Figure 10.6 is intended to indicate the extent of gaps in present orientation as well as past. It should be noted that, with advancing dementia, future projection may well reduce to little or none as this degree of debilitation is reached. Again, such a proposal is subject to test and verification or rejection.

In late dementia orientation has become almost complete disorientation, with its increasing dependence on another to assure the common adaptations necessary to social functioning. In Figure 10.7 the Present contains many barriers, indicating that few, if any, stimuli from the environment will be apprehended and responded to by the patient. These barriers are reflections of cellular change in the limbic system, initially, with the disease process spreading effects to other areas of the brain. As depicted, their nature is solely to reflect an interference in stimulation receptivity in the Present. It may still be possible that emotional behavior may be aroused as the equilibrium of the patient is disturbed, but this should be due to a loss in degree in the dependency relationship rather than directly related to danger signs in the environment. This outcome is easily recognized if the patient, particularly in a strange place, is left alone by the caregiver even with a sympathetic third person.

Once dementia has progressed to such a significant degree, even though the physical state of the patient may be healthy, the inability to recognize and deal with a Present leads to marked decline on use of Past memories. These are likely to be selective and rehearsed over and over. Their accuracy cannot always be determined, but that is probably less important than the fact that they remain the only link of the patient of today with the adequately functioning adult of past years. The Future now has become meaningless so far as time awareness is concerned.

THE EFFECTS OF DISORIENTATION

The meaning of Past, Present, and Future among healthy adults remains an obscure issue, as illustrated by the above section. Among demented patients there is somewhat more relevant evidence (particularly from case studies) but no greater comprehension since models and systems are lacking. In consequence, speculation (albeit as educated guesses) must serve to set the stage for a more directed research strategy. To conclude this book, such speculation will be the basis for consideration. Some of what will follow results from research data, but more results from analysis of case studies, personal observation, and reports of caregivers and patients. What is presented is not a template but a prospectus, subject to test, modification, and refinement. Attention to Table 10.1 will assist in understanding and explaining these comments.

The Present in Dementia

The most commonly reported changes associated with dementia, and the earliest perceived as problematic, involve operations in the present. Memory loss, notably short-term and involving day-to-day behaviors, is cited as the culprit—and this has generated an impressive body of research both of brain areas involved and practical results on behavior. The focus, then, has been on retention as a phenomenon, not on disorientation as a cause. Being unable to encode stimuli and to act effectively on them is certainly a major problem. It may, however, be more superficial than explanatory and leaves the need to demonstrate that the behavioral malfunction of the dementia patient is crucial to the progress of the disease and basic to the nature of dementia.

There are several items that introduce difficulty in resolving the role of short-term memory loss in dementia. For one thing, there is abundant evidence (largely observational but widely accepted) that "slippage" in memory function occurs in normally aging adults. In fact, there is evidence that some "slippage" begins in young adulthood. So the inability to encode stimulation and act upon it effectively is something less than a benchmark for determining malfunction. There is even the issue of whether such memory loss is an indication of cell damage or loss in the hippocampus or merely a tendency to lack of concentration or intent in the face of other motives perceived by the person.

The typical point in life when behavior is so disrupted as to force a consideration of a major dilemma usually focuses on a "critical incident." That is, some event is serious enough that the nagging doubts and worries of a caregiver now can be concentrated on what makes the event critical. Then there may be consultation with a physician to determine cause for the effects and solution for the stresses. Unless the doctor can find a treatable condition, the step is too little and too late.

There is a compelling need for such issues as those above to be investigated, cataloged, and systematized. Only then can we begin to move from the situation of men describing the nature of an object from one feature to an objective realization of a complex mosaic.

In the meantime we must depend on what we have: the cataloging of behaviors reported by patients, caregivers, and professionals; the results from medical and psychological tests administered at various times in the development of the disease; the inferences of those trained and capable to interpret the meaning of data and behaviors. In this light there must be some reference to the time before such evidence actually comes to hand.

One of these is the "natural history" of the condition. How does it begin, and how does it express itself when no one is aware that a disease process is at work? Such speculation is risky, at best, and dangerous for preconceived notions. But there are some indications that may warrant a cautious guess. Subsequent to diagnosis, a gradual decline is the usual outcome. It seems likely that this same process should be found before diagnosis—that is, a gradual change in the physical (neuronal) and intellectual status of the person that accumulates over a period of time. That period may likely be several years, meaning that the condition began expression at least three to four years before reaching a critical stage. Most such changes, by retrospective reports, are reflected in memory loss of a short-term nature. But surely there are losses in normal routine that could be identified if future caregivers were alerted to the possibility.

These early "signs" of a disease such as Alzheimer's and its result of dementia are most often cited in terms of their arousal of exasperation followed by fear of their meaning. Yet they are seldom interpreted for their possible relationship to dementia due to a lack of knowledge by the general public. Instead, the interpretation is most apt to be a personalized one, focusing on the disruption in interpersonal relations and "explained" as some form of revenge for a feeling of being slighted or abused. We hear this reaction from those with later awareness that the eventual patient ignored some request or deliberately spoiled some situation as a means of causing an argument or picking a fight. With hindsight the caregiver is aware that the misinterpretation was unjustified and avoided the real problem. Perhaps this is an argument for teaching more adults problem-solving skills (and developing other "executive" functions) that can be widely applied and lead to more positive behavioral outcomes.

Adults today are not taught such skills and frequently have no basis for seeking a more objective explanation of behavior than that developed over years of interaction with others. So things rock along, becoming progressively but slowly more complex until a particular event occurs that brings the frustration and aggression to a head, with an awareness that something is badly wrong and needs to be treated. Most often this will involve seeking the professional opinion of a physician, although other professionals may be consulted first, and in some cases, no action will be taken. There is always hope that something can be done, there is a treatment that will correct the situation, but in true cases of dementia caused by Alzheimer's or other conditions the hope is a futile one in current conditions.

The kinds of behaviors that eventually lead to diagnosis are usually assigned to memory, as stated above, and seldom even indirectly to orientation. Yet the caregiver will speak of incidents that directly affect the spatial awareness of the patient. Statements such as "She forgets to turn off the stove" or "He gets lost when he's going to his own office" or "He is careless in his workshop and I'm afraid he'll have an accident" are common. Certainly the memory function is involved, but to leave it at that level overlooks the more basic ramifications. These are essentially problems in awareness of space and one's relation to it.

There are also references to time disorientation, although they are not as typical as spatial references. The patient may report: "I can't seem to remember when I'm supposed to do certain things." Or the caregiver may say, "She's slower and slower at getting ready when we're going out." Again, memory is certainly the theater within which the aberrant behavior occurs, but its basis is more deeply related to the disorientation in time that is developing and will eventually result in a loss of contact with reality as we perceive it.

With a referral to a physician, diagnosis becomes possible and imminent. This opens the door to a variety of physical tests that are increasingly becoming more precise and useful. First, the doctor will gather evidence on conditions that are treatable and reversible. Should these prove unpropitious, there can be a move to the most refined of current-day examinations. Scans are usable today in a way not possible before. Meanwhile, research is proceeding in genetics, with viruses and prions, and with external causes such as aluminum. What may be only promising today is a certainty in the future so that earlier diagnosis will be possible and accurate. This opens the door to interventions and even treatment that is impossible under present conditions. Treatment options are an active focus by pharmaceutical firms today. At least two dozen drugs to treat symptoms are being developed and tested currently.

The diagnostic procedure will include intellectual assessment as well. Memory loss will be evaluated, measures may be used that disclose sources of confusion in the life of the patient, and limited tests of disorientation will be administered. These evaluations will be extended into executive functions, such as planning and problem solving, and breakdowns and errors can be identified, noted, and evaluated for their impact and correction.

For the patient and caregiver, emotional and social behaviors are as important as the physical and intellectual ones. There must be some evaluation of personality since there can be changes here as well. Many complaints contain references to the negative behaviors that are now found in the patient, sometimes new to the person and sometimes an enlargement of past maladjustments. But there may also be changes in the opposite direction: The patient may show positive changes in personality. These can only be disclosed by probing in the area by an experienced professional since caregivers are more commonly focused on the difficulties that exist in interpersonal relationships than on the positive instances of behavior. It is as important to identify these changes as it is to document the negative ones. At least some speculation should be applied here in order to better understand the condition and its effects.

One area of concern to many patients and caregivers involves social interaction and correctness. As the disease process develops and dementia increases, there is the possibility that the patient may say and do things that are embarrassing. Misinterpretation by outsiders can lead to difficulty in continuing relationships. It is important to most adults to continue their contacts in social situations, to enjoy the company of other persons, and to engender positive relationships. The unpredictability of behavior in a patient may strain such efforts and sometimes leads to increasing withdrawal and isolation of two individuals (patient and caregiver) who need as much, perhaps more, social support and respite than ever. Evaluation and recommendations from persons trained in sociology and psychology can be of immense benefit during and following the diagnostic period.

Essentially, the procedures involved in the physical, intellectual, and social evaluations are directly related to the changes that occur in orientation. As dementia increases, the effects on spacetime awareness and response become greater. For the person who suffers increasing time disorientation, there will be less ability to maintain contact with the reality of the rest of the world. Now reality will involve greater dependence on the caregiver, often with a willingness to avoid the unpleasant by insisting on rigidity in social and physical circumstances. Space and time thus become constricted and personalized. As the caregiver responds to the demands by joining the patient in avoiding the unpleasant and taxing, life becomes more burdensome.

There are exceptions and variations to all the observed outcomes cited above. Almost inevitably, however, the burdens outweigh the reliefs, and the constriction is more common than the expansion in social horizons. We need more explicit information on all such effects in patient and caregiver, although there is a strong literature on burden that does identify causes and sources of relief (see Zarit, 1998; Zarit, Orr, and Zarit, 1985, as examples).

The Past

There is less evidence available on the role of the Past in the thought processes of persons with dementia. A considerable attention to references to the Past by patients has been popular in the literature, with a once widely held belief that dementia patients increasingly moved from the Present (and Future) to a mode of "living in the Past." That view has not been lost, but it has been questioned and amended. A better explanation may be the physical and mental roles (see Table 10.1) played by the Past in directing behavior. As the roles deteriorate, the consequent actions are adversely affected. Particularly is this true for the so-called executive functions.

Aging persons have been said to move toward a stronger Past orientation as they grow older. This seems a probable event, if for no other reason than that there is an apparent shortfall to planning into the Future. Research indicates that older persons continue to live in the Present to the necessary degree for functioning in society, despite some slippage in short-term memory. There may even be somewhat greater concentration on the Past as a means of reliving both the best and worst of times. With dementia, what is retrieved from the Past is a sort of residue remaining in an increasingly dysfunctional mind. The Future is not entirely neglected, however. There is instead a realistic focus on the immediate Future, with decreasing emphasis on a future that extends beyond a year or so.

With the dementia patient, the rehearsal of Past events has been observed and reported by those close to the individual. There seems to be a selective element in the reliance on Past experiences, however. Perhaps the choice is based upon the more emotionally tinged elements in the Past (a factor also to be considered in Past reports from those aging normally). Observers relate that the events are limited in number and rehearsed so often that they become wearying. One caregiver reported, "He tells the same story about his World War I experience over and over, regardless of who he is talking to. I've tried to get him to stop, but he doesn't seem to even be aware that he has told the story before. I wish I could find some way to help him remember something else of interest, but it's as though this was the only big thing that ever happened." An analysis of such behavior could be interpreted as due to considerable loss of memory for other Past events, as a successful means of covering up deficiencies intellectually that would prove embarrassing, even as the central event in the life of this person. When one considers that children may no longer be recognized or there may be confusion about one's spouse or that the most basic physical needs are unrecognized by the patient, the context seems to merit some explanation beyond a reliance on the Past.

As the dementia progresses the patient will even begin to lose the capability to repeat the old and favored story over and over. There comes a time when it seems that, almost animallike, the person is living in a perpetual Present but without the ability to recognize and respond to most of the stimulation impinging on the individual. The dependency relationship in this case is so strong that the caregiver must literally live first for the patient and only secondarily for self. The whole process is gradual and uneven, perhaps, in its progression, but it represents the decrement of spacetime awareness with its loss of contact with reality as we define it.

The Future

Little is reported, and less has been added to the literature, about the role of the Future in the dementia patient. As must be expected from the losses cited in the sections above, projection into the Future becomes more dubious and less credible as the dementia progresses. In fact, Future reference is seldom reported, nor can it be cited, by caregivers. This is a function of decline, even absence, in executive functions (Table 10.1). Before the patient has reached the dependency state, there seems no evidence that the Future is a meaningful concept. By the time of dependency, awareness of the Future and any reference to future events has deteriorated. A Future orientation is strong during young adulthood and middle age, less often found in older persons, particularly of a long-range projection, and absent in most cases of dementia.

Present, Past, and Future are useful concepts when dealing with temporal relationships during most of the lifetime of the individual. Because spacetime awareness is so affected by the process (undefined at this point) that leads to dementia, they must be viewed in a different light, probably even from early in the process. As is so often stated in psychological literature: "Further study is needed." That study is well under way, in several directions, and should produce increasing evidence that can be used to build a model meeting the stringent demands for scientific testing.

Bibliography

Acredolo, Curt (1989). Assessing children's understanding of time, speed and distance interrelations. In Iris Levin and Dan Zakay (Eds.), *Time and human cognition: A life-span perspective*. Amsterdam: North-Holland, pp. 219–257.

Alzheimer, Alois (1907). Über eine eigenartige Erkrankung der Hirnrinde. *Allgemeine Zeitschrift für Psychiatrie und Psychisch-Gerichtliche Medizin*, 64, 146–148. (See Jarvik and Greenson, 1987, for an English translation)

American Psychiatric Association (1994). *Diagnostic and statistical manual of mental disorders* (4th ed.). Washington, DC: American Psychiatric Association.

Amyx, Douglas, and Mowen, John C. (1995). Advancing versus delaying payments and consumer time orientation: A personal selling experiment. *Psychology and Marketing*, 12, no. 4, 243–264.

Arlow, Jacob A. (1992). Altered ego states. *Israel Journal of Psychiatry and Related Subjects*, 29, no. 2, 65–76.

Baillie, G.H., Clutton, C., and Ilbut, C. A. (1956). *Britten's old clocks and watches and their makers* (7th ed.). New York: Bonanza Books.

Bascue, L.O., and Lawrence, R.E. (1977). A study of subjective time and death anxiety in the elderly. *Omega*, 8, no. 1, 81–90.

Bates, Elizabeth, Elman, Jeffrey, and Li, Ping (1994). Language in, on, and about time. In Marshall M. Haith (Ed.), *The development of future-oriented processes*. Chicago: University of Chicago Press.

Beer, Robert E., and Ulrich, Jurg (1993). Alzheimer plaque density and duration of dementia. *Archives of Gerontology and Geriatrics*, 16, no. 1, 1–7.

Beiser, Morton, and Hyman, Ilene (1997). Refugees' time perspective and mental health. *American Journal of Psychiatry*, 154, no. 7, 996–1002.

Bennett, David A., Cochran, Elizabeth J., Saper, Clifford B., Leverenz, James B., Gilley, David W., and Wilson, Robert S. (1993). Pathological changes in frontal cortex from biopsy to autopsy in Alzheimer's disease. *Neurobiology of Aging*, 14, no. 6, 589–596.

Benton, A.L., van Allen, M.W., and Fogel, M.L. (1964). Temporal orientation in cerebral disease. *Journal of Nervous and Mental Disease*, 139, 110–119.

Bergson, Henri (1965). *Duration and simultaneity.* Indianapolis, IN: Bobbs-Merrill.

Betz, Andrew L., and Skowronski, John J. (1997). Self-events and other-events. *Memory and Cognition*, 25, no. 5, 701–714.

Bierer, Linda M., Hof, Patrick R., Purohit, Dushyant P., Carlin, Linda, Schmeidler, James, Davis, Kenneth L., and Perl, Daniel P. (1995). Neocortical neurofibrillary tangles correlate with dementia severity in Alzheimer's disease. *Archives of Neurology*, 52, no. 1, 81–88.

Blessed, G., Tomlinson, B.E., and Roth, M. (1968). The association between quantitative measures of dementia and of senile change in the cerebral gray matter of elderly subjects. *British Journal of Psychiatry*, 114, 797–811.

Block, Richard A. (1996). Psychological time and memory systems of the brain. In J.T. Fraser and M.P. Soulsby (Eds.), *Dimensions of time and life: The study of time* (Vol. 8). Madison, CT: International Universities Press, pp. 61–76.

Block, Richard A. (1989). A contextualistic view of time and mind. In J.T. Fraser (Ed.), *Time and mind: Interdisciplinary issues.* Madison, CT: International Universities Press, pp. 63–72.

Block, Richard A. (1974). Memory and the experience of duration in retrospect. *Memory and Cognition*, 2, 153–160.

Boltz, Marilyn G. (1994). Changes in internal tempo and effects on the learning and remembering of event durations. *Journal of Experimental Psychology: Learning, Memory and Cognition*, 20, no. 5, 1154–1171.

Boltz, Marilyn G. (1993). Time estimation and expectancies. *Memory and Cognition*, 21, no. 6, 853–863.

Boorstin, Daniel J. (1983). *The discoverers.* New York: Random House.

Boris, Howard N. (1994). About time. *Contemporary Psychoanalysis*, 30, no. 2, 301–322.

Boscolo, Luigi, and Bertrando, Paolo (1993). *The times of time: A new perspective in systemic therapy and consultation* (Stephen Thorne, Trans.). New York: Norton.

Bouffard, Leandre, and Bastin, Etienne (1994). La perspective future des personnel ages en function de la perte d'autonomie et du type d'habitation. *International Journal of Psychology*, 29, no. 1, 39–53.

Bouffard, Leandre, Bastin, Etienne, and Lapierre, Sylvie (1996). Future time perspective according to women's age and social role during adulthood. *Sex Roles*, 34, nos. 3–4, 253–285.

Bouras, Constantin, Hof, Patrick R., Giannakopoulos, Panteleimon, Michel, Jean Pierre, and Morrison, J.H. (1994). Regional distribution of neurofibrillary tangles and senile plaques in the cerebral cortex of elderly patients: A quantitative evaluation of a one-year autopsy population from a geriatric hospital. *Cerebral Cortex*, 4, no. 2, 138–150.

Brandstädter, Jochen, and Wentura, Dirk (1994). Veränderungen der Zeit- und Zukunftperspektive im Übergang zum höheren Erwachsenenalter: Entwicklungspsychologische und differentielle Aspekte. *Zeitschrift und Pädagogische Psychologie*, 26, no. 1, 2–21.

Brandstädter, Jochen, Wentura, Dirk, and Schmitz, Ulrich (1997). Veränderungen der Zeit- und Zukunftperspektive im Übergang zum höheren Alter: Quer- und Längsschnittliche befunde. *Zeitschrift für Psychologie*, 205, no. 4, 377–395.

Brannigan, Gary G., Shahon, Amy J., and Schaller, Juli A. (1992). Locus of control and time orientation in daydreaming: Implications for therapy. *Journal of Genetic Psychology*, 153, no. 3, 359–361.

Brennan, Richard P. (1997). *Heisenberg probably slept here: The lives, times, and ideas of the great physicists of the 20th century*. New York: Wiley.

Brotchie, Janet, Brennan, James, and Wyke, Maria A. (1985). Temporal orientation in the pre-senium and old age. *British Journal of Psychiatry*, 147, 692–695.

Brown, Jason W. (1990). Psychology of time awareness. *Brain and Cognition*, 14, no. 2, 144–164.

Brown, Norman R. (1997). Context memory and the selection of frequency estimation strategies. *Journal of Experimental Psychology: Learning, Memory, and Cognition*, 23, no. 4, 898–914.

Brown, Scott W., Newcomb, Damon C., and Kahrl, Kathleen G. (1995). Temporal-signal detection and individual differences in timing. *Perception*, 24, no. 5, 525–538.

Buehler, Roger, Griffin, Dale, and Ross, Michael (1994). Exploring the "planning fallacy": Why people underestimate their task completion times. *Journal of Personality and Social Psychology*, 67, no. 3, 366–381.

Bueno Martinez, Belen (1994). The role of cognitive changes in immediate and remote prospective time estimations. *Acta Psychologica*, 85, no. 2, 99–121.

Burke, James (1985). *The day the universe changed*. Boston: Little, Brown.

Burns, Alistair, Howard, Robert, and Pettit, William (1995). *Alzheimer's disease: A medical companion*. Cambridge, MA: Blackwell.

Burt, Christopher D.B. (1993). The effect of actual event duration and event memory on the reconstruction of duration information. *Applied Cognitive Psychology*, 7, no. 1, 63–73.

Burt, Christopher D.B., and Kemp, Simon (1994). Construction of activity duration and time management potential. *Applied Cognitive Psychology*, 8, no. 2, 155–168.

Burt, Christopher D.B., and Popple, Jennifer S. (1996). Effects of implicit action speed on estimation of event duration. *Applied Cognitive Psychology*, 10, no. 1, 53–63.

Butler, Robert N. (1990). Senile dementia of the Alzheimer type (SDAT). In William B. Abrams and Robert Berkow (Eds.), *The Merck manual of geriatrics*. Rahway, NJ: Merck Sharp and Dohme Research Laboratories, pp. 933–998.

Butler, Robert N. (1963). The life review: An interpretation of reminiscence in the aged. *Psychiatry*, 26, 65–75.

Byram, Stephanie J. (1997). Cognitive and emotional factors influencing time prediction. *Journal of Experimental Psychology: Applied*, 3, no. 3, 216–239.

Calaprice, Alice (1996). *The quotable Einstein*. Princeton, NJ: Princeton University Press.

Cameron, Paul, Desai, K.G., Sahador, Darius, and Dremel, G. (1978). Temporality across the life span. *International Journal of Aging and Human Development*, 8, no. 3, 229–259.

Cannon, Susan Faye (1978). *Science in culture: The early Victorian period.* New York: Dawson and Science History Publications.

Cantor, Norman F. (1993). *The civilization of the Middle Ages.* New York: HarperCollins.

Caplan, Louis L. (1990). Cerebrovascular disease. In William B. Abrams and Robert Berkow (Eds.), *The Merck manual of geriatrics.* Rahway, NJ: Merck Sharp and Dohme Research Laboratories, pp. 948–973.

Carrillo de la Peña, M.T., and Luengo, M.A. (1994). Time estimation and juvenile delinquency. *Perceptual and Motor Skills,* 79, no. 3, 1559–1565.

Carrillo de la Peña, M.T., Luengo, M.A., and Romero, Estrella (1994). Antisocial youth behavior and future time perspective: A study of the influence of institutionalization. *Anuario de Psicologia,* 62, no. 3, 67–80.

Casini, Lawrence, and Macar, Françoise (1993). Behavioural and electrophysiological evidence for the specific processing of temporal information. *Psychologica Belgica,* 33, no. 2, 285–296.

Casson, Lionel (1965). *Ancient Egypt.* New York: Time-Life Books.

Chastain, Garvin, and Ferraro, F. Richard (1997). Duration ratings as an index of processing resources required for cognitive tasks. *Journal of General Psychology,* 124, no. 1, 49–76.

Chui, Helena C. (1989). Dementia: A review emphasizing clinico-pathologic correlation and brain-behavior relationships. *Archives of Neurology,* 46, no. 7, 806–814.

Clark, Ronald W. (1984). *Einstein: The life and times.* New York: Avon.

Constantinidis, Jean (1985). Pick dementia: Anatomoclinical correlations and pathophysiological correlations. In F. Clifford Rose (Ed.), *Modern approaches to the dementias. Part I: Etiology and pathophysiology.* New York: Karger, pp. 72–97.

Cooke, Robert A., Rousseau, Denise M., and Lafferty, J. Clayton (1988). Personal orientations and their relation to psychological and physiological symptoms of strain. *Psychological Reports,* 62, no. 1, 223–228.

Cooper, Brian, and Bickel, Horst (1984). Population screening and the early detection of dementing disorders in old age: A review. *Psychological Medicine,* 14, no. 1, 81–95.

Creasey, Helen, Schwartz, Michael A., Frederickson, Harold, Haxby, James V., and Rapaport, Stanley I. (1986). Quantitative computed tomography in dementia of the Alzheimer type. *Neurology,* 36, no. 12, 1563–1568.

Cremer, Roel, Snel, Jan, and Brouwer, Wiebo H. (1990). Age-related differences in timing of position and velocity identification. *Accident Analysis and Prevention,* 22, no. 5, 467–474.

Cummings, Jeffrey L., and Benson, Frank (1988). Psychological dysfunction accompanying subcortical dementia. *Annual Review of Medicine,* 39, 53–61.

Cutting, John, and Silzer, Herta (1990). Psychopathology of time in brain disease and schizophrenia. *Behavioral Neurology,* 3, no. 4, 197–215.

Damasio, Antonio R., Van Hoesen, Gary W., and Hyman, Bradley T. (1990). Reflections on the selectivity of neuropathological changes in Alzheimer's disease. In Myrna F. Schwartz (Ed.), *Modular deficits in Alzheimer-type dementia: Issues in the biology of language and cognition.* Cambridge, MA: MIT Press, pp. 83–100.

Danziger, Kurt (1990). *Constructing the subject: Historical origins of psychological research*. New York: Cambridge University Press.

Dapkus, Marilyn A. (1985). A thematic analysis of the experience of time. *Journal of Personality and Social Psychology*, 49, no. 2, 408–419.

DeKosky, Steven T. (1996). Advances in the biology of Alzheimer's disease. In Myron F. Weiner (Ed.), *The dementias: Diagnosis, management and research* (2nd ed.). Washington, DC: American Psychiatric Press, pp. 313–330.

Dennett, Daniel C. (1995). *Darwin's dangerous idea: Evolution and the meanings of life*. New York: Simon and Schuster.

Dickson, Dennis W., Crystal, Howard A., Bevona, Caroline, Honer, William, Vincent, Inez, and Davies, Peter (1995). Correlations of synaptic and pathological markers with cognition of the elderly. *Neurobiology of Aging*, 16, no. 3, 285–302.

Dieudonne, L. (1984). Maladie de Parkinson et troubles psychiques. *Feuillets Psychoatriques de Liege*, 17, nos. 1–2, 124–128.

Dobbs, Betty Jo Teeter, and Jacob, Margaret C. (1995). *Newton and the culture of Newtonianism*. Atlantic Highlands, NJ: Humanities Press.

Droit, Sylvie (1994). Temporal regulation of behavior with an external clock in 3-year-old children: Differences between waiting and response duration tasks. *Journal of Experimental Child Psychology*, 58, no. 3, 332–345.

Dube, Laurette, and Schmitt, Bernd H. (1996). The temporal dimensions of social episodes: Position effect in time judgment of unfilled intervals. *Journal of Applied Social Psychology*, 26, no. 20, 1816–1826.

Duncan, David Ewing (1998). *Calendar: Humanity's epic struggle to determine a true and accurate year*. New York: Avon.

Dworetsky, John P. (1991). *Psychology* (4th ed.). St. Paul, MN: West.

Ebbinghaus, H. (1913). *Memory: A contribution to experimental psychology* (H.G. Ruger and C.E. Bussenius, Trans.). New York: Teachers College, Columbia University Press.

Eco, Umberto (1994). *The island of the day before*. New York: Harcourt Brace.

Edwards, Allen Jack (1998). Standardization of the Edwards Scale of Temporal Orientation. Unpublished manuscript. Springfield, MO: Edwards.

Edwards, Allen Jack (1994). *When memory fails: Helping the Alzheimer's and dementia patient*. New York: Plenum Press.

Edwards, Allen Jack (1993). *Dementia*. New York: Plenum Press.

Einstein, Albert (1963). *Ideas and opinions by Albert Einstein*. New York: Crown.

Einstein, Albert (1916). Die Grundlage der allgemeinen Relativitätstheorie. *Annalen der Physik*, 49, no. 4, 769–822.

Einstein, Albert (1905). On the electrodynamics of moving bodies. *Annalen der Physik*, 17, no. 4, 891–921.

Eisler, Anna D., and Eisler, Hannes (1994). Subjective time scaling: Influence of age, gender, and Type A and B behavior. *Chronobiologia*, 21, nos. 3–4, 185–200.

Emirbayer, Mustafa, and Mische, Ann (1998). What is agency? *American Journal of Sociology*, 103, no. 4, 962–1023.

Fagg, Lawrence W. (1995). *The becoming of time: Integrating physical and religious time*. Atlanta, GA: Scholars Press.

Fang, Ge, Feng, Gang, Fang, Fuxi, and Jiang, Tao (1994). Preschoolers' estimation of time duration and their cognitive strategies. *Psychological Science China*, 17, no. 1, 3–9.

Fang, Ge, Feng, Gang, Jiang, Tao, and Fang, Fuxi (1993). Time duration estimated by preschoolers and their strategies. *Acta Psychologica Sinica*, 25, no. 4, 346–352.

Ferris, Timothy (1992). *The mind's sky: Human intelligence in a cosmic context.* New York: Bantam Books.

Fingerman, Karen L., and Perlmutter, Marion (1995). Future time perspective and life events across adulthood. *Journal of General Psychology*, 122, no. 1, 95–111.

Fisk, Albert A. (1981). *A new look at senility: Its causes, diagnosis, treatment and management.* Springfield, IL: Charles C. Thomas.

Fivush, Robyn, and Mandler, Jean M. (1985). Developmental changes in the understanding of temporal sequence. *Child Development*, 56, no. 6, 1437–1446.

Flaherty, Michael G. (1991). The perception of time and situated engrossment. *Social Psychology Quarterly*, 54, no. 1, 76–85.

Flaherty, Michael G., and Meer, Michelle D. (1994). How time flies: Age, memory, and temporal compression. *Sociological Quarterly*, 35, no. 4, 705–721.

Fleeson, William, and Heckhausen, Jutta (1997). More or less "me" in past, present, and future: Perceived lifetime personality during adulthood. *Psychology and Aging*, 12, no. 1, 125–136.

Foglia, P., Perini, Michele, and Vanzulli, F. (1991). Pure amnesia in a case of right thalamic lesion. *Italian Journal of Neurological Sciences*, 12, no. 2, 211–213.

Folstein, Marshal F., and Folstein, Susan E. (1990). Mental status examination (MSE). In William B. Abrams and Robert Berkow (Eds.), *The Merck manual of geriatrics.* Rahway, NJ: Merck Sharp and Dohme Research Laboratories, pp. 929–932.

Folstein, M.F., Folstein, S.E., and McHugh, P.R. (1975). "Mini-mental state": A practical method for grading the cognitive state of patients for the clinician. *Journal of Psychiatric Research*, 12, 189–198.

Fraisse, Paul (1981). Cognition of time in human activity. In Guy d'Ydewalle and Willy Lens (Eds.), *Cognition in human motivation and learning.* Hillsdale, NJ: Erlbaum, pp. 233–259.

Fraisse, Paul (1963). *The psychology of time* (Jennifer Leith, Trans.). New York: Harper and Row.

Fraser, J.T. (1987). *Time: The familiar stranger.* Amherst: University of Massachusetts Press.

Fraser, J.T. (1982). Time's rite of passage: From individual to society. In Ephraim H. Mizruchi, Barry Glassner, and Thomas Pastorello (Eds.), *Time and aging: Conceptualization and application in sociological and gerontological research.* Bayside, NY: General Hall, pp. 153–177.

Friedman, William J. (1992). Children's time memory: The development of a differentiated past. *Cognitive Development*, 7, no. 2, 171–187.

Friedman, William J. (1991). The development of children's memory for the time of past events. *Child Development*, 62, no. 1, 139–155.

Friedman, William J. (1989). The representation of temporal structure in children, adolescents and adults. In Iris Levin and Dan Zakay (Eds.), *Time and human cognition: A life-span perspective.* Amsterdam: North-Holland, pp. 259–304.

Friedman, William J. (1986). The development of children's knowledge of temporal structure. *Child Development,* 57, no. 6, 1386–1400.

Friedman, William J., and Wilkins, Arnold J. (1985). Scale effects in memory for the time of events. *Memory and Cognition,* 13, no. 2, 168–175.

Fromholt, Pia, and Larsen, Steen F. (1991). Autobiographical memory in normal aging and primary degenerative dementia (dementia of Alzheimer type). *Journal of Gerontology: Psychological Sciences,* 46, no. 3, P85–P91.

Fuster, Joaquin M. (1995). Memory and planning: Two temporal perspectives of frontal lobe function. In Herbert H. Jasper and Silvana Riggio (Eds.), *Epilepsy and the functional anatomy of the frontal lobe. Advances in Neurology* (Vol. 66). New York: Raven Press, pp. 9–20.

Gadow, Sally (1986). Time and the body in geriatric rehabilitation. *Topics in Geriatric Rehabilitation,* 1, no. 2, 1–7.

Ganesan, Shankar (1993). Negotiation strategies and the nature of channel relationships. *Journal of Marketing Research,* 30, no. 2, 183–203.

Garrett, Henry E. (1941). *Great experiments in psychology* (Rev. and enlarged ed.). New York: Appleton-Century.

Gibbs, C.J., and Gadjusek, M. (1978). Subacute spongiform virus encephalopathies: The transmissable virus dementia. In R. Katzman, R.D. Terry, and K.L. Bick (Eds.), *Alzheimer's disease: Senile dementia and related disorders.* New York: Raven Press, pp. 119–120.

Gjesme, Torgrim (1983). On the concept of future time orientation: Considerations of some functions' and measurements' implications. *International Journal of Psychology,* 18, no. 5, 443–461.

Gjesme, Torgrim (1981). Some factors influencing perceived goal distance in time: A preliminary check. *Perceptual and Motor Skills,* 53, no. 1, 175–182.

Gjesme, Torgrim (1975). Slope of gradients for performance as a function of achievement motive, goal distance in time and future time orientation. *Journal of Psychology,* 91, no. 1, 143–160.

Glicksohn, Joseph, and Ron-Avni, Ruth (1997). The relationship between preference for temporal conceptions and time estimation. *European Journal of Cognitive Psychology,* 9, no. 1, 1–15.

Golander, Hava (1995). Chronically ill, old, and institutionalized: Being a nursing home resident. *Family and Community Health,* 17, no. 4, 63–74.

Gould, Stephen Jay, and Shearer, Rhonda Roland (1999–2000). Boats and deckchairs. *Natural History,* 108, no. 10, 32–44.

Green, Miranda J. (1997). *The world of the Druids.* New York: Thames and Hudson.

Green, Robert C., Goldstein, F.C., Mirra, S.S., Alzraki, N.P., Baxt, J.L., and Bakay, R.R. (1995). Slowly progressive apraxia in Alzheimer's disease. *Journal of Neurology, Neurosurgery and Psychiatry,* 59, no. 3, 312–315.

Greene, Brian (1999). *The elegant universe.* New York: Norton.

Greenfield, Susan A. (1995). *Journeys to the center of the mind: Toward a science of consciousness.* New York: Freeman.

Grewal, Raji P. (1995). Awareness of time in dementia of the Alzheimer type. *Psychological Reports,* 76, no. 3, pt. 1, 717–718.

Grskovich, Janet A., Zentall, Sydney S., and Stormont-Spurgin, Melissa (1995). Time estimation and planning abilities: Students with and without mild disabilities. *Behavioral Disorders*, 20, no. 3, 197–203.

Grun, Bernard (1991). *The timetables of history* (3rd ed.). New York: Simon and Schuster.

Gurland, Barry J., Wilder, David E., Cross, Peter, Teresi, Jeanne, and Barrett, Virginia W. (1992). Screening scales for dementia: Toward reconciliation of conflicting cross-cultural findings. *International Journal of Geriatric Psychiatry*, 7, 105–113.

Gustafson, Lars (1987). Frontal lobe degeneration of non-Alzheimer type: II. Clinical picture and differential diagnosis. *Archives of Gerontology and Geriatrics*, 6, no. 3, 209–223.

Gutwinski-Jeggle, Jutta (1992). Trauma and temporal perception: Theoretical reflections. *Jahrbuch der Psychoanalyse*, 29, 167–214.

Guy, Bonnie S., Rittenburg, Terri L., and Hawes, Douglas K. (1994). Dimensions and characteristics of time perceptions and perspective among older consumers. *Psychology and Marketing*, 11, no. 1, 35–56.

Hackett, David A. (1995). *The Buchenwald report*. Boulder, CO: Westview Press.

Hambrecht, M. (1987). Gedachtnisstorungen bei Frontalhirnlasionen. *Nervenartz*, 58, no. 3, 131–136.

Hancock, Peter A., Arthur, E.J., Chrysler, S.T., and Lee, J. (1994). The effects of sex, target duration, and illumination on the production of time intervals. *Acta Psychologica*, 86, no. 1, 57–67.

Hawking, Stephen (1996). *The illustrated brief history of time*. New York: Bantam.

Hayflick, Leonard (1994). *How and why we age*. New York: Ballantine.

Heilman, Kenneth M., and Fisher, Waldo R. (1974). Hyperlipidemic dementia. *Archives of Neurology*, 3, no. 1, 67–68.

Hellström, Christina, and Carlsson, Sven G. (1996). The long-lasting now: Disorganization in subjective time in long-standing pain. *Scandinavian Journal of Psychology*, 37, no. 4, 416–423.

Herrera, Charles O. (1990). Sleep disorders. In William B. Abrams and Robert Berkow (Eds.), *The Merck manual of geriatrics*. Rahway, NJ: Merck Sharp and Dohme Research Laboratories, pp. 128–140.

Heston, Leonard L., White, June A., and Mastri, Angeline R. (1987). Pick's disease: Clinical genetics and natural history. *Archives of General Psychiatry*, 44, no. 5, 409–411.

Hilberg, Raul (1992). *Perpetrators, victims, bystanders*. New York: HarperCollins.

Holland, Audrey L., McBurney, Donald H., Moosy, John, and Reinmuth, O.M. (1985). The dissolution of language in Pick's disease with neurofibrillary tangles: A case study. *Brain and Language*, 24, no. 1, 36–58.

Holland, Lynn (1987). Life review and communication therapy for dementia patients. *Clinical Gerontologist*, 6, no. 3, 62–65.

Holzer, M., Holzapfel, H.P., Zedlick, D., Brückner, M.K., and Arendt, T. (1994). Abnormally phosphorylated tau protein in Alzheimer's disease: Heterogeneity of individual regional distribution and relationship to clinical severity. *Neuroscience*, 63, no. 2, 499–516.

Huber, Steven J., and Paulson, George W. (1985). The concept of sub-cortical dementia. *American Journal of Psychiatry*, 142, no. 11, 1312–1317.

Hughes, C.P., Berg, L., Danziger, W.L., Cohen, L.A., and Martin, R.L. (1982). A new clinical scale for the staging of dementia. *British Journal of Psychiatry*, 140, 566–572.

Hussian, Richard A. (1987). Wandering and disorientation. In Laura L. Carstensen and Barry A. Edelstein (Eds.), *Handbook of clinical gerontology*. New York: Pergamon, pp. 177–189.

Huttenlocher, Janellen, Hedges, Larry V., and Bradburn, Norman (1990). Reports of elapsed time: Bounding and rounding processes in estimation. *Journal of Experimental Psychology: Learning, Memory and Cognition*, 16, 196–213.

Huttenlocher, Janellen, Hedges, Larry V., and Duncan, S. (1991). Categories and particulars: Prototype effects in estimating visual spatial position. *Psychological Review*, 98, 352–376.

Huttenlocher, Janellen, Hedges, Larry V., and Prohaska, Vincent (1992). Memory for day of the week: A 5 + 2 day scale. *Journal of Experimental Psychology: General*, 121, no. 3, 313–325.

Huttenlocher, Janellen, Hedges, Larry V., and Prohaska, Vincent (1988). Hierarchical organization in ordered domains: Estimating the dates of events. *Psychological Review*, 95, 471–484.

Hyman, B.T. (1994). Studying the Alzheimer's disease brain: Insights, puzzles, and opportunities. *Neurobiology of Aging*, 15, suppl. 2, 579–583.

Jackson, Janet L. (1989). The processing of temporal information: Do we indeed time our minds? In J.T. Fraser (Ed.), *Time and mind: Interdisciplinary issues*. Madison, CT: International Universities Press, pp. 43–57.

Jarvik, L., and Greenson, H. (1987). About a peculiar disease of the cerebral cortex. *Alzheimer Disease and Associated Disorders*, 1, no. 1, 7–8. (See Alzheimer, 1907, for the original citation)

Jason, Leonard A., Schade, Jennifer, Furo, Louise, Reichler, Anne, and Brickman, Clifford (1989). Time orientation: Past, present, and future perceptions. *Psychological Reports*, 64, no. 3, pt. 2, 1199–1205.

Jaspers, Karl (1959). *General Psychopathology* (J. Hoenig and M.W. Hamilton, Trans.). Manchester, England: Manchester University Press.

Johanson, Aki, and Hagberg, Bo (1989). Psychometric characteristics in patients with frontal lobe degeneration of non-Alzheimer type. *Archives of Gerontology and Geriatrics*, 8, no. 2, 129–137.

Johnson, Colleen L., and Barer, Barbara M. (1993). Coping and a sense of control among the oldest old: An exploratory analysis. *Journal of Aging Studies*, 7, no. 1, 67–80.

Johnson, Colleen L., and Barer, Barbara M. (1992). Patterns of engagement and disengagement among the oldest old. *Journal of Aging Studies*, 6, no. 4, 351–364.

Jones, Alan W., and Richardson, J. Steven (1990). Alzheimer's disease: Clinical and pathological characteristics. *International Journal of Neuroscience*, 50, nos. 3–4, 147–168.

Jones, Mari Riess, and Yee, William (1997). Sensitivity to time change: The role of context and skill. *Journal of Experimental Psychology: Human Perception and Performance*, 23, no. 3, 693–709.

Josephs, Robert A., and Hahn, Eugene D. (1995). Bias and accuracy in estimates of task duration. *Organizational Behavior and Human Decision Processes*, 61, no. 2, 202–213.

Joslyn, Dan, and Hutzell, R.R. (1979). Temporal disorientation in schizophrenic and brain-damaged patients. *American Journal of Psychiatry*, 136, no. 9, 1220–1222.

Kadlub, Eugene A. (1996). Time: Language and substance. *Perceptual and Motor Skills*, 83, no. 3, pt. 1, 903–913.

Kahn, R.L., Goldfarb, A.I., Pollack, M., and Peck, R. (1960). Brief objective measures for the determination of mental status in the aged. *American Journal of Psychiatry*, 117, 326–328.

Kawata, Akihiro, Suga, Masakazu, Oda, Masaya, Hayashi, Hideaki, and Tanabe, Hitoshi (1992). Creutzfeldt-Jakob disease with congophilic kuru plaques: CT and pathological findings of the cerebral white matter. *Journal of Neurology, Neurosurgery and Psychiatry*, 55, no. 9, 849–851.

Kazee, A.M., Eskin, T.A., Lapham, L.W., Gabriel, K.R., McDaniel, K.D., and Hamill, R.W. (1993). Clinicopathologic correlates in Alzheimer disease: Assessment of clinical and pathologic diagnostic criteria. *Alzheimer Disease and Associated Disorders*, 7, no. 3, 152–164.

Kiernat, Jean M. (1983). Retrospective as a life span concept. *Physical and Occupational Therapy in Geriatrics*, 3, no. 2, 35–48.

Kirchmeier, Kathleen, Lee, Nora, and Schwartz, William J. (1988). Disorientation to place. *Archives of Neurology*, 45, no. 12, 1299.

Klapow, Joshua C., Evans, Jovier, Patterson, Thomas L., and Heaton, Robert K. (1997). Direct assessment of functional status in older patients with schizophrenia. *American Journal of Psychiatry*, 154, no. 7, 1022–1024.

Koenig, Fredrick, Swanson, William, and Harter, Carl (1981). Future time orientation, social class and anomia. *Social Behavior and Personality*, 9, no. 2, 123–127.

Koivula, Nathalie (1996). Estimation of time: Effects of locus of control, mental arithmetic and length of target interval. *Personality and Individual Differences*, 20, no. 1, 25–32.

Koriat, Asher, and Fischhoff, Baruch (1974). What day is today? An inquiry into the process of time orientation. *Memory and Cognition*, 2, no. 2, 201–205.

Kraepelin, Emil (1910). Das senile und präsenile Irresein. In *Psychiatrie: Ein Lehrbuch für Studierende und Ärzte*. Leipzig: Verlag von Johann Ambrosius Barth, pp. 533–554, 593–632.

Kramer, Samuel Noah (1967). *Cradle of civilization*. New York: Time-Life Books.

Krupp, E.C. (1983). *Echoes of the ancient skies: The astronomy of lost civilizations*. New York: Harper and Row.

Kuhs, Hubert (1991). Time experience in melancholia: A comparison between findings based on phenomenology and experimental psychology. *Comprehensive Psychiatry*, 32, no. 4, 324–329.

Larsen, Steen F., and Thompson, Charles P. (1995). Reconstructive memory in the dating of personal and public news events. *Memory and Cognition*, 23, no. 6, 780–790.

Larsen, Steen F., Thompson, Charles P., and Hansen, Tia (1996). Time in autobiographical memory. In David C. Rubin (Ed.), *Remembering our past: Studies in autobiographical memory*. New York: Cambridge University Press, pp. 129–156.

Laszlo, Janos (1995). The role of affective processes in reading time and time experience during literary reception. *Empirical Studies of the Arts*, 13, no. 1, 25–37.

Lehmann, Heinz E. (1967). Time and psycopathology. *Annals of the New York Academy of Science*, 138, 798–821.

Leonard, B.E. (1990). Research strategies for the treatment of Alzheimer's disease. *Medical Science Research*, 18, 663–665.

Lepage, Toussaint Jacqueline (1979). Collective graphic test for 5 to 6 year old children. *Psychologica Belgica*, 19, no. 2, 177–191.

Lewkowicz, David J. (1989). The role of temporal factors in infant behavior and development. In Iris Levin and Dan Zakay (Eds.), *Time and human cognition: A life-span perspective*. Amsterdam: North-Holland, pp. 9–62.

Libman, E., Creti, L., Levy, R.D., Brender, W., and Fichten, C.S. (1997). A comparison of reported and recorded sleep in older poor sleepers. *Journal of Clinical Geropsychology*, 3, no. 3, 199–211.

Loewenstein, David A. (1990). Objective assessment of functional status in Alzheimer's disease and related disorders. *Clinical Gerontologist*, 10, no. 1, 61–64.

Lomranz, Jacob, Shmotkin, Dov, Zechovoy, Amnon, and Rosenberg, Eliot (1985). Time orientation in Nazi concentration camp survivors: Forty years after. *American Journal of Orthopsychiatry*, 55, no. 2, 230–236.

Low, Jaclyn F. (1987). Time perspective and rehabilitation in the elderly. *Physical and Occupational Therapy in Geriatrics*, 5, no. 4, 17–30.

MacNay, Sterling K. (1995). The influence of preferred music on the perceived exertion, mood, and time estimation scores of patients participating in a cardiac rehabilitation exercise program. *Music Therapy Perspectives*, 13, no. 2, 91–96.

Mahon, Noreen E., and Yarcheski, Thomas J. (1994). Future time perspective and positive health practices in adolescents. *Perceptual and Motor Skills*, 79, no. 1, pt. 2, special issue, 395–398.

Mann, D.M.A. (1992). The neuropathology of the amygdala in ageing and in dementia. In John P. Aggleton (Ed.), *The amygdala: Neurobiological aspects of emotion, memory, and mental dysfunction*. New York: Wiley-Liss, pp. 575–593.

Marcus, Edward E. (1978). Effects of age, sex, and status on perception of the utility of educational participation. *Educational Gerontology*, 3, no. 4, 295–319.

Marmaras, Nikos, Vassilakis, Panayotes, and Dounias, George (1995). Factors affecting accuracy of producing time intervals. *Perceptual and Motor Skills*, 80, no. 3, pt. 1, 1043–1056.

Mattis, S. (1976). Mental status examination for organic mental syndrome in the elderly patient. In L. Bellack and T.B. Karasis (Eds.), *Geriatric psychiatry*. New York: Grune and Stratton, pp. 77–121.

McGaugh, James L., Introini-Collison, Agnes B., Cahill, Larry, Munsoo, Kim, and Liang, K.C. (1992). Involvement of the amygdala in neuromodulatory influences on memory storage. In John P. Aggleton (Ed.), *The amygdala: Neu-*

robiological aspects of emotion, memory, and mental dysfunction. New York: Wiley-Liss, pp. 431–451.

McGilchrist, Iain, Wolkind, Stephen, and Lishman, Alwyn (1994). "Dyschronia" in a patient with Tourette's syndrome presenting as maternal neglect. *British Journal of Psychiatry,* 164, 262–263.

McKee, A.C, Kosik, K.S., and Kowall, N.W. (1991). Neuritic pathology and dementia in Alzheimer's disease. *Annals of Neurology,* 30, no. 2, 156–165.

Meier, Christian (1995). *Caesar: A biography* (David McLintock, Trans.). New York: Basic Books.

Melges, Frederick T. (1989). Disorders of time and the brain in severe mental illness. In J.T. Fraser (Ed.), *Time and mind: Interdisciplinary issues.* Madison, CT: International Universities Press, pp. 99–119.

Montangero, Jacques (1996). *Understanding changes in time: The development of diachronic thinking in 7- to 12-year-old children* (Tim Pownall, Trans.). London: Taylor and Francis.

Montangero, Jacques (1993). From the study of reasoning on time to the study of understanding things in time. *Psychologica Belgica,* 33, no. 2, 185–195.

Morris, John C., McKeel, D.W., Storandt, M., Rubin, E.H., Price, J.L., Grant, E.A., Ball, M.J., and Berg, L. (1991). Very mild Alzheimer's disease: Informant-based clinical, psychometric, and pathologic distinction from normal aging. *Neurology,* 41, no. 4, 469–478.

Nagaratnam, Nages, and McNeil, Catriona (1999). Dementia in the severely aphasic: Global aphasia without hemiparesis—a stroke subtype simulating dementia. *American Journal of Alzheimer's Disease,* 14, no. 2, 74–78.

Nowotny, Helga (1994). *Time: The modern and post-modern experience.* Cambridge, MA: Polity Press.

Nurmi, Jari Erik (1991). How do adolescents see their future? A review of the development of future orientation and planning. *Developmental Review,* 11, no. 1, 1–59.

Osato, Eiko, Ogawa, Nobuya, and Takaoka, Nobuyuki (1995). Relations among heart rate, immediate memory, and time estimation under two different instructions. *Perceptual and Motor Skills,* 80, no. 3, 831–842.

Owen, Alma J. (1991). Time and time again: Implications of time perception theory. *Lifestyles,* 12, no. 4, 345–359.

Pandey, Sushma, and Agarwal, Adesh (1990). Future orientation and temporal coding: A developmental study. *Indian Journal of Current Psychological Research,* 5, no. 1, 24–32.

Papolla, Miguel A., and Robakis, Nikolaos K. (1995). Neuropathology and molecular biology of Alzheimer's disease. In Marvin Stein and Andrew Baum (Eds.), *Chronic diseases: Perspectives in behavioral medicine.* Mahwah, NJ: Erlbaum, pp. 3–20.

Park, Denise C., Morrell, Roger W., Hertzog, Christopher, Kidder, Daniel P., and Mayhorn, Christopher B. (1997). Effect of age on event-based and time-based prospective memory. *Psychology and Aging,* 12, no. 2, 314–327.

Parkin, Alan J., Walter, Brenda M., and Hunkin, Nicola M. (1995). Relationships between normal aging, frontal lobe function, and memory for temporal and spatial information. *Neuropsychology,* 9, no. 3, 304–312.

Parnetti, Lucilla, Ciuffetti, Giovanni, Signorini, Enrico, and Senin, Umberto (1985).

Memory impairment in the elderly: A three-year follow-up. *Archives of Gerontology and Geriatrics*, 4, no. 2, 91–100.

Pattschul-Furlan, Angela, and Retschitzki, Jean (1990). Approche cognitiviste de la rehabilitation de la desorientation temporelle chez les personnel atteintes de deménce senile. *Schweizerische Zeitschrift für Psychologie*, 49, no. 1, 27–36.

Paulman, Ronald G., Koss, Elizabeth, and MacInnes, William D. (1996). Neuropsychological evaluation of dementia. In Myron F. Weiner (Ed.), *The dementias: Diagnosis, management and research*. Washington, DC: American Psychiatric Press, pp. 211–232.

Petty, Richard G., Bonner, Deidre, Mouratoglou, Vassilis, and Silverman, Marisa (1996). Acute frontal lobe syndrome and dysfunction associated with bilateral caudate nucleus infarctions. *British Journal of Psychiatry*, 168, 237–240.

Philipp, Steven F. (1992). Time orientation and participation in leisure activities. *Perceptual and Motor Skills*, 75, no. 2, 659–664.

Piaget, Jean (1969). *The child's conception of time* (A.J. Pomerans, Trans.). New York: Basic Books.

Pilkington, J.G. (Trans.) (n.d.). *The confessions of St. Augustine*. Garden City, NY: International Collectors Library.

Pinker, Steven (1994). *The language instinct: How the mind creates language*. New York: Morrow.

Planck, Max (1968a). The meaning and limits of exact science. In Max Planck, *Scientific autobiography and other papers*. New York: Greenwood, pp. 80–120.

Planck, Max (1968b). *Scientific autobiography and other papers*. New York: Greenwood.

Pouthas, Viviane, Paindorge, Beatrice, and Jacquet, Anne Yvonne (1995). Learning to measure time: Studies with 4- to 7-year-old children. *Année Psychologique*, 95, no. 4, 593–619.

Powers, Charles B., Wisocki, Patricia A., and Whitbourne, Susan K. (1992). Age differences and correlates of worrying in young and elderly adults. *The Gerontologist*, 32, no. 1, 82–88.

Predebon, John (1996). The effects of active and passive processing of internal events on prospective and retrospective time estimation. *Acta Psychologica*, 94, no. 1, 41–58.

Pruchno, Rachel A., and Resch, Nancy L. (1989). Aberrant behaviors and Alzheimer's disease: Mental health effects on spouse caregivers. *Journal of Gerontology*, 44, no. 5, S177–S182.

Rakowski, William (1979). Future time perspective in later adulthood: Review and research directions. *Experimental Aging Research*, 5, no. 1, 43–88.

Rammsayer, Thomas H. (1997a). Effects of body core temperature and brain dopamine activity on timing processes in humans. *Biological Psychology*, 46, no. 2, 169–192.

Rammsayer, Thomas H. (1997b). On the relationship between personality and time estimation. *Personality and Individual Differences*, 23, no. 5, 739–744.

Rammsayer, Thomas H. (1994). A cognitive-neuroscience approach for elucidation of mechanisms underlying temporal information processing. *International Journal of Neuroscience*, 77, nos. 1–2, 61–76.

Ratzan, Scott C. (Ed.) (1998). *The mad cow crisis: Health and the public good.* New York: NYU Press.

Raynor, Joel O., and Entin, Elliott E. (1983). The function of future orientation as a determinant of human behavior in step-path theory of action. *International Journal of Psychology,* 18, no. 5, 463–487.

Read, Anthony, and Fisher, David (1992). *The fall of Berlin.* New York: Norton.

Richter, Jean Paul (Ed.) (1970). *The notebooks of Leonardo da Vinci* (Vol. II). New York: Dover.

Rifkin, Jeremy (1998). *The biotech century.* New York: Putnam.

Robinson-Whelen, Susan, and Kiecolt-Glaser, Janice (1997). The importance of social versus temporal comparison appraisals among older adults. *Journal of Applied Social Psychology,* 27, no. 11, 959–966.

Rosenfield, Israel (1992). *The strange, familiar, and forgotten: An anatomy of consciousness.* New York: Knopf.

Rothspan, Sadina, and Read, Stephen J. (1996). Present versus future time perspective and HIV risk among heterosexual college students. *Health Psychology,* 15, no. 2, 131–134.

Ryff, Carol D., and Heidrich, Susan M. (1997). Experience and well-being: Explorations on domains of life and how they matter. *International Journal of Behavioral Development,* 20, no. 2, 193–206.

St. Pierre, Josée, and Dubé, Micheline (1993). La competence temporelle des personnel âgées. *Canadian Journal of Aging,* 12, no. 3, 311–323.

Samuel, William, Masliah, Eliezer, Hill, L.R., Butters, Nelson, and Terry, Robert D. (1994). Hippocampal connectivity and Alzheimer's dementia: Effects of synapse loss and tangle frequency in a two-component model. *Neurology,* 44, no. 11, 2081–2088.

Samuel, William, Terry, Robert D., DeTeresa, Richard, Butters, Norman, and Masliah, Eliezer (1994). Clinical correlates of cortical and nucleus basalis pathology in Alzheimer's dementia. *Archives of Neurology,* 51, 772–778.

Sandifer, Cody (1997). Time-based behaviors at an interactive science museum: Explaining the difference between weekday/weekend and family/nonfamily visitors. *Science Education,* 31, no. 6, 689–701.

Sawyer, Thomas F., Meyers, Peter J., and Huser, Stacy J. (1994). Contrasting task demands alter the perceived duration of brief time intervals. *Perception and Psychophysics,* 56, no. 6, 649–657.

Schafer, Edward H. (1967). *Ancient China.* New York: Time-Life Books.

Scheltens, Ph., Hazenberg, G.J., Lindeboom, J., Volk, J., and Wolters, E.Ch. (1990). A case of progressive aphasia without dementia: "Temporal" Pick's disease? *Journal of Neurology, Neurosurgery and Psychiatry,* 53, no. 1, 79–80.

Shaw, C., and Aggleton, J.P. (1994). The ability of amnesia patients to estimate time intervals. *Neuropsychologia,* 32, no. 7, 859–873.

Shmotkin, Dov (1991). The role of time orientation in life satisfaction across the life span. *Journal of Gerontology: Psychological Sciences,* 46, no. 5, P243–P250.

Shomaker, Dianna J. (1989). Age discrimination, liminality and reality: The case of the Alzheimer's patient. *Medical Anthropology,* 12, 91–101.

Shoulson, Ira (1990). Huntington's disease: Cognitive and psychiatric features.

Neuropsychiatry, Neuropsychology and Behavioral Neurology, 3, no. 1, 15–22.

Shoulson, Ira (1978). Dementia in Huntington's disease and cognitive effects of muscimal therapy. In Kalidis Nandy (Ed.), *Senile dementia: A biomedical approach.* New York: Elsevier, pp. 251–258.

Siegler, Robert S., and McGilly, Kate (1989). Strategy choices in children's time-telling. In Iris Levin and Dan Zakay (Eds.), *Time and human cognition: A life-span perspective.* Amsterdam: North-Holland, pp. 185–218.

Sims, Andrew (1988). *Symptoms in the mind: An introduction to descriptive psychopathology.* Philadelphia: Saunders.

Skowronski, J.J., Betz, A.L., Thompson, C.P., and Larsen, S. (1995). Long-term performance in autobiographical event dating: Patterns of accuracy and error across a two-and-a-half year span. In A.F. Handy and L.E. Bourne (Eds.), *Learning and memory of knowledge and skills.* Hillsdale, NJ: Erlbaum, pp.206–233.

Staats, Sara, Partlo, Christie, and Stubbs, Kathy (1993). Future time perspective, response rates, and older persons: Another chapter in the story. *Psychology and Aging,* 8, no. 3, 440–442.

Strube, Gerhard, and Weber, Angelika (1988). The development of temporal ordering and dating of events. *Zeitschrift für Entwicklungpsychologie und Pädagogische Psychologie,* 20, no. 3, 225–238.

Strumpf, Neville. (1987). Probing the temporal world of the elderly. *International Journal of Nursing Studies,* 24, no. 3, 201–214.

Sunderland, Trey (1990). Non-Alzheimer dementias. In William B. Abrams and Robert Berkow (Eds.), *The Merck manual of geriatrics.* Rahway, NJ: Merck Sharp and Dohme Research Laboratories, pp. 944–948.

Sutherland, Stuart (1989). *The international dictionary of psychology.* New York: Continuum.

Suto, Melinda, and Frank, Gelva (1994). Future time perspective and daily occupations of persons with chronic schizophrenia in a board and care home. *American Journal of Occupational Therapy,* 48, no. 1, 7–18.

Taulbee, L.A., and Folsom, J.C. (1966). Reality orientation for geriatric patients. *Hospital and Community Psychiatry,* 17, no. 5, 133–135.

Thomae, Hans (1989). Veränderungen der Zeitperspective in höheren Alter. *Zeitschrift für Gerontologie,* 22, no. 2, 58–66.

Thomae, Hans (1981). Future time perspective and the problem of cognitive/motivation interaction. In Guy d'Ydewalle and Willy Lens (Eds.), *Cognition in human motivation and learning.* Hillsdale, NJ: Erlbaum, pp. 261–274.

Thompson, C.P., Skowronski, J.J., and Betz, A.L. (1993). The use of partial temporal information in dating personal events. *Memory and Cognition,* 21, 352–360.

Thompson, C.P., Skowronski, J.J., Larsen, S., and Betz, A.L. (1996). *Autobiographical memory: Remembering what and remembering when.* Mahwah, NJ: Erlbaum.

Thorn, Beverly E., and Hansell, Patricia L. (1993). Goals for coping with pain mitigate time distortion. *American Journal of Psychology,* 106, no. 2, 211–225.

Thorndike, E.L., Bregman, Elise O., Tilton, J.W., and Woodyard, Ella (1928). *Adult learning*. New York: Macmillan.

Thorne, Kip S. (1994). *Black holes and time warps: Einstein's outrageous legacy*. New York: W.W. Norton.

Tismer, Karl Georg (1991). Subjective time experience: Methodological procedures and conceptual considerations. *Zeitschrift für Gerontologie*, 24, no. 3, 146–153.

Travis, John (1996, February 17). Biological stopwatch found in brain. *Science News*, 149, 101.

Treisman, Michael (1993). On the structure of the temporal sensory system. *Psychologica Belgica*, 33, no. 2, 271–283.

Trommsdorff, Gisela, Lamm, Helmut, and Schmidt, Rolf W. (1979). A longitudinal study of adolescents' future orientation (time perspective). *Journal of Youth and Adolescence*, 8, no. 2, 131–147.

Tufte, Edward R. (1990). *Envisioning information*. Cheshire, CT: Graphics Press.

Unger, J.W., Lapham, L.W., McNeill, T.H., Eskin, T.A., and Hamill, R.W. (1991). The amygdala in Alzheimer's disease: Neuropathology and Alz50 immunoreactivity. *Neurobiology of Aging*, 12, no. 5, 389–399.

Usher, Marius, and Zakay, Dan (1993). A neural network model for attibute-based decision processes. *Cognitive Sciences*, 17, no. 3, 349–396.

Valax, M.F., Tremblay, E., and Sarocchi, F. (1996). What month is it? The process of temporal orientation as a unit of the year scale. *Acta Psychologica*, 94, no. 3, 309–317.

Vanneste, Sandrine, and Pouthas, Viviane (1995). Estimation temporelle prospective et retrospective chez la personne agée: Comparison avec le jeune adulte. *Bulletin de Psychologie*, 48, no. 420, 539–543.

Venable, Sheryl D., and Mitchell, Marlys M. (1991). Temporal adaptation and performance of daily living activities in persons with Alzheimer's disease. *Physical and Occupational Therapy in Geriatrics*, 9, nos. 3–4, 31–51.

Verma, Neelam (1992). Time orientation and work behavior. *Psychological Studies*, 37, nos. 2–3, 142–150.

Vriezen, Ellen R., and Moscovitch, Morris (1990). Memory for temporal order and conditional associative learning in patients with Parkinson's disease. *Neuropsychologia*, 28, no. 12, 1283–1293.

Wearden, John H. (1993). Decisions and memories in human timing. Special issue: Temporal processes. *Psychologica Belgica*, 33, no. 2, 241–253.

Webb, R. Mark, and Trzepacz, Paula T. (1987). Huntington's disease: Correlates of mental status with chorea. *Biological Psychiatry*, 22, no. 6, 751–761.

Webster's *New Universal Unabridged Dictionary* (1996). New York: Barnes and Noble.

Weinberger, Daniel R., Berman, Karen F., Iadarola, Mary, Driesen, Naomi, and Zec, Ronald F. (1988). Prefrontal cortical blood flow and cognitive function in Huntington's disease. *Journal of Neurology, Neurosurgery and Psychiatry*, 51, no. 1, 94–104.

Weiner, Myron F. (Ed.) (1996). *The dementias: Diagnosis, management and research* (2nd ed.). Washington, DC: American Psychiatric Press.

Weist, Richard M. (1989). Time concepts in language and thought: Filling the Piagetian void from two to five years. In Iris Levin and Dan Zakay (Eds.),

Time and human cognition: A life-span perspective. Amsterdam: North-Holland, pp. 63–118.

Whitrow, G.J. (1991). *Time in history: Views of time from prehistory to the present day.* Oxford: University Press.

Whitrow, G.J. (1972). *The nature of time.* New York: Holt, Rinehart and Winston.

Williams, J. Michael, Medwedeff, Catherine H., and Haban, Glenn (1989). Memory disorder and subjective time estimation. *Journal of Clinical and Experimental Neuropsychology,* 11, no. 5, 713–723.

Winokur, George, and Clayton, Paul J. (1994). *The medical basis of psychiatry* (2nd. ed.). Philadelphia: Saunders.

Wundt, W. (1862). Die Geschwindigkeit des Gedankens. *Gartenlaube,* 263–265.

Zakay, Dan (1993a). Relative and absolute duration judgments under prospective and retrospective paradigms. *Perception and Psychophysics,* 54, no. 5, 656–664.

Zakay, Dan (1993b). Time estimation methods: Do they influence prospective duration estimates? *Perception,* 22, no. 1, 91–101.

Zakay, Dan, and Block, Richard A. (1997). Temporal cognition. *Current Directions in Psychological Science,* 6, no. 1, 12–16.

Zakay, Dan, Tsal, Yehoshua, Moses, Masha, and Shahar, Itzhak (1994). The role of segmentation in prospective and retrospective time estimation processes. *Memory and Cognition,* 22, no. 3, 344–351.

Zarit, Steven H. (1998). Methodological considerations in caregiver intervention and outcome research. In Enid Light, George Niederehe, and Barry D. Lebowitz (Eds.), *Stress effects on family caregivers of Alzheimer's patients.* New York: Springer, pp. 351–369.

Zarit, Steven H. (1980). *Aging and mental disorders.* New York: Free Press.

Zarit, Steven H., Orr, Nancy, and Zarit, Judy (1985). *The hidden victims of Alzheimer's disease: Families under stress.* New York: New York University Press.

Zimbardo, Philip G., Keough, Kelli A., and Boyd, John N. (1997). Present time perspective as a predictor of risky driving. *Personality and Individual Differences,* 26, no. 6, 1007–1023.

Index

About the Author

ALLEN JACK EDWARDS is an emeritus professor of psychology at Southwest Missouri State University in Springfield. He has worked extensively with caregivers of Alzheimer's patients, including both professionals and families. His publications include books on dementia and on caring for the dementia patient.